THE POLAR ADVENTURES

OF A *Rich American Dame*

THE POLAR ADVENTURES

OF A *Rich American Dame*

A LIFE OF LOUISE ARNER BOYD

JOANNA KAFAROWSKI

DUNDURN
TORONTO

Cover image: Associated Press Image #100101016655; istock.com/nicholas belton (map)
Printer: Webcom

Library and Archives Canada Cataloguing in Publication

Kafarowski, Joanna, 1962-, author
        The polar adventures of a rich American dame : a life of Louise Arner Boyd / Joanna Kafarowski.

Includes bibliographical references and index.
Issued in print and electronic formats.
ISBN 978-1-4597-3970-3 (softcover).--ISBN 978-1-4597-3971-0 (PDF).--ISBN 978-1-4597-3972-7 (EPUB)

        1. Boyd, Louise Arner, 1887-1972. 2. Women explorers--United States--Biography. 3. Women adventurers--United States--Biography. 4. Philanthropists--United States--Biography. 5. Rich people--United States--Biography. 6. Arctic regions--Discovery and exploration--American. I. Title.

G585.B35K34 2017   919.804092   C2017-904947-X
                                                      C2017-904948-8

1 2 3 4 5   21 20 19 18 17

 Conseil des Arts   Canada Council
                    du Canada   for the Arts
 Canada
 **ONTARIO ARTS COUNCIL**
                     CONSEIL DES ARTS DE L'ONTARIO
                     an Ontario government agency
                     un organisme du gouvernement de l'Ontario

We acknowledge the support of the **Canada Council for the Arts**, which last year invested $153 million to bring the arts to Canadians throughout the country, and the **Ontario Arts Council** for our publishing program. We also acknowledge the financial support of the **Government of Ontario**, through the **Ontario Book Publishing Tax Credit** and the **Ontario Media Development Corporation**, and the **Government of Canada**.

Nous remercions le **Conseil des arts du Canada** de son soutien. L'an dernier, le Conseil a investi 153 millions de dollars pour mettre de l'art dans la vie des Canadiennes et des Canadiens de tout le pays.

Care has been taken to trace the ownership of copyright material used in this book. The author and the publisher welcome any information enabling them to rectify any references or credits in subsequent editions.
                                                      — *J. Kirk Howard, President*

The publisher is not responsible for websites or their content unless they are owned by the publisher.

Printed and bound in Canada.

VISIT US AT

dundurn.com | @dundurnpress | dundurnpress | dundurnpress

Dundurn
3 Church Street, Suite 500
Toronto, Ontario, Canada
M5E 1M2

For my parents

Pamela Elizabeth Maud Loweth Kafarowski (1928–2010) shared with me the delights of reading and visiting libraries and bookshops and introduced me to the magical worlds of Noddy, the Andrew Lang Fairy books, and the Famous Five. Dreamer, dancer, singer, kindred spirit.

Zygmunt Kafarowski (1924–2006) encouraged me and showed me how to set my goals high and then achieve them through perseverance, a solid work ethic, and sheer bloody-mindedness. Risk-taker, philosopher, perfectionist, family man.

With all my love

Far north, hidden behind grim barriers of pack ice, are lands
that hold one spellbound. Gigantic imaginary gates, with
hinges set in the horizon, seem to guard these lands. Slowly the
gates swing open, and one enters another world where men are
insignificant amid the awesome immensity of lonely mountains,
fiords and glaciers. Five times have the gates opened for me.
May they do so many times again!
— LOUISE ARNER BOYD

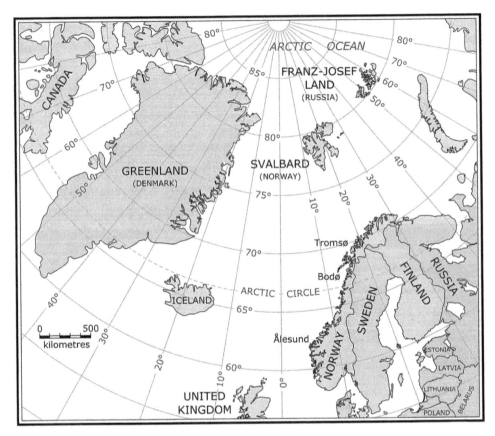

The area of Louise Arner Boyd's expeditions.

Contents

Illustrations

MAPS

All maps were created by Duncan Payne, and were derived from a composite map outlining the route of all Louise Arner Boyd's expeditions, as well as maps published in Boyd's books. The composite map was designed by William Briesemeister of the American Geographical Society in 1954 (revised 1956) according to her exact specifications, and hung proudly on a wall in her home. It is currently housed in the San Francisco Maritime National Historical Park.

Author's Note

Although this is a comprehensive biography, it is my hope that it provides a springboard for future researchers to uncover the mysteries that still need to be revealed about Miss Boyd's life. There is also scope for a scholarly investigation into her scientific contributions. There is so much still to learn and she is a rewarding subject.

The research I conducted for this biography revealed a treasure trove of letters, documents, and artifacts related to Miss Boyd that are scattered across the globe. It highlighted the fact that the majority of her precious Greenland photographs and her expedition journals and logbooks are missing. In addition, although I was able to interview many people who graciously shared their personal experiences of Miss Boyd, there are still many others with Boyd stories to tell. I should be grateful if anyone with knowledge of Louise Arner Boyd photographs, logbooks, artifacts, or letters not noted in this book, or anyone with stories to share, would contact me through the publisher.

PROLOGUE

A sheltered life can be a daring life as well.
For all serious daring starts from within.
— EUDORA WELTY

She gripped the ship's railing tightly with both rough-gloved hands while gazing sombrely into the sprawling darkness of the frozen night. Tall for a woman, broad-shouldered, wavy brown hair tucked under a snug cap framing a handsome face with piercing blue eyes, she could easily have been mistaken for one of the crew. Beneath her feet, the *Hobby* juddered and jarred as it made its way through the icy waters of the Arctic Ocean. The air was a constant thrum of men's guttural voices, the clang of thick cables and ropes, the bursting swell of the ocean as the ship slammed through the seething waves, moving forward on its perilous mission. Though unaccustomed to life onboard ship, and only recently acquainted with northern waters, California native Louise Arner Boyd found herself profoundly moved and invigorated by the experience — and more than a little unsettled. Whether above or below deck, she was never alone. There were always experienced seamen keeping a watchful eye on the gently bred

American socialite who had somehow become an integral part of one of the most desperate quests in polar history — the 1928 search for missing famed Norwegian explorer Roald Amundsen.

She caught herself as the ship yawed abruptly to starboard. *What was she thinking?* Only a few weeks before, she had been dressed in a bejewelled gown, dining on lobster at Claridge's in London, England, and dancing the quickstep at the Ritz. And yet here she was, wearing stiff leather boots and rough woollen trousers that itched like the dickens, standing unsteadily on the slippery bow of a ship sailing northward. There was so much for her to absorb — so much that the male crew members just took for granted. Louise spent hours poring over detailed nautical charts, checking the *Hobby's* position with a sextant, and quizzing the officers; more than might be expected of a respectable society lady of a certain age. But if she was going to contribute and really make a difference to this expedition, then she had to learn, and quickly, too. As *Hobby's* hull rose and fell rhythmically, she mused to herself that this was not the trip to Greenland that she had originally intended. Who knew what winding, dreary path her life would have taken if the Amundsen tragedy had not intervened and disrupted her travel plans? As unlikely as it seemed, Miss Louise Arner Boyd of San Rafael, California, was never supposed to be discussing weighty matters with naval commanders on the high seas, recognized by all onboard as one of the leaders of a daring rescue mission of international significance.

During that summer of 1928, far above the frigid Arctic Circle, the weathered schooner *Hobby*, Louise, and the Norwegian crew, including Captain Kristian Johannesen and Captain's Mate Astrup Holm, were sailing north in search of one of the greatest explorers of all time. Renowned for his bold exploits, geographic contributions, and endless brushes with death, Roald Amundsen had inexplicably vanished on June 18 during an effort to rescue the Italian explorer Umberto Nobile, who had himself gone missing in the airship *Italia* on its return flight from the North Pole. A Norwegian journalist noted tersely in a local Oslo paper, "It's a terrible thought that the rescue of one explorer might end with the death of another."[1]

Louise's first trip north had been an idyllic pleasure cruise a few years earlier. She had sailed with some intrepid friends around the rugged coast of Spitsbergen, Norway, and farther north, close to elusive Franz Josef

Land. It was the fulfillment of a childhood dream. During her earlier trip to Spitsbergen, she had been overcome by joy at her first sight of the Arctic Ocean. She was entranced by the deepening silence late at night that was broken only by the heaving and jostling of the massive icebergs, the harsh crispness of the cold air that seared the lungs, that sense of absolute oneness with the primal core of the world. It stirred her blood just to think of it. To be honest, it was also the thrill of the mighty polar bear hunt that attracted her. Like many adventurous women of her class, she craved the chase, the adrenalin-pumping rush that comes from sighting, stalking, and shooting one of the most fearsome beasts on earth. And she desired the kill as much as any man, when the blood-lust was upon her and the animal fell dead beneath her still-smoking rifle. But more than that, she went north because she wanted to know what was out there. She had to see it for herself. But *leading* a polar expedition and joining the ranks of fellow American polar explorers such as Elisha Kent Kane, Robert E. Peary, and Richard Byrd? Well, that happened by coincidence — or perhaps it was her destiny.

Just as the ship left Tromsø harbour at the start of the rescue mission, newspaper headlines heralded, "Woman Joins Arctic Search — Miss Boyd To Assist Rescue" and "Miss Boyd Confident of Rescue Outlook. Californian Going in Search of Amundsen Is Huntress and Business Woman." Were they really referring to her — a forty-year-old sophisticated woman-about-town? Forty! It had taken her quite by surprise.

She thought long and hard that year about what she wanted out of life. She wasn't married and had no children — no ties at all. Her mother and father had passed away a few years earlier and she'd lost both of her brothers when she was young. No family then to judge or criticize or offer loving guidance and support. She was quite alone. There was no one to really care about what she did so she just went ahead and did it. In the spring of 1928, her plans to hire a ship and travel north of Norway once more were well under way. But fate intervened when Amundsen was lost. Louise thought about the people closest to her and the pivotal events leading to this critical junction in her life.

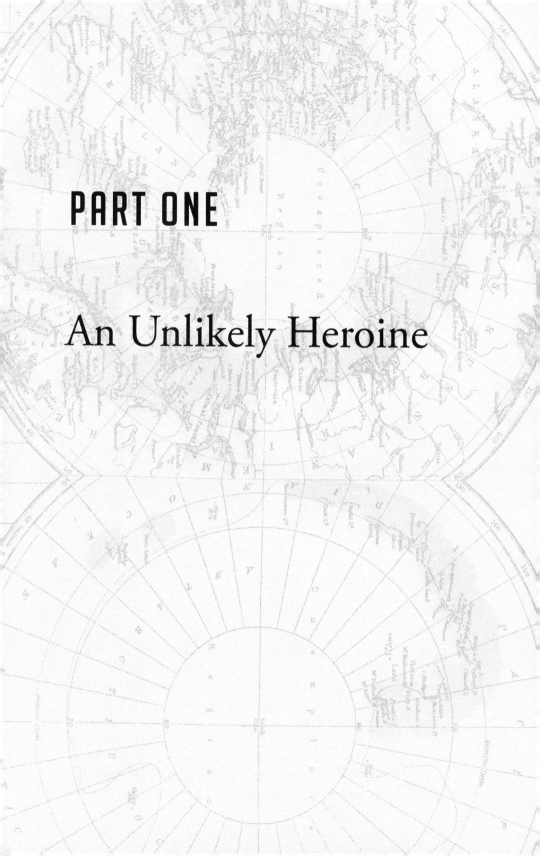

PART ONE

An Unlikely Heroine

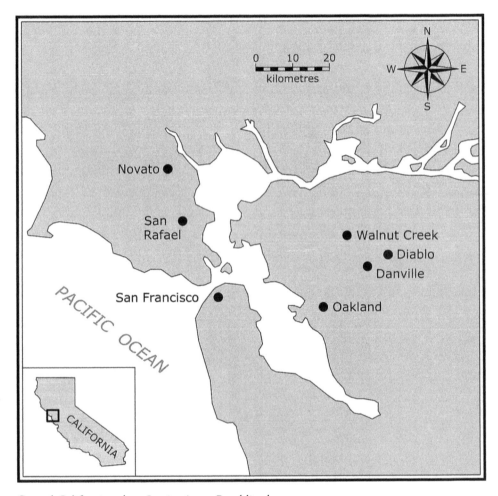

Central California, where Louise Arner Boyd lived.

CHAPTER ONE

AN ADVENTURESS IS BORN

To strive, to seek, to find, and not to yield.
— ALFRED, LORD TENNYSON

She always considered herself to be a true-blue American girl. Sheltered from the gritty hardships of life, Louise Arner Boyd was set free as a child to explore her world. Independent. Curious. Adventurous. Her wealthy parents, Louise and John Franklin Boyd, shuttled her and her older brothers Seth and Jack between lavish homes in San Rafael in Marin County near bustling San Francisco and rural Diablo near Danville in Contra Costa County, California. All the wonders of country and city life were theirs. When balmy June days arrived, their noisy household was packed up and shipped off to their summer home, where life proceeded at a more leisurely pace. Nestled into a sprawling pastoral estate overlooked by Mount Diablo, the Oakwood Park Farm hummed with the comings and goings of busy adults and rambunctious children. Peopled by childhood playmates, her father's boisterous business colleagues and government associates, and chattering society women with whom her mother worked on philanthropic events, this is where her bold spirit developed and flourished. Unshackled from the constraints of citi-fied ways, Louise responded joyously.

Known as the "Colton" or "Cook Ranch," Louise's childhood summer home was uniquely connected to California history. At the peak of railway fever, in the 1870s, the two-thousand-acre property was acquired by the Central Pacific and Southern Pacific Railroads. One of the early owners was David Doughty Colton, a rough-and-tumble miner, lawyer, and railway baron. Colton's property passed to his son-in-law, Daniel Cook, and then to Daniel's brother Seth. Louise's mother inherited it in 1888 following the untimely death of her favourite uncle, Seth Cook. How overwhelming it must have been for her to inherit such wealth at the age of twenty-seven. Executors conducting a property appraisal documented the spacious two-storey Italianate mansion replete with lush gardens, a billiard hall with bowling alley to which the Cook brothers had retired in the evenings with their business cronies, a training barn for show horses, an elegant carriage house, a dairy, barns, and farm stock, including 102 thoroughbred horses and 319 head of dairy cattle. Louise's parents christened the property "Oakwood Park Farm."

Oakwood Park Farm near Danville, California, the Boyd summer residence until 1912. Photograph taken in 1913.

From his beginnings on a Pennsylvania farm, John Boyd's love of horses had remained constant. He improved the mile-long race track built by Daniel Cook, erected a viewing stand, and applied his astute managerial skills toward improving the estate. Over the years, Oakwood Park Farm gained a stellar international reputation and won him the admiration of his neighbours:

> Look straight down from Mt. Diablo and behold a sight! That dozen or more houses you see belong to John F. Boyd, the largest stock rancher in the world. He owns 6,000 acres of land and you couldn't buy his place and its holdings for less than $1,000,000.00.... Nowhere in California or perhaps in the world is there a spot so admirably adapted to the purpose of stock-raising as the little valley setting off from the San Ramon and occupied by the Oakwood Park Stock Farm. It is a beautiful little valley surrounded by rolling hills that protect it from invading winds and sudden atmospheric changes ... and the herds of cattle and horses that roam in the luxuriant fields and on the hills know of but one season, and that is summer.[1]

Oakwood Park Farm was the ideal place for Louise and the boys to play. The children would have paid scant attention to the notable men and women who passed through their doors or who affectionately cuffed her brothers around the ears when they got in the way. They were oblivious to the reputation of Oakwood Park Farm and their father's growing stature in the state of California as a man of financial acumen. During her childhood years, there would have been madcap indoor games accompanied by wild shrieking and teasing by her two brothers, gentle remonstrances by her mother as she watched over her high-spirited children, whiskery kisses and being flung high into the air and back again by her laughing father, and bedtime stories about California gold prospectors and daring settlers travelling west in their carriages. The imagination of the three children was fired up by tales of adventure and intrepid explorers risking life and limb to reach a distant land, before the children knelt on the polished floorboards for prayers with their mama before the lights were dimmed.

Louise and the boys were tutored during the summer months at Oakwood Park Farm. A young girl's education would have included being taught to play the piano, to draw and sing, and while Louise likely enjoyed these pursuits and the praise of her parents, her mind would have drifted off to whatever harum-scarum games Seth and Jack were planning. Whether fair weather or foul, her father spent much of his time walking the land. As a good stockman, he would have been checking on an ailing horse with hoof disease, reviewing auction lists, purchasing the latest piece of innovative farm equipment, or monitoring race-course results. One can imagine an energetic John Boyd striding to the door each morning with Louise and her brothers imploring him to take them along. As the youngest child and only girl, it was natural that Louise was treated differently. Their mother would have nodded approvingly to the boys, who would be gone in the blink of the eye. After all, they would inherit the estate one day and had to learn how to manage it. Louise, on the other hand, was expected to marry well and adorn the life of her husband. She would have been encouraged to stay behind with her mother and do needlework or some other womanly task. But lively young Louise would have caught her Papa's arm as he strode out the door. His brown eyes twinkling, he likely shrugged his shoulders and exchanged an amused, knowing glance with his despairing wife. Then with an exasperated nod from her mother, Louise would race out the door after her brothers, past the trailing wisteria and fragrant honeysuckle vines and across the grass, always keeping her father and brothers in sight.

Once they had left the safe environs of the manicured family garden, their adventure truly began. Out the back door and across the rustic bridge that spanned the creek behind the house, trudging up over the grassy ridge, then past the dairy and across the fields to the mighty eucalyptus trees ringing the horse-racing track. Then, reaching the viewing stand, the three children would have clambered up the wooden steps and watched excitedly as those beauties were put through their paces, thundering down the course, tails twitching, nostrils flaring, beads of sweat hanging suspended in the air. Louise loved those horses, whether it was watching them trackside or riding them alongside Seth and Jack.

When duties at Oakwood were finished, the weary, grim-faced ranch workers would have returned to staff quarters, lit a roaring fire out back, and swapped tales of the glory days. Perhaps John Boyd joined them on occasion. He would have settled easily amongst these rough and sunburnt men. He was a gruff and plain-speaking man, and with them he was just himself. He would rummage in his pockets distractedly, pull out a stout, worn pipe, and puff away contentedly. One can imagine Seth, Jack, and Louise snuggled up next to his rough leather jacket, gazing at their father with delight while listening avidly to the men's stories of derring-do; Louise waiting breathlessly for her father to recount his own thrilling adventures as a California gold rush pioneer. The boys were perhaps content just to listen, but not Louise. Forever interrupting with probing questions about how he had set snares for rabbits or helped battle a fire after a terrifying mining explosion, Louise absorbed everything. The ability to ask the right questions and remember the answers regarding any number of subjects stood her in good stead later in life.

John Franklin Boyd was not a garrulous man. A self-made man raised in rural Valley Forge, Pennsylvania, he had left home as a teenager to strike out on his own. Short and stocky, with a kind rather than handsome face, he possessed the heart of a lion. Likely leaving home with only a few dollars, the fervent blessing of his mother, and the ambition to succeed in life any way he could, he took up hard, dirty work that covered his room and board and little else. He followed a southwesterly route, eventually meeting some hardbitten fellows who worked the placer mines. Their tales of skirmishes with "Indians," of hiding out in abandoned caves from the law, and of seeking gold that would bring riches beyond his wildest dreams appealed to his adventurous nature, so he travelled onward with them, finally ending up in Virginia City, Nevada.

Virginia City was notorious as a raucous, rough, and lawless town where fortunes could be made and lost in the roll of a die. Virginia City attracted all types, including a cocky young journalist named Mark Twain, who worked for the *Territorial Enterprise* during the 1860s. Twain wrote:

> I discovered some migrant wagons going into camp on
> the plaza and found that they had lately come through

the hostile Indian country and had fared rather roughly. I made the best of the item that the circumstances permitted and felt that if I were not confined within rigid limits by the presence of reporters of the other papers I could add particulars that would make the article much more interesting. However, I found one wagon that was going on to California and made some judicious inquiries of the proprietor. When I learned, through his short and surly answers to my cross-questioning, that he was certainly going on and would not be in the city next day to make any trouble, I got ahead of the other papers, for I took down his list of names and added his party to the killed and wounded. Having more scope here, I put this wagon through an Indian fight that to this day has no parallel in history. My two columns were filled. When I read them over in the morning I felt that I had found my legitimate occupation at last. I reasoned within myself that news, and stirring news, too, was what a paper needed, and I felt that I was peculiarly endowed with the ability to furnish it.[2]

It was while in Virginia City that Louise's father's staunch Quaker work ethic paid off. He compensated for his lack of formal training by being industrious, conscientious, and determined. An 1871 phrenological study of John Boyd noted:

Mechanical ingenuity, Sir, is your predominant gift and is remarkably developed. Your natural place is putting up, repairing and working machinery and setting men to work advantageously. I advise you to connect yourself with some mining operations as a practical engineer for I find every mechanical and intellectual attribute in your brain necessary for ensuring success.[3]

John Boyd likely met and joined forces with Seth and Daniel Cook in Virginia City. Working together, they found success in the mines at last. Boyd and the Cook brothers were raw farm boys from rural America. Hailing from Genessee County, New York, Seth and his younger brother Daniel toiled in the placer mines of Idaho, Montana, and California, where the mining life was "nasty, brutish, and short."

Eventually, their hard work was rewarded, and they attained higher-paying positions within the mines. Seth became superintendent of the Sierra Nevada mine in Nevada, Daniel worked as secretary of the Chollar-Potosi Mining Company in Virginia City, and John Boyd became manager of the Eureka mine. The Cook brothers had notorious reputations as men unafraid of risking it all. Like John Boyd, Seth and Daniel literally clawed their way through muck and mire on their way to the top. When they finally got there, they revelled in their success. Men who were less fortunate openly displayed their envy, as is evident in this poem about the Cooks:

"Yachts and Lots," by D. O'C.

Jones sold out on Friday
A homestead which he prized
Jones had found in Alta
His pile badly sized.
Jones felt sore and sorry,
Cursed his wretched lot
Blasphemed more when Monday
He learned Dan had bought a yacht.

Smith was much disgusted;
Thought it rather hard
Dan and Seth should rastle
Thus their ancient pard.
Said he'd live no longer —
Things were getting hot —
Foamed and frothed on learning
Of Daniel's pleasure yacht.

Jenks (one of the inside)
Bore it rather well
Said that he could stand it.
Cooks could go to _____
Jenks, though taciturn,
Shrieked, "The devil here's my pot
Raked in to buy this pirate
A handsome pleasure yacht."

Seth and Daniel, bully!
Go it while you're young,
Slosh the coin round fully,
Spite of envious tongue.
But don't you think it rash, boys,
After those garrotes
To splurge so soon, so wildly,
Into yachts and lots?[4]

Word reached the Cook brothers of a low-producing mine for sale in Bodie, California, that had been passed over by other mining surveyors. By the 1870s, John Boyd had become a mining engineer known for his shrewdness and integrity. Seth and Daniel dispatched him to investigate the claim. John Boyd had a hunch about the mine, but knew there were no guarantees. Mining on this scale was not for the faint-hearted. After sleepless nights and heated discussions between Boyd and the Cooks, likely bolstered by the finest whisky money could buy, John Boyd took the greatest risk of his life. In September 1876, Boyd, Seth and Daniel Cook, and another partner purchased the property later known as the Bodie mine. The price for the legal claim, explosives, dented mining and blacksmithing tools, tallow candles, and two careworn ponies was $75,000.

John Boyd's insight and sound technical expertise regarding Bodie's potential proved fortuitous. News that miners had struck it rich at Bodie spread like wildfire throughout the state. Miners, storekeepers, gamblers, entrepreneurs, lawmen, prostitutes, preachers, bankers, and all manner of ne'er-do-wells flocked to Bodie. In less than a year, the population swelled from fewer than ten to more than 1,200. The price for building lots escalated from $100 to $1,000. The town of Bodie was bursting at the seams, and during its heyday boasted seventeen saloons, six restaurants, fifteen brothels, four barbershops, four lodging houses, one bakery, two blacksmiths, two drug stores, one jewellery shop, three doctors, four lawyers, two daily stage lines, and a post office. In December 1877, a share of Bodie stock was worth $3.75 but skyrocketed to $53.00 per share only eight months later. The fortunes of John F. Boyd and the Cook brothers were secure. According to the *Bodie Standard* of November 7, 1877:

> But a few short months ago Bodie was an insignificant little place, now she is rapidly growing in size and importance and people are crowding in upon her from far and near, and why? Because of the rich discoveries of gold, "yellow, glittering, precious gold," the bane of man and yet his antidote, his blessing and his curse; his happiness and his misery.[5]

After he had made his millions in the Bodie mine, John Boyd was no longer a down-on-his-luck miner scrabbling out a hard day's pay in the filthy sluice pits or dank caverns below ground. There was no need for him to travel long, dusty hours from one godforsaken hole in the ground to another, overseeing desperate miners who just wanted to give it one more try. He was living proof that any red-blooded American male with perseverance could make it against all odds. By the early 1880s, John Boyd was a man of means. He and the Cook brothers sold the Bodie mine at just the right time and relocated to San Francisco, where they were wined and dined as befitting their status as successful California gold rush pioneers. Once described as "a sea of sin, lashed by the tempests of lust and passion," over the years Bodie faded into an eerie ghost town. Today, set amidst scrubby sagebrush and tumbleweed, the rickety buildings and rusting artifacts are the only remnants of this once-thriving boomtown. Now known as the Bodie State Historic Park, it is maintained in a "state of arrested decay." With its evocative landscape and haunting atmosphere, the park attracts thousands of visitors each year. The stamp mill, assay office, and other sites where John Boyd toiled to strike it rich are still an imposing sight on the rolling hillside overlooking the historic town.

Like many young girls, Louise would have enjoyed hearing about how her parents met, their courting days, and their wedding. In her childish fantasies, she would imagine this was what lay in her own future. Her mother, Louise Cook Arner, had been introduced to John Boyd by the Cook brothers as their niece. She had been orphaned as a teenager. Although almost twenty years her senior, John Boyd was beguiled by the petite, attractive young woman with the heart-shaped face. In John Boyd, Louise Cook Arner encountered a pleasant-faced older man who seemed steady, kind-hearted, and a good provider. Perhaps most importantly, he was a man trusted by her uncles — the two people closest to her in the world.

Louise's mother, Louise Cook Arner, as a young woman. Photograph likely taken around 1883.

Romance blossomed, and a wedding was planned. Sadly, one of Louise's uncles, fifty-eight-year-old Daniel Cook, died suddenly just two weeks before the event. As fulsomely described in the *San Francisco Examiner* on April 29, 1883, Miss Louise Cook Arner married her uncles' business partner and mining crony in a lavish, although still subdued, society wedding at the Colton mansion in San Francisco:

> It would require the pen of Washington Irving, with all his descriptive talent at its zenith, to correctly describe the scene at the elegant Cook mansion on Wednesday evening last. The occasion was the wedding of Miss Louise Arner, niece of the late Daniel Cook and ward of Seth Cook, to John F. Boyd, the mining millionaire. The effect upon entering the house was that of dazzling brilliancy, and as the sound of soft music, mingled with the fragrant odors of sweet-scented flowers, was heard coming as if from a distance, the senses seemed to be stealing away from their

Louise's father, John Franklin Boyd, as a young man. Photograph likely taken around 1883.

accustomed abode — one might suppose to keep following passing strains. It was Fairy Land in real life.[6]

If John Boyd's beginnings were humble and modest, the origins of Louise's mother were, in comparison, decidedly high-brow and patrician. Louise Cook Arner was the only child of Theodocia Cook Arner and Dr. Thomas Arner of Rochester, New York. Both Arner grandparents passed away before Louise was born but she felt she knew them quite well from the romantic stories her mother shared with her and from their distinguished portraits that still graced the walls of Maple Lawn, the family home in San Rafael. Dr. Thomas Arner had a shock of wild dark hair above a high, pale forehead, an unruly beard, and a steady gaze. He served heroically as assistant surgeon with the 108th New York Infantry Regiment during the Civil War, but tragically died of tuberculosis at thirty-five. The daughter of Ira and Louisa Cook and the sister of Seth and Daniel, Theodocia Cook Arner was a teacher at the Rochester Female Academy. A portrait painted later in her life depicts her as a self-assured woman of quiet humour who was reluctant to shed her widow's weeds despite losing her husband when she was only thirty-three. The *Rochester Union Advertiser* described her as "a lady of rare intellect and thorough refinement, she was a bright ornament in the social circle and by her uniform friendly spirit and good nature she endeared herself to all who knew her."[7]

Theodocia Cook Arner was a staunch patriot. Although her husband served in the Civil War for less than a year, she ensured his body was interred in Rochester's Mount Hope Cemetery, where more than two thousand Civil War soldiers were buried. This love of country was passed on to her daughter, Louise Cook Arner (mother of Louise). Louise Cook Arner was an early member of both the National Society of the Daughters of the American Revolution and the National Society of the Colonial Dames of America, whose members claimed direct descent from leaders in the original thirteen colonies. As an adult, she was inordinately proud of her lineage. She maintained an extensive correspondence with genealogical researchers who provided her with evidence of her prestigious forebears. Her children, Seth, Jack, and Louise, were raised on tales of the exploits of these early Americans. When she grew up and began exploring remote polar regions, Theodocia's granddaughter Louise was a proud American who represented her country with a fierce ardour that never abated.

After the tragic death of her husband in 1865, Theodocia Cook Arner was left desperate and alone with her four-year-old daughter Louise. The bitterly divisive Civil War had just ended, President Abraham Lincoln had been assassinated, and her hometown of Rochester, New York, was in upheaval. Following the mining successes of her brothers Daniel and Seth and hearing their stories of sunny California, Theodocia Cook Arner, her daughter, Louise, and Theodocia's father, Ira Cook, left Rochester, jostling and bumping thousands of miles overland in an arduous and bone-jarring carriage journey. This unlikely threesome — the old man, the young, cultured widow grieving for her lost husband, and the bewildered child — arrived in the flourishing community of San Rafael in Marin County, California, with abundant relief and sky-high expectations. It was a thrilling time but it was also a period of great tumult since they had left their home, their friends, and all that was familiar to them to move across the country in hopes of a promising future.

Since moving to San Francisco a few years earlier with his brother Daniel and partner John Boyd, Seth Cook had had his eye on San Rafael in Marin County. Like many of the gold rush pioneers, the Cook brothers and Boyd wasted no time in joining the ranks of real estate speculators. While Boyd and Daniel Cook primarily bought property in San Francisco, Seth Cook purchased a small home on a ten-acre plot in San Rafael. Located within a warm valley and surrounded by gently rolling hills, San Rafael offered endless opportunities for growth, as well as proximity to San Francisco. Upon their arrival in California, Seth moved his father, sister, and niece to his new property. But Theodocia had not borne the rigours of the journey well. Shortly thereafter, she fell ill with tuberculosis — the same disease that had killed her husband. The Cook family had always been close and Seth did everything he could to care for his only sister. According to *The Hospital Review*, "The last years of her life, a brother's love and affection provided her with every comfort and luxury that wealth could procure or heart desire."[8] Sadly, the dry climate failed to improve Theodocia's health and she died in June 1876.

Mourning the sudden loss of his daughter, Ira Cook and his fifteen-year-old orphaned granddaughter Louise Cook Arner sought comfort through engaging in brisk activity. Earlier that year, Seth had hired an arborist to plant magnificent trees and gardens. The San Rafael house was enlarged and renovated and an elaborate Gothic Revival gatehouse was built to accommodate guests. In 1879, the *Marin Journal* reported, "The work being done by Mr. Ira Cook at the corner of Sixth (current Mission Ave.) and B Street and on the face of the hill to the north, is unique and grand and when completed, the place will be one of the most beautiful to be found on this coast."[9] Ira Cook's plans were never finished — he passed away in August, 1880, at the age of eighty. Having lost both her mother and her

An interior view of Louise's home, Maple Lawn, in San Rafael, California, with portraits of her mother (centre) and maternal great-grandparents on the wall. Photograph taken by Ansel Adams in the late 1960s.

grandfather within four short years, a bereft nineteen-year-old Louise Cook Arner became the ward and heir of her Uncle Seth.

Three years later, Louise Cook Arner (hereafter referred to as Mrs. Boyd) married John Boyd. Seth Cook generously gave the newly refurbished San Rafael home to his favourite niece as a wedding gift. John Boyd spared no expense in importing diverse native and exotic species of flowers, shrubs, and trees to delight the eye of his young bride. As an enduring and public testament to his love for her, a floral tribute spelling out "Louise A. Boyd" was prominently located in a garden located at the eastern side of the house. Now recognized as one of the finest abodes in San Rafael, the Boyd family home was officially named Maple Lawn, because of the splendid Japanese maples that adorned the estate.

The happy couple soon started a family. In August, 1884, their first child was born, and was named Seth Cook Boyd after Louise's uncle who had shown them such kindness. John Franklin Boyd Jr., known as "Jack," arrived two years later. Their third child and only daughter, Louise Arner

LEFT: Louise's brother Seth Cook Boyd.
RIGHT: Louise's brother John "Jack" Franklin Boyd Jr. Both photographs taken around 1900.

Boyd, was born on September 16, 1887. Seth, Jack, and Louise were all born at Maple Lawn.

Although a busy young mother, Mrs. Boyd became a leading society woman in thriving San Rafael. In 1874, San Rafael had become an incorporated town with a population of 600, which rose to 2,665 by 1899. Both Mr. and Mrs. Boyd were prominent philanthropists and supported causes including the first San Rafael library, and St Paul's Episcopal Church. A self-described capitalist, John Boyd formed the Boyd Investment Company to manage his burgeoning real estate and stock interests. His offices were located in the prestigious Nevada Block in the financial district of San Francisco, and he was praised as a man with a promising future:

> The writer suggests the name of Mr. Boyd for the next Governor of the State.... We speak without authority,

Louise and her mother, Louise Cook Arner Boyd. Photograph taken in 1888.

simply from our knowledge of the man. He has no political ambition. He is satisfied with the prizes already won.
He has done much hard work, has realized his hopes and is
taking things easy. He is still young and vigorous in health.
He has a lovely family to whom he is all devotion.... His
investments and interest in paying mines give him just
enough business to defy ennui. Do you suppose you could
tempt such a level headed, happy man to become the petty
office distributor of the State?[10]

Louise's childhood, whether in San Rafael or at Oakwood Park Farm
near Danville, was spent investigating the joys of the natural world. For six
months of each year, the Boyd family lived at Maple Lawn in San Rafael.
John Boyd was likely absent much of the time as he travelled to San Francisco
on business. In San Rafael, there were myriad delights to tempt the inquisitive children. Often, Seth, Jack, and Louise hiked up the dry manzanita
slopes of nearby Mount Tamalpais, or hunted squirrels at the Freitas Ranch.
Louise was a crack shot with a steady hand. Unlike her brothers, she had no
gun of her own, but was a skilled and enthusiastic markswoman by the time
she reached adulthood. One of her treasured possessions as an adult was her
father's .44 derringer pistol, which she kept all her life. Weather permitting,
the three children would swim lazily in the San Rafael Canal or wander
aimlessly through the B Street Marsh looking for frogs. When Seth, Jack,
and Louise returned from a day out running helter-skelter around the wilds
of San Rafael, their cuffs torn, dirt smeared across their cheeks, exhausted
but happy, her mother would likely chide Louise for her carelessness while
her brothers got off scot-free.

Family outings were always anticipated with glee. In the early days,
before the San Rafael roads were paved, the children would climb up into
the carriage next to their mother and travel sedately down Mission Ave. to
B Street. There at the corner was a favourite candy store, where Mrs. Hoover
would serve them delicious ice cream sodas. Every Sunday, they attended
the regular services at St Paul's Episcopal Church, where the Boyd family
had a front pew. After the service, they might drive down Fourth Street past
the Opera House Block, where Louise would wave merrily to kind Mr.

Wolfe the druggist. Then past Mr. Magne's Dry Goods Store, down C Street past the Bay View Carriage Factory, Murray's Livery Stable, and Cochrane Brothers' Horseshoes, where they sometimes were allowed to stop and feed the horses. There might also be an obligatory social visit to their mother's friends, the Menzies or the Dollars. Then down B Street past Hertzog and Co. Butchers, and home again to Maple Lawn.

Reading was another of Louise's passions. Her mother had inherited a magnificent library from her uncles and grandfather, and Louise enjoyed reading stories about polar exploration the most. As the dutiful daughter of patriotic parents, young Louise was keen to learn about American exploits in the polar world. She read about George Washington De Long's tragic voyage on the *Jeannette* while searching for the open polar sea. She was haunted and intrigued by grisly tales of the disastrous Greely Expedition, which began as a scientific and rescue mission but ended with sensational charges of cannibalism among the surviving crew. For imaginative Louise, the hours would have flown by while she dreamed about the men daring enough to brave this remote and mysterious region.

John Franklin Boyd's .44 derringer pistol.

The thought that a woman could be a polar explorer would have been too far-fetched for her to consider.

Louise attended Miss Stewart's School in San Rafael and then Miss Murison's in San Francisco, where she would have made friends with girls from other *nouveau riche* families. Miss Murison's was a progressive and academically rigorous educational institution; unlike others, which were mere stepping-stones toward European finishing schools. Seth and Jack entered the newly opened Mount Tamalpais Military Academy in San Rafael, where students were groomed for West Point and military careers of distinction. As Louise grew older, she was gradually introduced to the social milieu in which her mother circulated. Following the example of her own mother, who had worked ardently on behalf of women in Rochester, Mrs. Boyd was one of a coterie of wealthy San Rafael women engaged in working for the social good. Young Louise would soon be joining this elite group.

Louise and her brothers led idyllic lives, cared for by their loving parents, and their bright futures seemed secure. In the late summer of 1901, Louise was approaching her fourteenth birthday. Her eldest brother, Seth,

Louise with her mother and brothers. Photograph likely taken around 1894.

had turned seventeen a few weeks previously, and they would have had a jolly celebration. On Tuesday, August 13, the Boyd family spent a happy day in San Francisco, and returned to Maple Lawn in the early evening. Later, Louise was to recall that Seth had felt restless and unwell that day. The following morning Louise awoke to pandemonium outside her bedroom door. Shockingly, Louise's eldest brother Seth had died unexpectedly in the night. According to the *Marin Journal*:

> He retired at about 10 o'clock and the next morning at about a quarter to nine, when his mother went to his room to call him, she could get no response, but discovered the odor of gas coming from the room. She at once called Mr. Boyd who attempted to force the door open, but being unable to do so, one panel was broken and a younger son, John F. Boyd Jr., crawled through and opened the door. They found the young man lying on the floor face downward, dressed in his nightshirt and with his slippers on. He was lying with his head about two feet from a gas stove with his face toward the stove. The gas for the stove was about one-quarter turned on. It was his custom to get up during the night, warm and drink some milk. He had evidently been in bed and gotten up to heat the milk.... The death was purely accidental.[11]

Louise's parents were struck down with grief from the loss of their first-born child and heir. Young Jack and Louise were deprived of their older brother, their playmate and comrade-in-arms. Later, the family learned that Seth's death had been caused by a weak heart, aggravated by rheumatic fever. Alarmingly, Jack was known to have a weak heart, too.

The new school term began the following month and Louise's mother was determined that life would carry on as normally as possible for her children. In September, Louise returned to Miss Murison's and Jack entered The Thacher School in Ojai, California, as a new pupil. Founded by Yale graduate Sherman Day Thacher, it had a sound reputation as one of the leading educational institutions for boys in California. According to the school application completed by his mother, Jack was a truthful, straightforward boy, somewhat behind in his classes due to absences for health reasons. His transition to a new school, so soon after the loss of his older brother, was somewhat eased by the knowledge that his beloved horse Piker would be accompanying him. Louise's mother wrote to Headmaster Thacher, "He is young and perhaps easily lead and any advice or guidance you can give him towards strengthening his character and inculcating good moral principles into him will meet with our approval. Should Jack displease you or be disobedient, let me know and I will admonish him. We want an honest, manly, Godfearing man and work to that end."[12] From the day he started attending his new school, Louise's mother was in constant correspondence with Headmaster Thacher about Jack's progress and about his health. On Feb. 25, 1902, Headmaster Thacher wrote to her:

> Enclosed please find Jack's report. His eighteen late marks
> are a few too many: but for one fortnight he made an effort,
> and got on the Honor List, as you know. His record in
> his lessons is, on the whole, excellent. He is taking a good
> many subjects and doing very well. He is one of the boys
> we all depend upon for right doing and as a help in the
> school in every way.[13]

Jack was one of the most popular boys, although he was among the youngest. He entered into Thacher school life with vigour and became captain of the cavalry drill. In late March, Mrs. Boyd received the disquieting news that Jack was confined to bed with a chill after over-exerting himself during a school outing. The doctor was called and reported that Jack was expected to make a full recovery. Unbelievably, another harsh blow was delivered to the family. Jack passed away at school, four weeks from his eighteenth birthday:

> Every hope was entertained of his recovery, when suddenly
> his heart, which had been weak before he was taken ill,
> broke down completely, and a week later he passed away,

mourned by forty classmates and teachers, whose respect and love he had so thoroughly won in the few months he dwelt among them. On the same afternoon, the troop of which he had been the commander, in cavalry formation, escorted the hearse and Mr. and Mrs. Boyd to the special train which awaited them. For the next thirty days, the flag at half-mast and a small knot of black on every coat were the only outward signs of the deepest grief.[14]

Jack's death, coming a mere eight months after Seth's, brought the family low. Like Seth's, his death was due to endocarditis. The loss of a child is the single most devastating blow a parent can experience. It is hard to grasp the strength of will that must have been required by parents Louise and John Boyd to continue on. Fourteen-year-old Louise's feelings following these tragedies have not been recorded. Still only a child herself, she knew only that she had lost her protectors, her best friends, and perhaps the only people who truly understood her. It is likely that young Louise did everything in her power to ease the heavy burden that had been placed upon her parents. Although only tender in years herself, she was doubtless aware what the loss of his sons and male heirs meant to her father. As loving as he always was to Louise, his boys were his pride and joy, as well as his assurance that the Boyd bloodline, and all he had worked for, would live on.

It was Louise's mother who saved them. She made sure that their rhythm of life and daily routine continued despite their overwhelming grief. She assumed responsibility for family and business matters as a heartbroken John Boyd retreated into himself. Mrs. Boyd's poignant correspondence with Headmaster Thacher following Jack's death emphasizes her steely resolve. Louise never really knew at what personal cost she did this. It was tragic enough to be a mother who had lost two children, but to maintain composure throughout that ordeal and for years afterward must have required extraordinary courage. In an eleven-page letter written to the school, Louise's mother expressed gratitude to the students and faculty of Thacher for the care they had shown the Boyds:

Be always assured dear Mr. Thacher of our sincere and earnest good wishes for the school and the entire Thacher family. We are proud to have made such friends in spite of the sadness connected with everything. I am glad to say that I have kept remarkably well and Mr Boyd is growing stronger daily and feels less broken. We pick up the threads of life as best we may, and working for each other helps us individually to be brave. But oh, the heartache! I suppose time may assuage the pain and soften the awful sense of separation.... Louise is well and the sorrow develops many womanly qualities. She helps both her father and me very much. Louise and Mr. Boyd add their best remembrances to mine to be shared amongst your family and members of the school and faculty.[15]

Mr. and Mrs. Boyd channelled their suffering into ensuring that the memory of their boys would live on. The Jack Boyd Clubhouse was established for the use and enjoyment of young people in nearby Ojai Valley. The Jack Boyd Memorial Prize in English was endowed at The Thacher School, and the Seth Cook Boyd Memorial Medal for Proficiency in English was set up at Mount Tamalpais Military Academy. Two stained-glass windows at St. Paul's Episcopal Church in San Rafael were commissioned in memory of Seth and Jack. Of the eight windows currently gracing St. Paul's, the stunning Boyd memorial window is remarkable for its nature images depicting the San Rafael hills and the oak trees that the boys had loved so dearly. These windows never failed to provide comfort when Mr. and Mrs. Boyd and Louise attended Sunday services. For Louise, it was a constant reminder for the rest of her life of the dear brothers who were lost to her.

But Louise's parents wanted to do even more to honour their boys. What grand gesture could they make? Eventually, Mr. and Mrs. Boyd donated twenty acres of their expansive Maple Lawn estate to the town of San Rafael for use as a public park — a fitting memorial to the two boys who had played there with such abandon.

Louise likely suffered deeply as a result of her parents' decision to donate part of the Boyd property to the town of San Rafael, as so much of the land where she, Seth, and Jack had played was carved up and given away. Louise was bereaved as only a child who loses all her siblings can be. Her big brothers had been her near-constant companions and playmates, both at Maple Lawn in San Rafael and at their summer home at Oakwood Park Farm. She had relied on them for guidance and advice. After their deaths, she often found solace amongst the great oaks and eucalyptus trees, and would tramp up and down the hills of the Boyd family estate at Maple Lawn. But the decision to donate the land was not hers to make. In late April 1905, Boyd Memorial Park was dedicated, and the whole town came out to celebrate. The *Daily Independent* reported:

> Last Saturday was a day long to be remembered by the residents of San Rafael. It was a day set apart by the City to receive a most munificent gift from a noble man and woman. By eight o'clock in the morning the flags were floating to the breeze from all of the public buildings and the City presented an appearance of real holiday attire.

Boyd Memorial Park, with the original Boyd Gate House, in San Rafael, California. Photograph taken in 2015.

Nature was exceedingly kind in giving us an almost perfect day. The main streets presented an unusually busy appearance and towards noon, the trains brought many visitors who came to participate in the ceremonies. By two o'clock both sides of the street along the entire line of the march were thronged with a grateful people.[16]

Promptly at two o'clock, a cavalry detachment from the Mount Tamalpais Military Academy headed the procession, starting from E and Fourth Streets with all the pomp and circumstance demanded by the occasion. They were followed by the 5th Regiment band and Company D, the cadets of Mt. Tamalpais Military Academy, the St. Vincent Orphan Asylum band, members of the San Rafael Fire Department, Hitchcock's Academy band and students, children from the local Parochial school, twelve girls from Miss Stewart's School, and city officials. Louise and her parents rode in the last carriage. Heartfelt speeches of thanks were given by dignitaries and then Mr. and Mrs. Boyd were called upon to say a few words. While her husband sat ashen-faced beside her, Mrs. Boyd rose and asked that three cheers be given for the good people of San Rafael, and especially for the children.

Several months later, the family travelled to Europe in search of some much-needed peace and quiet. They visited friends and enjoyed the local attractions. Then, quite unexpectedly, their fragile sense of calm was suddenly ruptured by devastating news from home. On Wednesday, April 18, 1906, a powerful earthquake struck San Francisco and the coast of northern California. The massive quake and resulting fires — caused primarily by ruptured gas mains — destroyed more than 80 percent of the buildings in San Francisco. The flames raged for four days and nights before being brought under control. One journalist wrote:

To those who make occasional visits to San Francisco and are familiar only with the more notable buildings and famous places, the best idea can be gained when they realize that every theater, every widely known store, every wholesale house, every downtown hotel, every famous building including the residences on Nob Hill are either prostrate in ashes or gutted wrecks. The blocks of wooden buildings are leveled to nothing.[17]

Marooned in Europe, the Boyds were distraught, particularly since they were so far from home. *How was San Rafael affected? Was their home Maple Lawn still standing? What had happened to their friends?* Within days, John Boyd had booked passage home. They travelled to Cherbourg, France, and there, with other concerned Americans, boarded the ocean liner *Kronprinz Wilhelm* for the long journey home.

No words could capture the family's devastation at seeing that changed landscape when they arrived in San Francisco. Mr. Boyd hustled his wife and daughter as quickly as possible to San Rafael. They were relieved to discover that their home and community had miraculously avoided most of the damage.

Thousands of San Franciscans who had been left homeless flooded into neighbouring towns. Refugee camps were set up all over. San Rafael's first hospital, incorporated only the year before, was soon overwhelmed with the most critically injured victims of the fire and quake. Louise and her mother joined forces with the Ladies Relief Committee, along with their good friends Mrs. Menzies and Mrs. Kent. Eighteen-year-old Louise learned firsthand about the importance of teamwork during a time of crisis. Operating under difficult circumstances and having to think on her feet, Louise enjoyed the camaraderie. Meanwhile, preparations and plans were soon under way for the rebuilding of San Francisco. Although they responded to this new challenge with energy and zeal, Louise would have wondered how much more her poor mother and father could take. They had suffered such trauma over the past few years that it seemed tranquility would never be restored to their family. It was not until the summer of 1906 that happier times would visit them once again.

CHAPTER TWO

SHAPED BY ADVERSITY

Character is best formed in the stormy billows of the world.
— JOHANN WOLFGANG VON GOETHE

On October 21, 1906, throngs of elated San Franciscans gathered eagerly on Telegraph Hill and along the wooden wharves still bearing the scars of the quake and fire. Hearty cheers rang out and a sea of arms waved furiously as local citizens, including perhaps nineteen-year-old Louise and her parents, welcomed the official arrival of the battered Norwegian sloop *Gjøa* as she sailed through the Golden Gate into San Francisco Bay. A few months previously, captained by Norwegian explorer Roald Amundsen, the *Gjøa* had successfully navigated the fabled Northwest Passage from east to west during an epic three-year voyage that some compared to the discovery of America by Columbus and his sailing fleet. A *San Francisco Chronicle* journalist reported:

> The *Gjøa* is not a beautiful specimen of naval architecture and unless one knows the history of the splendid little craft, it is not likely that a second thought would be

bestowed upon her. She is a tubby, unwieldy-looking boat measuring seventy-three feet over all, twenty feet beam and twenty feet deep. Her rig is unusual. Technically she is a sloop but a large yard has been added enabling the settling of a square sail when sailing before the wind. At present the vessel sets high out of the water and is painted green and yellow.[1]

For a few heady weeks while Amundsen was in town, San Francisco put aside its woes. Amidst the charred buildings and the rubble left from what is still considered the worst natural disaster in United States history, high society revolved around receptions and banquets given in the explorer's honour. John Boyd and his wife would quite likely have attended one of these, as John was a prominent local businessman. At the very least, talk of Amundsen and his accomplishment in being the first to find and traverse a route between Europe and Asia, linking the Atlantic and Pacific Oceans, would have dominated conversation in the Boyd household. Given her childhood interest in polar exploration, Louise would have wanted to meet the weather-beaten and craggy-faced Norwegian hero who had been

The *Gjøa* on display in Golden Gate Park, San Francisco, California. Photograph taken after 1906.

Statue of Roald Amundsen in Tromsø, Norway.

glimpsed at society occasions or seen striding through the San Francisco streets. But Mr. and Mrs. Boyd made sure that Louise was safe at Maple Lawn, the primary Boyd residence in San Rafael, just north of San Francisco — away from the potential hazards of the devastated city and in a protective environment where they could keep a watchful eye on her. As a diligent mother, Mrs. Boyd surely did her best to harness her daughter's vitality and restless spirit by encouraging Louise to attend lively parties and dances. She also regularly took part in fundraising occasions organized by the worthy women of San Rafael.

Earlier that year, Mrs. Boyd had taken a risk by hosting Louise's official début into society. It was only four months after the earthquake and the city still lay in ruins, but Mrs. Boyd gambled that the right people would welcome a glamorous occasion amidst the gloom:

> The picturesque suburban home of John F. Boyd was the scene today of a notable event in social circles when Mr. and Mrs. John F. Boyd formally presented their charming and accomplished daughter, Miss Louise Boyd. From 3 to 6 this evening, there was a continuous line of carriages bringing hundreds of guests to greet the new debutante. The parlors were tastefully decorated for the occasion and many, taking advantage of the splendid weather, strolled about the beautiful grounds surrounding the Boyd home.[2]

Regrettably, it seems Louise did not make an indelible impression on the hearts of any of the potential suitors in attendance, despite her mother's best efforts. All society mothers knew that establishing lifelong friendships in those rarefied circles would ensure a young woman's social standing and find her the perfect mate. As a wealthy heiress and daughter of a well-respected California pioneer family, Louise was an attractive candidate for marriage. Poised and self-confident, with a vivacious nature — perhaps a trifle over-confident in expressing her opinions, some may have thought — she never lacked friends. This would serve her well later in life, when she needed all the support she could get.

A formal portrait of Louise taken in New York, likely in the early 1920s.

As the sole surviving child, she was the focus of her parents' attention whether she wanted it or not. Louise dutifully accompanied her mother to a constant stream of philanthropic events and her time was occupied attending one social function after another. As she grew older and the first flush of young womanhood faded, she would have been increasingly aware that many of her closest friends were marrying and moving on to the next stage in their lives. It seems that Louise hadn't yet found her soulmate, and her father's possessiveness whenever a man courted her didn't help.

Mrs. Boyd undoubtedly worked tirelessly to find Louise a husband. She would have taught her all the necessary skills required by a modern upper-class American woman at the turn of the twentieth century — how to effectively run a houseful of servants, how to graciously entertain visiting dignitaries, and how to adroitly assist one's husband in advancing his career. Yet Louise must have sensed her mother's underlying ambivalence. After all, both of her sons had died and Louise was the only child left to the still-grieving parents. It is possible they were fearful that Louise would be the target of an unscrupulous individual attracted only by her fortune. In none of Louise's surviving letters or diaries does she describe any particular male friends, so it is not known if any romantic liaisons were quashed by her parents. It is likely that, as her parents aged, Louise had no wish to leave them during the final years of their lives. They had all suffered enough loss. In any event, Louise never married.

John Boyd still travelled frequently between his Nevada Block office in San Francisco and Maple Lawn in San Rafael. After the deaths of his sons, he never regained his former vigour and strength. Increasingly, a pressing need arose to begin grooming Louise to assume control of her father's business. Now in his sixties, he was often unwell and his physician urged him to retire. Under her father's tutelage, and with the assistance of financial and legal advisors, Louise began managing her father's multimillion-dollar company while also caring for her increasingly enfeebled parents. It was a tremendous burden for one individual to assume. But it would have been while working for the Boyd Investment Company that Louise acquired valuable lessons she put to good use later on when planning an expedition: put everything in writing, no matter how mundane; be obsessively meticulous and detail-oriented; and delegate to those with greater technical skills and more experience. In that male-dominated world of high finance, she likely encountered discrimination on the basis of her gender for the first time. Even though she bore the golden name of "Boyd," Louise was venturing into privileged territory traditionally denied to women.

Over time, as she assumed control of her father's investment and real estate empire, she would have expressed her opinions more assertively and would have taken a greater role in decision-making. It would not be the last time she dared to challenge traditional gender stereotypes.

As her parents' world narrowed and they relied on her more, Louise found she had to bring the world to them. A voracious reader, Louise probably combed newspaper headlines for the most enthralling stories to capture their interest. It would also have been a way for her to temporarily escape from what must have been, at times, her stifling domestic responsibilities. Throughout 1908–09, the Peary-Cook North Pole controversy was splashed regularly across the front pages of American newspapers. Widespread coverage of this contentious issue — in which two noted explorers each claimed to have been the first man to conquer the North Pole — provided an ongoing and stimulating source of wonder and bemusement for households across the country, including the Boyds.

The turn of the twentieth century had been marked by a sensational race for the North and South Poles. Funded by thrill-seeking millionaires and media moguls, more Americans entered the world of polar exploration, which had once been dominated by the British, Norwegians, and Russians. The "American Onslaught" of 1898 through 1909 was led by American adventurer/explorers including Walter Wellman, Evelyn Briggs Baldwin, and Anthony Fiala, who launched their own attempts to conquer the North Pole during this period. Yet it was two larger-than-life Americans who dominated the stage at that time and whose exploits and bitter feud continue to stir passions today.

Within four days of each other, in September 1909, while travelling on separate expeditions, Dr. Frederick A. Cook and Commander Robert E. Peary each claimed the North Pole for the United States. With the *New York Herald* and the National Geographic Society backing Peary and the *New York Times* supporting Cook, the American public — and the Boyds — were riveted by this fascinating real-life drama as it unfolded. At the same time, Amundsen visited San Francisco again as part of a lecture tour. Polar enthusiast Louise would have been intrigued to discover that Amundsen was a colleague of Frederick A. Cook and had sailed with him a few years earlier on the Belgian Antarctic Expedition (1897–99). Amundsen seemed unstoppable, as he captured one elusive polar prize after another. The following year, on December 14, 1911, he planted the Norwegian flag at the South Pole, besting British naval officer Robert Falcon Scott by a mere thirty-four days. Scott and several of his party tragically perished in a storm shortly after discovering Amundsen's flag.

Louise was as enthralled by these contemporary tales of the North and South Poles as she had been as a child. The lure of the North only intensified as she grew older. Reading about these brave exploits likely sustained her during challenging times when she was required to stay close to home to care for her aging parents.

Oakwood Park Farm, the former Boyd residence in Diablo, California. It is currently a private home. Photograph taken in 2014.

In 1912, Louise's parents sold Oakwood Park Stock Farm, her beloved summer home near Danville in Contra Costa County. Completely unbeknownst to her, her mother had been trying to sell the property for years. Louise was nearly twenty-five by then and past the years of running wild and free across the land. Truth be told, after Seth's death eleven years earlier, the family had rarely returned there. But it would have been a hard thing for Louise to lose her childhood haunts and those special places that she most closely associated with her brothers.

Britain's declaration of war on Germany in 1914 did not greatly impact the Boyds' small world at Maple Lawn. President Woodrow Wilson's policy of neutrality was widely accepted in the United States and was one that the Boyds likely supported. However, this opinion shifted dramatically as news of German atrocities in Belgium and the German sinking of the *Lusitania* in 1915 with 128 American lives lost caused outrage amongst the American people. On April 6, 1917, the United States entered the war, participating until armistice was declared and the war ended in November 1918.

Unlike so many other families, the Boyds were spared the loss of a family member in the Great War. The virulent outbreak of Spanish influenza across the United States, and indeed worldwide, was much more significant and hit much closer to home. This highly contagious and often fatal illness had spread to southern California. Those individuals with compromised immune systems, such as her parents, were especially susceptible, so Louise would have taken every precaution necessary to keep her parents safe. At home in Maple Lawn, the Boyds restricted their movements out-of-doors as much as possible. A local ordinance was issued requiring citizens to wear preventative gauze masks when in public. Headlines such as "Citizens Indignant at Mask Slackers" and "Five Arrested as Flu Mask Slackers" were both alarming and comical, but underscored the dire health situation. By mid-November, doctors advised that the epidemic was under control and the number of cases began decreasing. That Christmas of 1918 was more subdued than usual as Louise and her parents reflected soberly on how they had escaped the clutches of the dreaded flu epidemic, and that the Great War was thankfully at an end.

The following summer, Louise grew increasingly concerned about her parents' health. During the fall of 1919, Mrs. Boyd was admitted to Adler's Sanatorium in downtown San Francisco. For the next several months, Louise hardly left her mother's side. As Mrs. Boyd's health deteriorated, so, too, did Louise's hopes for her mother's recovery. Mrs. Boyd passed away on October 2, 1919, at the age of fifty-eight:

> Mrs. Boyd has been one of the most beloved women for San Rafael for many years. To her and her husband the city's gratitude is due for the Memorial Park which bears the family name and which was donated to the municipality to commemorate the names of John Franklin and

Louise's mother in later years. Photograph likely taken around the early 1910s.

Seth Cook Boyd, the two sons whose untimely passing was a grievous blow to the parents some years ago.... Notwithstanding the fact that since she was stricken there has been but little hope of her recovery, the shock to her countless friends here when her death was announced caused them to suffer keen grief.[3]

Mrs. Boyd's funeral service was held at St. Paul's Episcopal Church in San Rafael. She was laid to rest next to Louise's brothers in the Boyd mausoleum at Mount Tamalpais Cemetery and Mortuary. The flag at San Rafael City Hall flew at half-mast that day.

Louise had no time to grieve; no time to reminisce, or berate herself for failing to see how ill her mother had been. She had to devote herself entirely to her father's care. He had borne up bravely until his wife's funeral, but then it seemed he no longer wished to live. Six months later, Mr. Boyd misstepped and fell down the long staircase at Maple Lawn. He

Louise's father in later years. Photograph likely taken around 1905.

was transported to the hospital in great agony after sustaining a fractured left leg and internal injuries. He died five days later, on May 3, at the age of seventy-seven:

> Mr. Boyd was highly respected in San Rafael and his large circle of acquaintances, both business and social. For the past dozen years he had passed his summers with his family in his home here, which sits near the gates of Boyd Memorial Park, his gift to the City of San Rafael to commemorate his dead sons both of whom died in early youth. Some years ago he retired from business, in which he had amassed a fortune estimated at about $3,000,000.00. He was preceded in death by his wife, Mrs. Louise Arner Boyd, just a few months ago and is survived by but one child, a daughter, Miss Louise Boyd.[4]

The Boyd family mausoleum, Mount Tamalpais Cemetery and Mortuary, San Rafael, California. Photograph taken in 2015.

Louise was bereft. The enormity of her grief weighed heavily upon her. Most tragic of all was the timing of the loss. Her brothers Seth and Jack had died within months of each other. For poor Louise, history repeated itself as both of her parents died within the same year. She had known her parents were unwell and would have prepared mentally for this day as best she could, but it had not been enough. Her friends rallied around her, but there was no escaping the fact that she was thirty-two years old, a millionairess, and completely alone.

Portrait of Louise Arner Boyd. Photograph likely taken in London, England, in 1925.

Months later one of Louise's closest friends, Sadie Pratt, persuaded her that she needed a complete change. Sadie was married to Lieutenant-Colonel (later Major-General) Henry Conger Pratt, who was also a good friend of Louise. In September 1920, Sadie and Louise boarded the transatlantic ocean liner SS *Olympic* for a three-month sojourn in Europe. This trip would have allowed Louise time to grieve, but also provided an opportunity to reflect on what the next steps on her life's journey would be. Louise related:

> I realized that for my own good I must disconnect myself from the past, and find and create new interests not associated in any way with the sadness that had so completely absorbed many years. They must be constructive interests upon which I could build not only pleasure but worthwhile accomplishments in the future. The most difficult mental obstacle I had to overcome was the fact that after being a definite part of other people's lives for so many years, I was no longer needed. There was nobody to come home for: my job which had been so all-absorbing was ended.[5]

But the trip seemed doomed to failure. Upon arrival in Europe, they travelled to France and Belgium, where they witnessed the horrifying results of war — devastated forests, mass graves as far as the eye could see, rubble-strewn and ruined buildings. Hardly a destination to raise the spirits. They travelled on to Switzerland, Italy, Yugoslavia, Luxembourg, Holland, and England.

Returning on the SS *Aquitania* from Southampton, the two women arrived in New York just in time for Christmas. It had been an unusual travel experience, but the memory of her parents had rarely been far from Louise's mind. Only time would heal those wounds.

Several years later, Louise's life was stagnating. She was still engaged in the same philanthropic work as before. She visited friends, threw convivial parties, attended prestigious gallery openings, and chaired important committee meetings. For many women, this would have been sufficient for a fulfilling life, but not for Louise. Not for the woman who dreamed of icy lands and heroic deeds. She led a comfortable life at her sumptuous home, Maple Lawn, and it was a life that offered her familiarity and security. It took four years after her parents' deaths before she was able to summon up the courage and take the first momentous step toward realizing *her* dreams.

In 1924, Sadie Pratt and Louise set off on another grand European adventure. But this time the real reason for the trip was Louise's desire to visit the land of her hero, Roald Amundsen. Louise was thrilled as she and Sadie travelled widely throughout Norway, Denmark, and Sweden. But the best was yet to come.

On August 8, 1924, they boarded the SS *Irma*, a sturdy passenger steamer, and sailed north along the western coast of Norway toward the stormy coast of Svalbard. The *Irma* stopped at several small Norwegian ports along the way, including Bodø and Tromsø, whose names were familiar to Louise as the bases from which many famous sealers and vessels bound for the Arctic had departed. But Louise was not content to idly observe from the comfort of *Irma*'s deck. She secured permission to board several of the ships in port, and she and Sadie, along with her new friends, fellow passengers the Count and Countess Ribadavia from Madrid, gingerly climbed the gangways and explored as much as they dared. Louise found it to be a stirring two weeks spent sailing the frigid waters of the Arctic Ocean. She remarked:

> Continuing northward beyond North Cape, our boat took us to Spitzbergen and the pack ice north of there. This was the part of the trip to which I had looked forward the most, because through my reading I had formed a very vivid impression of the appearance of pack ice. On the day when our small boat reached the edge of the ice, the weather was bad — both windy and foggy. In order not to miss anything I remained up and on deck all night. About six o'clock in the morning the skipper nosed the

boat into the outer edges of the ice and those of us who were up early had a brief glimpse of it.[6]

Louise was entranced. It was everything she had ever hoped for. The *Irma*'s captain was surprised by her enthusiasm. Her willingness to accept harsh conditions onboard ship and her intense desire to penetrate deep into the pack ice impressed him. He asked her what she thought of the ice, since she had waited her whole life to see it. Her response foretold the unusual path that she would soon adopt: "Captain," she replied. "I want to be in there some day, looking out; not here, looking in."[7]

Louise was true to her word, and noted that it was exactly two years later, to the day, when she landed several miles north at frozen and remote Franz Josef Land and gazed out over the polar ice fields.

The following year, newspapers throughout the world announced that Roald Amundsen was striving to accomplish another extraordinary goal — that of reaching the North Pole by air. This daring feat marked the beginning of a new era in polar exploration:

> The First World War interrupted exploration towards the North Pole, but neither that, nor the widespread belief that the Pole was already conquered by Peary, inhibited explorers from continuing to try to reach it. On the contrary, the war period, and the years immediately following it, brought major technological advances which completely changed the face of exploration and stimulated a whole new era of attempts to attain both the North and the South Poles. The object now was not to be the first to get there, but to be the first to get there by other means.[8]

Amundsen was determined to be at the forefront of these new adventurers. He wrote in his autobiography: "The future of Polar exploration lies in the air. I make bold to claim for myself the distinction of being the first serious Polar explorer to realize this fact, and the first to give a practical demonstration of its future possibilities."[9] Astonishingly, he learned to fly a mere eleven short years after the historic Wright Brothers' first flight at Kitty Hawk. His first daring aerial expedition would take place in 1925, when he and American millionaire explorer Lincoln Ellsworth proposed flying over the North Pole. Transported by ship to their base in King's Bay, Spitsbergen, and accompanied by esteemed pilots Hjalmar Riiser-Larsen (later to be well-known to Louise) and Leif Dietrichsen, and two mechanics, the intrepid team encountered poor weather, bad luck, and the catastrophic loss of one of their two German Dornier Wal airplanes. Given the pioneering nature of this flight, it was not unexpected that Amundsen, Ellsworth, and their team encountered grave difficulties and were lucky to return with their lives.

Halfway across the world, Louise Arner Boyd received an invitation she could not refuse. Along with seven other American women, Louise was invited to Buckingham Palace to be presented to Their Majesties King George V and Queen Mary:

> Popular in the smart set and particularly prominent in the society realm of California, Washington and New York, a host of ardent friends followed with intense acclaim the first news that brought word of Louise Boyd's formal presentation in Buckingham Palace. The presentation ceremony at the court of their majesties, King George and Queen Alexandra [sic], was one of the most brilliant events even of such magnificent affairs, which has ever been chronicled. Radiantly attired American women, present when Miss Boyd made her courtly bow to their royal majesties, accompanied the lovely California heiress in what has been rightly termed on of the most fascinating and elegant presentations in years. The elegant gown worn by Miss Boyd has been described as befitting her charms and loveliness. Silver tissue elegantly embroidered with pearls and sparkling stones was used as the texture of her gown. A court train of blue velvet lined with blue tissue and edged

Louise being presented at Buckingham Palace, London, England, on June 26, 1925.

with the rarest of chinchilla fell in graceful folds from the
gown and she carried the conventional feather fan required
by all who are presented at the British court.[10]

A court presentation represented the pinnacle of any woman's social
career, and particularly so for those few American women lucky enough to
receive an invitation. As Louise stepped forward to curtsey to their Majesties,
she had never felt prouder to be an American. Her father began life on a
humble Pennsylvania farm and, through sheer hard work and perseverance,
became a California gold rush pioneer, dying a wealthy man. And now, his
daughter, Miss Louise Arner Boyd, had met the reigning King and Queen
of England. While delighted to be there, Louise would have been painfully
aware that this honour was the result of her inherited wealth and status,
rather than her own accomplishments.

When she returned to Maple Lawn, Louise must have felt restless and
anxious, unable to settle. She had taken many precious photographs on her
last trip, and sifted endlessly through them. A significant change was on
the horizon for her. By the spring of 1926, she knew what her next course
of action would be. She was determined to follow where her heart led, no
matter what the cost.

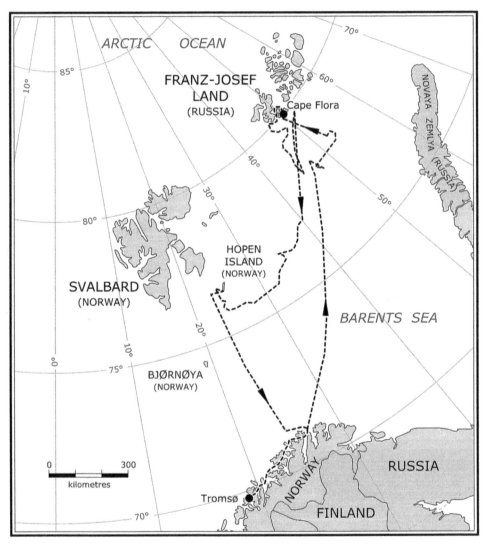

Route of Louise Arner Boyd 1926 Expedition.

CHAPTER THREE

"Diana of the Arctic"

She senses her life's compass
Has just set its pointed foot and the rest of her years
Will rotate around it.
— Elizabeth Bradfield [1]

During the summer of 1926, when the Norwegian polar ship *Hobby* was tied up at quayside in Tromsø harbour and bulging crates began accumulating on the sagging wooden pier, excited townspeople knew that another daunting Arctic voyage would soon be under way. But where would the ship be going, and who would be sailing on her? *Hobby* was a favoured maritime daughter of Tromsø and of all northern Norway. She had been Amundsen's base ship, transporting the two airplanes associated with his 1925 attempt to fly to the North Pole, and had also helped American explorer Richard Byrd. Following Byrd's pioneering 1926 flight to the North Pole, his base ship, the SS *Chantier*, had required *Hobby*'s assistance after becoming immobilized in the impassable ice.

Similar in size and capacity to many contemporary polar vessels, including Amundsen's *Maud*, which had successfully sailed through the

The *Hobby* docked at harbour in Tromsø, Norway.

Northeast Passage in 1924, *Hobby* measured 130 feet from bow to stern, 24 feet in width, with a gross tonnage of 300 and an average speed of 8 knots. Built in 1918 at Arendal, Norway, and refitted in 1921, *Hobby* was sturdy and stalwart rather than sleek and elegant. As a relatively new ship, she had not yet acquired the battle scars of older vessels, despite her critical role in polar history. But her mettle had already been tested in unforgiving Arctic waters.

The frenetic dock activity increased as, day after day, the people of Tromsø watched in gleeful anticipation. Gulls wheeled and dived as husky local lads lucky enough to be hired to help outfit *Hobby* staggered up and down her gangway, loading heavy fuel cans, sloshing water barrels, a bulky wireless radio, spare marine parts, a prized collection of Springfield rifles, sharp harpoons, overladen boxes, food, and finally the heavy leather chests and suitcases of the privileged passengers. This was a familiar sight at the harbour. But, as the departure date grew nearer, local citizens were in for a

Louise's suitcase (designed by Louis Vuitton).

surprise. *Hobby's* next trip out would be an unusual one and differed from all earlier trips in one key respect: when *Hobby* sailed proudly from Tromsø harbour, it would be as part of the 1926 Louise A. Boyd Expedition — the first Arctic sea voyage planned, organized, and financed by a woman — and an American, at that.

Months earlier, Louise had taken the first momentous step. She was tired of travelling aimlessly and longed to experience the freedom of the open polar sea once more. Like her countryman, explorer Robert Peary, she yearned to be "free from discussions, from entanglements, from social complications."[2] The trip she had in mind was unlike any she had undertaken before. Louise wanted to sail the Arctic Ocean again and return to that remote and mysterious region that had struck a chord in her heart. After much research, she decided on Franz Josef Land, that tantalizing region she had only heard about two years previously on her Norwegian pleasure cruise. Located due east of Svalbard and due north of the Russian island Novaya Zemlya, no Western woman had yet set foot there, and for good reason. Unwittingly, she had chosen a destination that was notoriously difficult to reach, because of treacherous ice and weather conditions that challenged the most knowledgeable seaman. Additionally, at that time, Franz Josef Land was a political hotspot.

Historically regarded as *terra nullius* or no man's land, Franz Josef Land had been seized by Russia only three months previously. Russia was a volatile country still reeling after the 1917 October Revolution, but it was considerably more powerful than Norway. There was no way of knowing how Russia might respond to a ship, flying the Norwegian flag and the American Stars and Stripes, landing on territory it claimed as her own.

But where to begin? What was the next step for Louise in planning this expedition? If a man had wished to undertake such an adventure, he would have contacted noted polar experts, technical advisors, and even male relatives with outdoor experience and fix-it skills. Louise Arner Boyd had recourse to none of these. She knew how to organize a lavish six-course dinner party for 150 guests, choose a winning thoroughbred for the next race, or even converse knowledgeably about the variations between the Western tree species *Pinus radiata* and *Pinus radiata* var. *binata*. Preparing for an Arctic expedition was quite another matter. Instead, Louise relied on her greatest assets — her impressive social network and the goodwill of friends in high places. She wrote to the Count and Countess Ribadavia, whom she had met on her 1924 Norwegian cruise. They shared Louise's passion for the North and were keen to join her proposed voyage. They also provided her with the name of Spanish mariner Francis J. de Gisbert. The initial contact between Louise and Gisbert was prickly:

> I wrote to Mr de Gisbert telling him of my desire to go into the far north. By return mail came an answer declining to take me because I was a woman. He had never taken a woman, and frankly said that he did not wish to do so. I was turned down but not defeated! I replied at once that I fully appreciated his point of view but that I was determined to go into the pack ice and to lands beyond it. I explained to him also what I had learned on my first trip north, told him that I had visited sealers with the idea of a trip in mind … Mr. de Gisbert was much surprised that I had not accepted his first letter as final. When he realized that I did know something about the project I had in mind, he wrote that he would be glad to meet me and talk the matter over.[3]

With this first critical choice of expedition leader, Louise demonstrated an unerring instinct for choosing the right person for the job despite her own inexperience. Previously, her only involvement in employing individuals had been confined to hiring domestic servants for her San Rafael home. This hardly prepared her for her current enterprise. Yet her innate qualities as an astute leader were slowly evolving. A distinct portrait of Gisbert emerges from the pages of *Modern Whaling and Bear Hunting: A Record of Present-day Whaling with Up-to-Date Appliances in Many Parts of the World, and of Bear and Seal Hunting in the Arctic Regions* by Scottish painter, travel writer, and explorer William Gordon Burn-Murdoch. In this account of an 1911–12 whaling cruise in the North Atlantic and a 1913 bear-hunting trip to East Greenland, Gisbert is presented as a consummate adventurer, a gifted musician, and a hearty raconteur. Of middling height, handsome, broad-shouldered, and with wavy hair and a bushy salt-and-pepper beard, Gisbert had sailed Arctic waters for twenty years and hoped to participate in an ambitious Spanish National Polar Expedition. The son of a former consul to Spain, Gisbert was charming and well-educated, and could play a mean mandolin and guitar. Louise shrewdly surmised that Gisbert offered the perfect combination of skills for what she had planned, and that he would be able to adroitly handle both *Hobby* and her cultured guests.

Francis J. de Gisbert and Louise. Unknown date and location.

Through ensuring that Gisbert signed a lengthy, iron-clad contract, she implemented business practices acquired while working for the Boyd Investment Company. This detailed contract was a requirement demanded of every expedition member, both at that time and in the future, and was designed to protect her own legal and personal interests. Gisbert's contract outlined the terms of the expedition as well as his specific roles and responsibilities. He agreed to "personally lead and direct the expedition according to the wishes of Miss Louise A. Boyd who will furnish him with instructions which he will execute with the utmost good will and dispatch."[4] Although the trip was due to last approximately six weeks, she reserved the right to extend the trip another three weeks in the event of unforeseen occurrences. Most importantly, Gisbert agreed that he "and all members of the Crew and Attendants shall do their best to please Miss Louise A. Boyd and make the expedition a great success in every way."[5]

The goal of the six-week 1926 expedition was to sail north to Franz Josef Land and, if possible, to nearby King Charles Land and North East Land. Louise's preparatory notes indicate a burgeoning scientific interest in visiting these islands. A meteorologist from the Institute of Geophysics in Tromsø named Backman was onboard to collect data, but few details exist about how he came to join the expedition or what he accomplished.

Louise adopted the role of expedition photographer with gusto. She was determined to capture all nuances of the trip through shooting both still photographs and cinematic film, which was considered an innovative process at the time. However, the trip was also planned as a "Shooting Expedition" in which Louise claimed exclusive rights over all "skulls and skins of bears, reindeer, seals and walrus." As was in evidence during this voyage, her zeal for hunting had continued unabated. Playfully referring to Louise as "Diana of the Arctic," a friend penned a rhyme about her.

> There was a young lady named Boyd
> Whom polar bears tried to avoid
> For when she fired shot
> They went where 'twas hot
> With a joy not unalloyed.[6]

With the ship secured and Gisbert's services engaged, Louise oversaw all further preparations to ensure that the trip would be comfortable for her guests. Like many aristocratic adventurers of the nineteenth century, Louise travelled in style. Accordingly, she ensured that the ship's provisions included enough liquid libations to see them through their journey. Along with twenty-one tins of Gold Flake cigarettes, the ship was stocked with twelve bottles of claret, twelve bottles of sauternes, twelve bottles of champagne, four bottles of whisky, four bottles of cognac, twelve bottles of sherry, and sixteen bottles of beer. As stipulated in Gisbert's contract, the wine, beer, and spirits were specifically for the enjoyment of Louise and her three guests.

⚜

Hobby slipped quietly away from the Tromsø pier at 6:00 a.m. on July 29, 1926, with all officers, crew, and passengers onboard. Much to Louise's annoyance, the wireless man managed to smuggle his powerful and bad-tempered German shepherd Basso onto the ship.

Their departure was noted by the Norwegian, American, and international press. According to a *San Francisco Chronicle* headline, "S.F. Woman in Arctic Hunt: Louise A. Boyd Included in Polar Film Trip Led by Spanish Engineer." That story likely irked Louise, since she was the one doing the organizing and, therefore, wasn't just being "included."

As Gisbert had arranged, the guest cabins were spacious and commodious. Louise settled into the sunny cabin at the stern while her friends Janet Coleman and the Count and Countess Ribadavia had cabins on the starboard side. Everyone onboard was happy to finally begin the journey. Like Louise, Janet Coleman was a member of an old California family and belonged to the exclusive San Francisco, Washington, and New York social sets. To her family's knowledge, this was the only trip of its kind that the more retiring and traditional Janet ever took. Louise's other guests were the darkly handsome couple Ignacio and Blanca, the Count and Countess Ribadavia. As members of the Spanish nobility, they circulated in more elevated social spheres. They shared Louise's taste for adventure and for game hunting on a grand scale.

Hobby sailed north, following the jagged Norwegian coastline, passing fishing trawlers whose grizzled seamen hailed them with a hearty "God Reise *Hobby*!" For the first day, grey clouds blanketed the sky, but the occasional splatter of rain did not dampen the spirits of those onboard. Gisbert had full confidence in the crew he had chosen. Captain Kristian Johannesen and mate Astrup Holm were both senior officers experienced in Arctic navigation and sailing these hazardous waters. Johannesen had been *Hobby*'s master only the previous year as part of Amundsen and Ellsworth's unsuccessful attempt to fly to the North Pole.

When the weather shifted and dense fog kept them entombed in one spot, Gisbert entertained all onboard with tales of his polar exploits. He was more garrulous than his Norwegian comrades, and his daring tales enthralled Louise and her guests. He and Louise suited each other fine, since he liked to talk about the Arctic and she liked asking questions. Although at this time Louise possessed a certain level of knowledge about polar matters, she was eager to learn more. She pressed Gisbert to talk about female explorers in the region. Gisbert replied:

> Lady Franklin had funded many Arctic expeditions to search for her long lost husband who had disappeared in the ice waters when he was trying to discover the Northwest Passage. I also believe that a princess funded another expedition but none of them took part in the trip. You are, without a doubt, the first woman, Miss Boyd, to freight and equip a ship in order to navigate the polar seas. These are trips that, before you, women had not embarked upon.[7]

His admiring words undoubtedly made Louise's cheeks glow. The respect Gisbert expressed toward her and her female guests could only have raised him in her estimation.

> The skipper went on deck, sniffed the air and said "I smell the ice. We'll soon meet it."... Needless to say, my untrained nose got no smell of ice — it only inhaled cold

air that pepped one up and made one feel very fit and fine. "Smell the ice," with its significance of meeting the pack ice, meant something to me! It meant the realization of two years of planning and I stayed up, outside on the bridge with the captain and de Gisbert, as the hours rolled by, in anticipation of a prelude to a new chapter in my life — the opening pages of my future years in the Arctic![8]

A few hours later, as *Hobby* sailed through the water, the first ice floes appeared all around. From the crow's nest, a crewman barked orders, directing *Hobby* through the ice fields: "Port side! Hard left! Straight ahead!" The helmsman steered the wheel to avoid hitting the ice, but sometimes impact was inevitable. As the ice collided with the ship's hull, *Hobby* jolted, shuddered, and then carried serenely on her way. Louise, Janet, and the Ribadavias were deeply moved by the spectacle. Louise confided in her journal: "So fascinated and interested was I in our entrance into the ice, it was 3:30 a.m. before I went to my bunk, and then only upon what almost amounted to compulsion by Captain Johannesen and de Gisbert, who wisely foresaw long days ahead of me."[9]

Early in the voyage, wildlife sightings were rare. They had seen only seals until, at last, they heard a shout, "Bjørn! Bjørn!" It was the first, momentous, polar bear sighting. It was still far in the distance and Louise and her guests watched breathlessly as the bear lumbered directly for the ship. There was no question about what to do. Louise dashed to her cabin, threw open her locker, and pulled out her rifle. Louise, Gisbert, Count Ribadavia, and a few crew members descended precariously to the ice. Louise related her excitement: "My brain left all of me that was feminine behind on the ship, and, with Army Springfield over my shoulder, with a man-size stride and will power, I set out with de Gisbert and two of the crew, bound on proving I belonged there just as much as the men!"[10]

Eyes trained on the approaching animal, nerves steeled, she waited as the old male bear plodded toward her. Then, lifting the gun resolutely to her shoulder, she fired the first shot. The bullet penetrated the bear's shoulder and was stopped only by his ribcage. Two more bullets did the trick and the bear fell dead. Crewmen Sverre Sørensen and Ivar Anstad approached the

Louise the huntress onboard the *Hobby* during the summer of 1926.

bear with ropes, tying them about the animal's neck and legs, and dragged it to *Hobby*. All crowded around and marvelled at its size. The bear was two metres long and weighed 372 kilograms. Back onboard, Louise received hearty congratulations from all and they celebrated the first kill with a champagne supper party. Count Ribadavia later wrote that not many things in life produced such intense exhilaration as being faced down by a magnificent polar bear. Gisbert, the crew, and the Ribadavias were amazed by the courage Louise had displayed and the vigour with which she participated in hunting the polar bear. She may have been a sophisticated socialite, but she was no shrinking violet.

Captain Johannesen set a northeasterly course for Cape Flora on Northbrook Island, one of the nearest islands in the Franz Josef archipelago. Louise nailed a map of the area on the galley wall and Mate Astrup Holm dutifully plotted their new position throughout the day.

For the next few days, *Hobby* sailed a perilous course through the ice. Visibility was poor and the wind blew relentlessly. Captain Johannesen spent anxious hours on the topmast scanning the horizon with his telescope. He was uneasy about what he saw before him. He later confided to Count Ribadavia: "The ice field is always treacherous. I'm 43 and I've been sailing these seas since I was 18. I know the ice and its malicious ways. Every year, seal hunters … get trapped in the ice. Some are able to free themselves, but many are lost. If the crew is able to free the ship, it is only after great effort and much terrible suffering."[11]

But Gisbert scoffed at Johannesen's pessimism, retorting that only seamen who were careless got caught in the ice. Count Ribadavia wrote that the two men complemented each other perfectly. Gisbert's daring nature was tempered by scientific knowledge, while Captain Johannsen represented prudence and experience.

With the dense fog and ominous ice conditions, *Hobby*'s progress toward Franz Josef Land continued to be slow and laborious. Louise had given orders to the captain that "nothing was to be met or passed without my being called, day or night."[12] Apart from bridge and chess games, hunting parties were a favourite pastime, particularly of Louise and Count Ribadavia. Ribadavia relates that, as a result of the successful bear hunts, the cook was able to expand his culinary repertoire. In his journal,

Ribadavia stated wryly that as more bears were killed, Johnson added fresh meat to his "more or less flavourful" meals.

It was at mealtimes that Gisbert revealed his lighter side. In a document found amongst Louise's papers, she relates how *Hobby*'s hard rocking and pitching created havoc in the kitchen galley. After only a few days into the journey, all the tablecloths were filthy. Learning that Louise used blankets on her bed but not sheets, Gisbert devised a unique solution to the problem of dirty tablecloths:

> The following morning, at an early hour, my ear detected sounds of a great deal of tearing — repeated sounds of "Rip, rip." "What's that?" I thought, and going in the direction of the sound, I found de Gisbert in the mess tearing white objects full length. Turning to me, he said, "Louise, don't tell the others, but you know, these sheets are not really dirty. I'm just tearing them in two so each will make two tablecloths. True to his word, a change in covers met our

Captain Kristian Johannesen. Unknown date and location.

eyes at the noonday meal. A clean-looking cover covered the mess table and in answer to comments of pleased surprise, de Gisbert and I avoided each other's glances, when he said to them, "There was a mistake. We have table cloths but not sheets." De Gisbert, himself, has passed from this world and the pack ice he loved so dearly, into that of the Great Unknown, and until that time, it remained between us, one of our secret memories, over which he and I had many a good laugh![13]

The weather seemed to be conspiring against them. No sooner had *Hobby* made slow progress for a few hours than Captain Johannesen would call a sudden halt and all was still. One morning, Louise woke to find the ship anchored and surrounded again by impenetrable fog. Now even Gisbert recognized that their objective of reaching Franz Josef Land was in jeopardy. This dismal news resulted in despondency, among the guests and crew alike. The heavy, dank fog enveloping *Hobby* caused their spirits to sink further.

After being confined to the ship for almost a week, Louise was desperate to relieve the monotony and provide a much-needed diversion. Despite the plummeting temperatures and poor visibility, Gisbert recklessly agreed to accompany Louise, Count Ribadavia, and two crewmen on a seal-hunting jaunt. Captain Johannesen, Janet Coleman, and the Countess Ribadavia would have watched in consternation as the hunting party set off in a row-boat in search of seals. The small boat was soon swallowed up in the fog. As an experienced leader, Gisbert should have known better. Seal-hunting on the water is challenging enough at any time, since the seal's head emerges only for a few seconds and seals rarely swim close to a rowboat. But in poor conditions, it was madness. After hours of searching, and with several crack hunters onboard, Louise and the others had succeeded in shooting only one seal. And, although Gisbert had paid close attention to their position with watch and compass, the rowboat had strayed much farther than they expected in search of their elusive prey. As time dragged on, returning to the *Hobby* after their jaunt proved difficult. The banks of fog had grown more dense, and Louise feared they were lost. For more than two anxious hours, the crewmen rowed toward what they thought was the *Hobby*, only to discover she was nowhere to be found:

> As time went by, one of the seamen blew on a whelk he had with him. There was no response to his sound and it was starting to get less and less amusing as the cold and hunger began to affect us. After calling again, we heard three gun shots that indicated the direction of the ship. This was opposite to the direction we had been heading towards. Guided by the shots and the siren of the *Hobby*, we moved closer to the ship until it suddenly appeared before us. It was so close that we could clearly hear the conversations onboard. Moral of the story: It is reckless imprudence to leave the ship on foggy days.[14]

Louise, Gisbert, and Count Ribadavia were overcome with relief at the sight and sound of the ship. All were well pleased to clamber onboard and no further escapades in the fog took place for the duration of the expedition.

Over the next few days, the level of tension on the ship as a result of their recent frightening incident was dissipated by the sighting of more bears. Louise and the Count and Countess were enlivened by the prospect of sport and more mighty polar bears fell to their guns. A female bear was shot and her two cubs were taken alive onboard. Gisbert wanted one for a zoological park in Hamburg and the Ribadavias wanted another to present to King Alfonso XIII of Spain. The cubs were lassoed and brought onboard while strong cages were constructed for them. Louise remarked:

> On coming on deck, I found all the crew and ship's officers in the bow in conference. Their faces were serious and very determined. Now and then a burst of laughter broke the tenseness of the situation. I asked what it was all about and learned that the polar bear cubs had to be named and it was bad luck to anyone to have such a cub named after him. No wife, sister or sweetheart must ever have her name given to a polar bear cub. If the men thought any man was

in love with a girl and suggested her name for the cub, they immediately found out in this way if he really loved the certain lady. I left them and returned to my diary writing in the mess room while various Norwegian names were suggested. When I returned on deck, Captain Johannesen told me, "Ve ho you don't mind, but ve have called one cub Louise and de other Blanca (after Blanca Ribadavia)." I had a good laugh and told him that was fine, that nobody loved me or cared for me or Blanca and that naming the cubs for us was fine. They were splendid specimens and I liked Polar bears anyway and Countess Ribadavia felt as I did. Captain Johannesen's face fell. He had completely forgotten what they had told me![15]

Despite the light tone in which Louise related this story, the underlying message that no one loved or cared for her was a hurtful one. It was a bitter reminder that, when the journey ended, there would be no loving partner or children waiting for her at home.

❧

As the weeks continued to pass, Louise settled into the ship's routine. Living with strangers in confined quarters in freezing temperatures with no privacy and a significant language barrier must have been quite an adjustment for a single woman used to living alone in a mansion. Additionally, sailing to Franz Josef Land was a dangerous undertaking at that time, regardless of the experienced crew and captain. And yet, Louise's correspondence and reminiscences about this expedition reflect only good humour, curiosity, and eternal optimism — and more than a touch of naïveté:

Under my bunk were two drawers and in them I stored my woolen underwear, sweaters, shirts, and woolen socks. Ordinarily this cabin was occupied by the skipper Astrup Holm. In the drawers I found sticks a foot or more long that looked so like sticks of Christmas candy ready to be tied up with holiday wrappings and hung on a Christmas tree, that I mentioned the fact to Astrup Holm. "What are they?" I asked. "Candy?"

With a look that pierced right through and down into me, he said, "No, not candy. They're dynamite!" He then asked me if I smoked. If so, for Almighty's sake, not to do so in the bunk or let ashes or any fire reach the sticks. Receiving a negative reply and assurance that I never smoked in bed, he requested me to leave them there so he would always know where they were and where to get them — it was a good safe place for them! As for a safe place for me, nothing was said…! And so, throughout that voyage northward through the ice fields of Barent Sea to Franz Josef Land, as well as that of two years later in search of Amundsen, the "Christmas Candy," in reality dynamite, and I shared a mutual small cabin![16]

Louise enjoyed learning about the crew she was sailing with as well as the region they were exploring. She was intrigued to discover a hidden side to the intelligent, level-headed Captain Johannesen.

August 13 fell on a Friday that year, and in the spirit of the day, Captain Johannesen sat down to dinner with Louise and her guests and shared superstitions held by Norwegian seamen. Louise might have been amused to learn that the seamen believed in leprechauns and omens and found prophetic significance in dreams. Cool and cautious Captain Johannesen turned out to be extremely superstitious, as he told them solemnly that the ghost of an old sailor roamed his seal-hunting vessel, the *Autumn*. He had also dreamed that the polar bear cubs they had captured freed themselves and were headed to his son's bedroom in Norway. Louise would have crossed her fingers that his superstitions didn't interfere with his duties onboard.

Traversing the Arctic was never easy. Navigating by the stars was often impossible, since the sky was almost always cloudy or shrouded by fog. The horizon was difficult to identify, behind the fluctuating ice floes.

After relentless foggy weather, the sun finally shone through, weakly, but enough for Gisbert and Johannesen to take sextant readings. Their calculations put them farther east than previously thought, but also showed that they could set a clear heading for Cape Flora. Their goal was in sight. After sailing over a hundred miles through the ice field, *Hobby* was travelling steadily toward Franz Josef Land.

Suddenly, the fog cleared, and it was as if a curtain had lifted. Cape Flora appeared, a ring of clouds crowning its summit. Louise and her guests gathered on the bridge, transfixed. Years earlier, explorers Weyprecht and Payer had been similarly enthralled:

> We beheld from a ridge of ice the mountains and glaciers of the mysterious land. Its valleys seemed to our fond imagination clothed with green pastures, over which herds of rein-deer roamed in undisturbed enjoyment of their liberty.... There was something sublime to the imagination in the utter loneliness of a land never before visited.[17]

Louise was overwhelmed by emotion after having travelled so far and nearly being turned away. Farther west, they could glimpse Bell Island and Cape Grant. As they anchored off the coast of Cape Flora and readied the rowboat for landing, the excitement level amongst the guests and crew was heightened. The weather had not been propitious. Until only a few hours ago, it seemed that Louise would be denied. But here she was, about to claim her prize.

Franz Josef Land is a foreboding and uninhabited island archipelago. Despite its remoteness and lack of access, or perhaps because of them, it has held a compelling attraction for Western explorers since the late nineteenth century. Military officers Carl Weyprecht and Julius Payer on the *Tegetthoff* officially "discovered" the islands during their 1871 Austro-Hungarian North Pole Expedition and named it for Austrian Emperor Franz Josef. In seeking to find the Northeast Passage, Weyprecht and Payer had believed that Franz Josef Land was a massive continent stretching to the North Pole. British expeditions led by Benjamin Leigh Smith of the *Eira* in 1880 and 1881–82 continued exploration in the southern region, but the *Eira* was caught in the ice and crushed. Forced to overwinter, the crew was rescued the following year. The Jackson-Harmsworth Expedition of 1894–97 on the *Windward* made an exhaustive survey of Franz Josef Land, and discovered that it was a series of islands rather than one extended land mass. Serendipitously, Jackson and his crew rescued the noted Norwegian explorer Fridtjof Nansen during his momentous 1895–96 journey on the *Fram*. Further expeditions by American journalist Walter Wellman in 1898–99, the Italian Duke of Abruzzi in 1899–1900, and the Baldwin-Ziegler Expedition of 1901–02 explored and mapped this region. Franz Josef Land had also long been a destination for Norwegian sealing captains who plundered the waters for walrus, seals, and bears.

Fierce winds whipped around *Hobby*'s landing party as they set foot on Cape Flora, on Northbrook Island, the most accessible island in the archipelago. The current had been vigorous, and it had not been easy for five brawny crewmen to row them ashore. Janet Coleman's diary relates: "The Captain's parting words to us were to return as soon as possible. It is not wise to linger long around Franz Josef Land."[18]

Captain Johannesen's warning was ambiguous. Ever-vigilant, he would not have wished to put *Hobby* or her passengers in any danger from shifting weather or treacherous ice conditions. However, due to his own experience of these Arctic waters and his close contact with other skippers eager to protect Norway's commercial interests in sealing and hunting in this area, he would have known that Russia had claimed Franz Josef Land only a few months previously. Most significantly, it is almost certain that he was aware that Russia had officially notified Norway and other foreign powers of its claim in May of that year. As a result of this formal declaration, Norway's engagement in hunting and other economic activities in the region should have ceased immediately.

One would have thought that Captain Johannesen's personal history would have made him averse to becoming embroiled in a potential Russian-Norwegian conflict. In 1918, Johannesen had been arrested by the Russians and accused of being a spy after his ship, the *Autumn*, broke down while hunting in the White Sea. But Norwegian captains sailing in Arctic waters were a law unto themselves and would disregard official territorial disputes when it suited them, as Louise would discover during a later expedition. While the captain and Gisbert were likely aware of the current situation with Franz Josef Land, it is not known if Louise had been informed, or if she herself was aware of the potential political ramifications of their visit. The *Hobby* was lucky this time, as no Russians were in evidence during their visit. But the situation could have been quite different.

After the precarious landing, Louise, Gisbert, Janet, the Ribadavias, and a few crewmen made their way over the snowy shores, greeted by the sharp yipping of white foxes dancing at their heels. Amidst the raucous cries of nesting guillemots and gulls, the group rambled at will. Most of Northbrook Island was covered by an ice cap, but Cape Flora was a rare exception. Despite the biting wind, Louise joyously collected samples of the diverse flora bursting with riotous colour, including bright green tangled mosses, waving Arctic poppies, white saxifrage, and low-lying yellow buttercups. Several of the species could be found only in that region. Botany was a newfound interest of hers. She hoped that her photographs and the botanical specimens she collected would complement other data collected during this voyage.

Following a short visit to the ship for a hurried lunch, Louise and her guests returned with great anticipation to Cape Flora in the early afternoon, searching for signs of earlier expeditions. Louise stated later:

> My thoughts were mixed between my personal delight and tremendous interest in being at Cape Flora, and at the same time, I was not blinded or numbed to the realities of the past, which here seemed so very present and so very alive, in a land where men had perished in the pursuit of science and exploration.... [Here] were the visible reminders and unspoken tell-tale signs of the hardships and sacrifices of the past.[19]

The group was lost in thought as they encountered stark evidence of the tragic fate of the explorers who had been there before. There was a roughly hewn wooden cross — "W. Mouatt, died June 17, 1895, *S. W. Windward*" — indicating the resting place of a Jackson-Harmsworth Expedition member. Further evidence of this expedition's camp lay all around them as they trod gingerly through the scattered ruins of abandoned sleighs, pieces of dog harness, weathered boots, broken bottles, and rusted pots and pans. A can of food cached for this 1894–97 expedition was opened and, unwisely, tasted by the group, who pronounced its flavour surprisingly good. Farther on, there was another cross covered with moss, on which were engraved the names "Foueroni H. Stokker F. Ollier *Stella Polare* 1900." These men had been members of the Italian Duke of Abruzzi's 1899–1900 Expedition on the *Stella Polare*.

Rummaging amongst a cache of rocks, Louise found a lead tube containing an old document. Sadly, that paper was damaged and impossible to read, but there were other documents there written in Norwegian and Italian. They added their visitor cards to the other papers and slid the tube back into place. Count Ribadavia wrote:

> Among the names that we were leaving there, three of them deserved to be placed next to those of the most famous explorers: Miss Louise A. Boyd, Miss Coleman, and the Countess Ribadavia, who are to this day the only women who ever set foot on these lands and to be first at something is usually so difficult to achieve that it deserves to be recorded and disclosed. But much of the glory goes to Miss Boyd, who was the first woman to freight a ship to be transported to the remote regions of the Arctic.[20]

But time was short, so after only three hours of exploration, the landing party returned to *Hobby* and settled down to a hearty meal. The weather was closing in, so the crew lifted anchor and set sail.

As she had throughout the entire voyage, Louise had been busy photographing. She had already amassed several canisters of cinema film and a growing collection of still pictures documenting the expedition to date. Although Johannesen and Gisbert were accustomed to their customers taking photographs, they noted that Louise's keenness for photography was unusual. Unlike other society ladies, who simply enjoyed posing for photographs, Louise demonstrated a dedication to photographing and filming every slight variation in ice patterns, every nook and cranny along the coastlines they explored, and every bear and seal they encountered. Gisbert later remarked to her admiringly:

> If ever anybody deserved a success for the amount of work put in a job, you certainly deserved one. For although I have had many professional operators on my trips, I have never had one as keen or taking as much trouble and care with the filming as you did. I am sure you edited the films very cleverly, and the titles! Well they are sure to be splendid, containing some of your wonderfully descriptive and nippy remarks like "from boots on till boots off!"! I am simply longing to see them and hope you will publish some soon.[21]

Louise's photographic skills would improve over time as she sought technical advice from professionals and bought more sophisticated equipment. Nevertheless, her instinct for the type of photograph required was sound. After the expedition was over and the film developed, Louise's hard work resulted in a fine collection of almost six hundred photographs focusing on different kinds of sea ice, terrain features, polar bears, and seals.

After leaving Franz Josef Land, the *Hobby* headed for Norway in a southerly direction. Passing through Nightingale Sound, Louise and her guests saw Bell Island, where Eira Lodge — the sturdy cabin built by Benjamin Leigh Smith in 1881 and still in excellent condition — was easily visible. After they searched fruitlessly for walrus and seals, stormy weather beset them, with large ice floes surrounding the ship. Temperatures plummeted.

Janet Coleman confided to her journal, "Excellent day for bridge and [working on] the tapestry. So cold at night that we indulged in a bit of brandy and hot water bottles."[22]

As the end of their expedition drew nearer, Janet shared a secret desire to shoot a bear. No one was more surprised than Louise, but, once alerted, all were on the lookout for an easy target. That opportunity soon presented itself. Count Ribadavia recounted the tale:

> I quickly went to get her to come down and I found her in her cabin at her usual work, wearing her beautiful pink slippers lined with white fur. She rapidly replaced them for enormous boots and left her cabin nervously without thinking about grabbing a gun. Somebody went to get it. The bear was swimming at about 40 meters from the front of the ship. Miss Coleman seized the weapon, shot and killed the animal with the first bullet. The novice huntress, very surprised with her performance, received a warm ovation from all of us.[23]

Although Janet Coleman was quietly pleased with her prize, polar bear hunting was not an activity in which she participated again.

Life proceeded quietly for the guests. They read or played cards. Louise classified the plants and flowers she had collected at Cape Flora and took photographs of the fluctuating sea ice during the last leg of the journey. Countess Ribadavia made an unusual model of *Hobby* out of cardboard boxes, which everyone admired, and Janet completed her tapestry. After encountering many enormous icebergs, they saw their first Norwegian ship and passed Hopen Island. The sea became even stormier and even stalwart sailors Count and Countess Ribadavia were forced to retire to their cabins. Count Ribadavia recalled that afternoon:

> Lying on my bed, the memory of the tender bear fillets tortures my stomach and the one of the seal meatballs makes it quiver. Two or three times, the door opened and Jonson, bracing himself against the walls, asked me if I

wanted anything to eat. "For God's sake! Don't talk about food!" This is how the day went. Blanca, in the cabin next to mine, was feeling the same way. However, the heroic Miss Boyd ate, smoked and went on deck. It is true that her arms went blue with bruises after constant bumping but how can it compare to what we endured?[24]

Although she sympathized with her indisposed guests, Louise confessed to an uncharitable feeling of glee that she was the only person apart from the crew who was capable of standing on the bridge at such a time. She felt she belonged there.

Finally, on September 9, they arrived at the pier in Tromsø, Norway. They were all saddened to leave *Hobby* and the fine crew. What a time they had shared. Louise bade goodbye to the Ribadavias, and shortly thereafter she and Janet travelled to London, England.

During their London visit, they stayed at her usual suite of luxurious rooms at Claridge's. They hosted parties for their friends, who marvelled at the exotic display of polar bear skins and seal pelts and admired Louise's photographs of glaciers and pack ice. Louise also granted interviews to several journalists who wanted to hear her Arctic tales.

Experienced polar hunters doff their hats to Miss Louise Arner Boyd of San Rafael, California, who has returned to London after a six weeks trip into the Arctic. To Miss Boyd belongs the distinction of having been the first woman to set foot upon desolate Franz Josef Land, to which she made the voyage up on Roald Amundsen's old supply ship *Hobby*. From the eightieth degree northern latitude, Miss Boyd returned with the pelts of twenty-nine polar bears, six of which she shot in one day. This, it is considered, is enough to turn envious any Arctic hunter. There was nothing in the appearance of the slim American girl, clad in modish knee-length dress of black georgette, to suggest tussles with Arctic beasts as she sat in the drawing-room of a West End hotel telling The Associated Press a story of

Louise and long-time chauffeur Percy Cameron. Unknown date and location.

Arctic exploits which would do credit to any male big game hunter.... Miss Boyd took 25,000 feet of film besides 700 photographs of Arctic scenery. She has sent her bearskins back to her home in California. She plans an extended tour of the Continent. "I shall be sailing for sunny California at the end of October or early November," said Miss Boyd, "but I revel in the cold. I have got the Arctic lure and will certainly go North again."[25]

Upon her return to Maple Lawn, Louise basked unabashedly in the attention and glory she received. Her exploits were splashed across the American newspapers and she participated in more interviews. She was also busy for many months developing her films and cataloguing the photographs. Her 1926 expedition had reached its primary objective of reaching Franz Josef Land. Louise was proud of what she had done and, recognizing their significance, donated most of her photographs, cinematic films, and a copy of *Hobby's* log to the American Geographical Society. But underneath it all there was an undercurrent of uneasiness. Had she really accomplished enough on the expedition, or would real polar explorers expose her as a fraud — a rich American dame who merely enjoyed gallivanting around the Arctic with her society pals? Time would surely tell, but it would be sooner than she imagined.

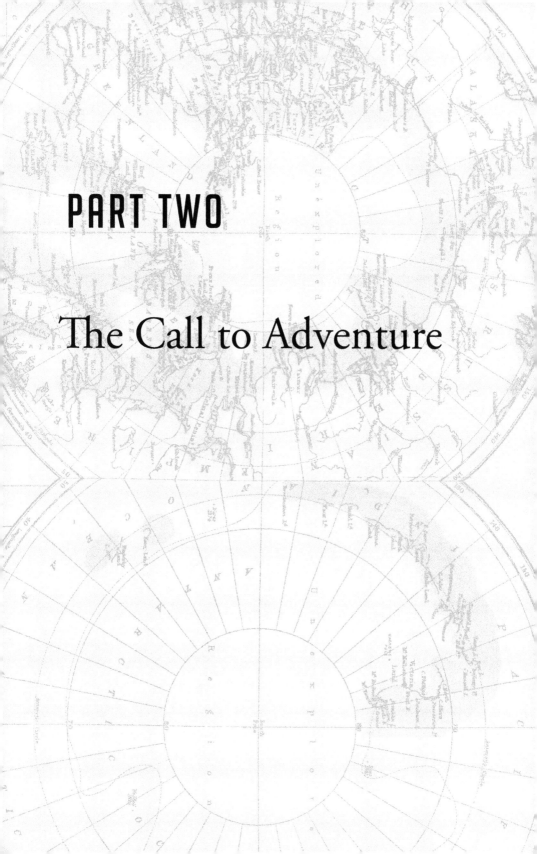

PART TWO

The Call to Adventure

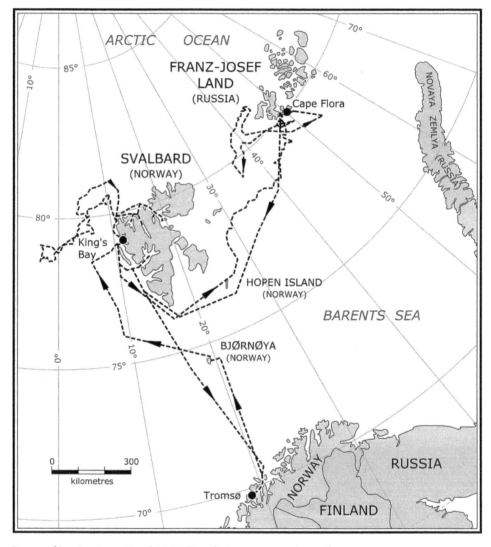

Route of Louise Arner Boyd 1928 Expedition to rescue Amundsen.

CHAPTER FOUR

CHASING AMUNDSEN

Well-behaved women rarely make history.
— LAUREL THATCHER ULRICH

Returning home to the United States was exhilarating. Louise was fêted by friends in New York and San Francisco who had read in the newspapers about her thrilling Franz Josef Land voyage. Settling into her customary routine at Maple Lawn must have provided contentment and security. It was the only home she had ever known, and there she was surrounded by the comforting memories of her blissful childhood and her now long-dead family.

There is no record of any culture shock experienced as a result of travelling abruptly from the rude hardships of life onboard *Hobby* to the gracious surroundings of her San Rafael home where she was cosseted by trusted servants. But the contrast could not have been starker. After returning to California, Louise resumed her active involvement in community affairs, maintaining the Boyd family legacy as well-known philanthropists and pillars of society.

As an outgoing, vivacious single woman with no family, Louise's social network was of paramount importance to her. Although many friends responded positively to her adventures, one may surmise that many others did not understand why she needed to go north, did not care, or did not approve. This time of her life marked the beginning of a lifelong struggle for Louise between the lure of the Arctic and the freedom it represented, and the pressure to conform to the rigid societal values imposed on a wealthy American woman in the 1920s. But Louise Arner Boyd was no ordinary woman, and she was unwilling to relinquish one world for another.

By 1927, Louise had made her mind up to return to the Arctic. She continued her extensive research on Franz Josef Land, Greenland, and Svalbard, and broadened her connections with professionals who could help her prepare for another expedition. It was around this time that she began corresponding with the American Geographical Society and its director, Isaiah Bowman. She also contacted botanist Alice Eastwood at the California Academy of Sciences. Eastwood is credited with saving the Academy's priceless plant collection when she rushed into a burning building during the 1906 San Francisco earthquake to retrieve it. Both Bowman and Eastwood would become important mentors in Louise's life.

In between her social engagements, Louise wrote to Captain Kristian Johannesen and Astrup Holm, the senior officers during her 1926 Expedition. Would they be interested in sailing with her to Northeast Greenland the following year? Was *Hobby*, the ship in which she had sailed previously, available? Astrup Holm replied:

> Dear Miss,
> Hereby I cordially will thank you for the Christmas greetings and the photographies from our well succeeded expedition to the Frantz Josefs Land the summer 1926. When I see these excellent pictures, it seems to me as if I again take share in the expedition, and again I am in your very pleasant company. My membership of your Arctic expedition 1926 is to me as one of my most well succeeded voyage to these regions. I should be very glad if I again could be able to service you on a new and similar expedition to the Artic regions next year.[1]

And *Hobby*, which had carried Louise so courageously into northern waters and then safely home again, was available as well. Planning began in earnest. As experienced skippers, Johannesen and Holm could be relied upon to look after *Hobby* and her needs. Lively and good-humoured Astrup Holm commanded the respect of his comrades while remaining ever-watchful of his shipboard charges. Along with Johannesen, he hired the crew, locating several men from the 1926 Louise A. Boyd Expedition, including ship's mate Lars Olsen and cook Johnson.

Hobby was fitted out with the necessary provisions as instructed. Louise and her guests might be travelling through unknown waters, but there was no need to deprive themselves of the finer things of life! As before, Louise ordered and shipped the heavy wooden crates of champagne, wine, and fine liquors to make sure that she and her guests remained in convivial spirits. She spent hours developing a detailed itinerary, planning the meals, readying the firearms, and securing the necessary permits. She invited her good friend Julia Calhoun and her husband. They were such fun and would make a wonderful addition to the group.

Italian engineer and explorer
Umberto Nobile in 1928.
Unknown date and location.

In the spring of 1928, Louise travelled to London for the busy social season. She continued on to Spain, where she visited the Count and Countess Ribadavia.

In April, all Europe was abuzz with the news of Italian aeronautical engineer Umberto Nobile's daring airship flight to the North Pole. On April 15, Nobile and a staunch crew of twenty capable men launched the airship *Italia* from Milan, Italy, on a perilous course toward Svalbard. Radio contact with the outside world was unexpectedly lost during the *Italia*'s return journey, sparking a monumental international rescue effort to find her and her crew. Because of a public feud between Nobile and Roald Amundsen, the Norwegian government asked Hjalmar Riiser-Larsen, not Amundsen, to spearhead that country's rescue activities. Two years earlier, Nobile had played a key role in the 1926 Amundsen-Ellsworth Transpolar Expedition. Amundsen had acted as co-leader with Lincoln Ellsworth while Nobile assumed the role of captain. Following the completion of this expedition, their cordial relationship ceased as Amundsen and Nobile jostled to claim the victory. Throughout his life, Amundsen was single-minded and zealous in his commitment to polar exploration. Unswervingly loyal to his friends, embittered and quarrelsome toward his enemies, Amundsen relentlessly pursued his goals, often at great personal cost. In 1928, at the age of fifty-six, Amundsen was deeply in debt and embroiled in controversy. He had championed the unpopular cause of Dr. Frederick A. Cook, who had claimed victory at the North Pole but who was languishing in an American federal penitentiary for mail fraud. Due to the bitter dispute with Nobile, Amundsen was *persona non grata* with the Italian government and its belligerent dictator Benito Mussolini.

Despite his personal animosity toward Nobile, Amundsen felt compelled to assist in the *Italia* rescue efforts. He obtained the use of a twin-engine Latham 47 flying boat, and, with Norwegian pilot Leif Dietrichsen and a French crew of four, departed from Tromsø, Norway, on June 18. Norwegian authorities lost contact with the Latham several hours after takeoff, but this did not cause immediate concern, given Amundsen's experience and his reputation for overcoming seemingly insurmountable odds. After a lifetime of polar accomplishments,

Amundsen had attained near-mythic status as one of the world's greatest explorers, a man who had cheated death time and again. Accomplishing one spectacular exploit after another, there seemed to be no stopping him. Eventually, Nobile and most of his crew were located, but the days dragged on with no contact or sightings of the Latham 47. Finally, the international rescue efforts for Nobile were redirected in a desperate attempt to locate Amundsen, the Latham, and its crew.

While this drama was unfolding on the international stage, Louise travelled to Norway just a few weeks before her expedition was due to begin. She knew that *Hobby* had been part of the Nobile search effort, but understood that it was now returning to Tromsø in readiness for her own trip. Louise held Amundsen in high regard and was aware of the international crisis, which she herself could help to alleviate — at least in a small way. Accordingly, she put her own plans aside and offered a fully equipped *Hobby* to the Norwegian government. All the necessary supplies, an experienced and hardy crew, and a sturdy, recently outfitted vessel were ready and waiting. Louise wrote to a friend, "My masterstroke was not my offer to Norway but the way I wrote it. They had to take the C's [the Calhouns] and me if they accepted *Hobby*."[2] Norwegian prime minister Johan Mowinckel accepted her gracious offer with alacrity. Incurring the considerable costs of hiring the ship, the crew's salaries, and all supplies, Louise Arner Boyd chartered the *Hobby* and, with that audacious step, joined the international rescue mission to find Amundsen. Rolf Tandberg later commented that once her offer was accepted, Louise was ready to leave immediately. He stated: "Miss Boyd was very eager to set out and fairly impatient when they did not get ready at American speed. She specified very strongly that when she put her expedition at their disposal, it was in hopes of contributing efficiently to the search, and in no way were they to be cautious in the use of *Hobby* … and that it was to be used as if there were only men onboard."[3]

The American press immediately broadcast news of Louise's involvement. Headlines such as "Woman Joins Arctic Search" and "American Woman Searching for Amundsen" suggest serious journalistic coverage of her participation. However, at this early stage in the rescue mission, the newspaper articles focused on her society connections and her physical appearance. A *New York Times* reporter stated fawningly that "Miss Boyd is a charming woman whose keen blue eyes give the impression of a strong will and a big heart."[4] Over time, press coverage would increasingly reflect her strong will and moral fibre rather than the colour of her eyes.

Hours before *Hobby*'s departure, Louise was giddy with excitement. She wrote to a friend: "I could write pages but if I am to be up and see us start and get this mailed, I must stop and get some sleep. We are at the dock for fresh water and the light in my cabin is so poor that I cannot see sufficiently well to write other than a bad scrawl. However, I wanted you to know that all goes well and that I enjoy obeying orders."[5]

Despite the light tone of her correspondence (perhaps to allay any concerns her friends might have), she could no longer think of her northern voyages as mere pleasure jaunts, nor herself an enthusiastic tourist observing her surroundings. Nor could she blind herself to the potential dangers that awaited *Hobby* and all who participated in the Amundsen rescue attempt. Her momentous decision to charter *Hobby* for this purpose meant that she was joining an elite group — almost exclusively male — with members from Russia, Italy, France, Sweden, Denmark, and Norway. She knew her ship. She knew Captain Johannesen, Astrup Holm, Gisbert, her friends the

The *Hobby* during the summer of 1928. Unknown location.

Calhouns, and several crew members, but what would happen on this risky adventure was unknown to her.

On July 3, 1928, after refuelling and taking on water, the crew of the *Hobby* hoisted anchor. Travelling northward along the Norwegian coast, Captain Johannesen set a course for windswept Bjørnøya, the most southerly island in the Svalbard archipelago. His instructions then were to continue on to King's Bay, which was the meeting place for the international rescue mission. Thus, they were retracing almost exactly the route Amundsen had taken after the Latham 47 took off from Tromsø a few weeks earlier. Passing the North Cape *Hobby* encountered dense fog, but managed to reach Bjørnøya on July 5. Louise was not impressed with this seemingly abandoned coal-mining colony. "Such a bleak and forlorn spot! The highest point of the island is Mount Misery, which we thought well named. The coal mines at its base are not running, the dock had burned and never been replaced and the three men in the wireless station were the sole care-takers."[6]

As expeditiously as possible, *Hobby*'s crew fulfilled their mission to unload twenty-four cans of oil and five two-hundred-pound barrels of petrol to be picked up later by the Italian fleet. But it was a dirty, hazardous, and time-consuming job, as each barrel had to be laboriously loaded into the rowboat, rowed to shore, and then hoisted onto the landing. As soon as the last barrel had been off-loaded, *Hobby* set off once more. Under low cloud cover, the ship sailed northwesterly through the churning grey-blue waters of the Barents Sea toward their next destination, King's Bay. All onboard were on the lookout for anything that would provide clues to Amundsen's whereabouts. Passing fishermen working those frigid waters were set on high alert for debris or, God forbid, wreckage. Sadly, no reputable sightings of Amundsen or the Latham 47 had been made for quite some time.

In the days leading up to their entry into King's Bay, it is likely that Louise felt daunted and uneasy about what lay ahead. King's Bay was the rendezvous point for the principal ships of the rescue mission and it was where Louise would meet notable figures in polar exploration. It was also where *Hobby*'s next task would take place — taking three aviators, their mechanics, and two airplanes onboard.

As they entered King's Bay, sailing past glistening glaciers, *Hobby*'s passengers were struck by the majestic vista. Four imposing ships were moored in the bay, set against a dramatic backdrop of the towering Three Crown Peaks. Louise remarked, "The harbor was a sight that we shall never forget. There lay the Norwegian battleship *Tordenskjold*, the French cruiser *Strasbourg*, the *Citta da Milano*, the *Braganza* and a collier. The *Strasbourg* and the *Tordenskjold* looked very formidable, very warlike in these Arctic parts and both of these ships were waiting for *Hobby*. Surely things here looked serious."[7]

In particular, Louise was thrilled by the flagship *Strasbourg*, commanded by Admiral Herr, who was coordinating the entire mission. Seeing the *Tordensjkold* and the *Strasbourg* anchored in the harbour emphasized the urgency of the undertaking. These were impressive vessels designed to withstand extreme temperatures; built to endure and to survive. In comparison, they made their own *Hobby* look small and insignificant.

The international rescue team involved at least fifteen important vessels and several airplanes representing six European countries. The ships included the *Krasin* and the *Malygin* from Russia; the *Quest* and the *Tanja* from Sweden; the *Quentin Roosevelt*, the *Pourquoi Pas?*, the *Heimland*, and the *Strasbourg* from France; the *Citta da Milano* and the *Braganza* from Italy; the *Gustav Holm* from Denmark; and the Norwegian contingent of the *Michael Sars*, the *Tordenskjold*, the *Svalbard*, the *Veslekari* (which Louise would later come to know well), and *Hobby*. Many of these ships and their illustrious captains were household names associated with momentous events in polar history. Jean-Baptiste Charcot of the *Pourquoi Pas?* was a polar scientist and medical doctor who had led two French Antarctic Expeditions between 1904 and 1910 (the second with the *Pourquoi Pas?*). Oscar Wisting of the *Veslekari* had worked with Amundsen for more than sixteen years and had travelled with him to both the South and the North Poles. The Russian icebreaker *Krasin* had helped to locate Nobile and several of his crew a few weeks earlier, and the *Tordenskjold* and *Michael Sars* had also participated in this mission. Truly an intimidating group of individuals and vessels!

Upon mooring in King's Bay, Louise and the senior officers spent hours meeting with other team members. By this time, *Hobby*'s Norwegian crew was more accustomed to the onboard presence of Louise and her friend Julia Calhoun. But at King's Bay, it was clear that some international team members thought that women had no place on such an important rescue mission. Louise confided to her diary:

> That to them, I was an object of curiosity, they did not hide. Did they expect me to look different from other women? Was I to have flippers of a seal, tusks of a walrus or horns of a muskox? Or was I to be some extremely eccentric, awful, hard-boiled old hag, sloppy and dirty-looking in appearance? This latter seemed evident, and my plain, well-made American tweed tailor suit and brown leather low-heeled shoes, well-shampooed and waved hair topped off with felt hat, gloved hands that were useful and seen doing all kinds of things, from moving things on the dock to trunks and cases, or wielding the hammer or screw driver, and yet, when not gloved, were seen to be not calloused or the quality of sand paper, all seemed absolutely incomprehensible to them. Their sphinx-like faces glared still harder on sight of my using face powder and lipstick as the sweat of the Arctic during long working hours rolled down my face and neck in rivulets.[8]

But to everyone's surprise, Louise would win them over in the end. Her stamina, optimism, and courage during this adventure would come to impress even the most skeptical of the men.

After instructions had been exchanged, *Hobby* prepared for the boarding of the aviators and their mechanics. This group included three of the world's most experienced polar aviators — Norwegians Captain Hjalmar Riiser-Larsen, Lieutenant Finn Lützow-Holm, and Lieutenant Finn Lambrechts.

Tall, rangy, and broad-shouldered, Riiser-Larsen towered over everyone on *Hobby*. A renowned polar aviator and explorer in his own right, he had flown on two North Pole expeditions with Roald Amundsen and accompanied him and Nobile on the 1926 airship *Norge*'s flight over the North Pole. He was also Amundsen's close personal friend.

Lützow-Holm was another highly respected pilot and colleague of Riiser-Larsen.

A skilled military pilot, Lieutenant Lambrechts had never been to the Arctic before. After watching him shiver continually, Louise handed him one of her oversized brown woollen sweaters. Although he was reluctant to take it, she was amused to see the sweater worn by both Lambrechts and Lützow-Holm during the course of the journey. These men, along with top mechanics Svein Myhre, Jarl Bastøe, and Lars Ingebriktsen, played a critical role in *Hobby*'s mission. Riiser-Larsen later wrote in his

Captain Hjalmar Riiser-Larsen. Unknown date and location.

autobiography, *Femti År for Kongen*, "I was a little anxious about what it would be like to have ladies onboard for the type of voyage we were to make. Let me quickly add: it was perfectly fine, despite the fact that this was not a pleasure trip."

Then came the arduous task of hoisting the two airplanes and all the supplies for the aviators onto *Hobby*'s deck. The two Hansa-Brandenburg W.33 seaplanes, marked "F.36" and "F.38," were thirty-six feet long with a wingspan of fifty-two feet. Louise related how this was accomplished:

> Soon the planes came alongside the *Hobby*, one on one side, one on the other. Loading them on our little hatch looked like an impossibility; they looked far too big. After lunch the airship going on the hatch by the galley was hoisted and after some difficulty was finally adjusted to its place. Then the one on the hatch by the bow was hoisted onboard and went into place very easily. They really did not look large at all once they were on the

Lieutenant Finn Lützow-Holm onboard *Hobby* during the summer of 1928.

Hobby for all the passageways were free, and the planes were not in the way.[9]

Despite the size of the airplanes, *Hobby* was able to accommodate them comfortably since her engine was located aft. Riiser-Larsen stated that it was preferable to have three fliers along so that, when two were in the air, one would still be on *Hobby* to take command should the planes not return.

After the aviators were onboard, *Hobby* was contacted by Einar Lundborg, the young, heroic captain of the Swedish ship *Quest*, who had located Umberto Nobile but who had then himself crashed during the dangerous rescue attempt. The *Quest* had a particularly illustrious history as she had previously been under the command of Sir Ernest Shackleton during his last expedition to Antarctica in 1921–22.

At Captain Lundborg's invitation, a group from *Hobby*, including Louise, rowed over to *Quest*. Everyone crowded into the small mess room where Louise and Julia Calhoun were the only women present. The men shared their personal accounts of hazardous polar flights and daring

Loading the airplanes on *Hobby* during the summer of 1928.

rescues, tales that often featured their own aviators, Riiser-Larsen and Lützow-Holm. The meeting continued until the early hours of the morning as the smoke from pipes and cigarettes became thicker and thicker. Louise related how, finally, the officers all burst spontaneously into song. "Conversations up until now had been carried on in five tongues — Norwegian, Swedish, German, French and English. Now, in song, it was concentrated in Scandinavian only. As we took our departure, the Swedes rose to their feet and said, 'We will now sing a song in honour of the Americans.' And with the full blasting power of their lungs, the Swedes sang, 'For They Are "Yolly" Good Fellows' and the *Hobby* team 'yollied' with them. The refrains of 'yollies' ringing in our ears followed us to our anchored ship."[10] In the midst of the despair and the uncertainty, it was good for the international team members to bond over their common purpose. Tragically, Captain Einar Lundborg would be dead three years later, as he perished at the age of thirty-five during a test flight of a Jaktfalken airplane in Sweden.

Hobby lifted anchor and set out shortly after. They had received their orders from Admiral Herr of the *Strasbourg*:

> The specific mission entrusted to the Boyd Expedition is to rally at the ice fields north of Svalbard (Spitsbergen) and explore the region towards the south-west until the *Hobby* meets the whaler *Heimland* which will also be exploring the ice fields in the northern regions towards the 75° parallel. I would be very happy if this mission allows you the satisfaction and honour of finding Amundsen, Guilbaud and their companions.[11]

Years later, the *Strasbourg*'s first officer, Gunnar Hovdenak, wrote about the Amundsen rescue mission. He conveyed the disquiet that many onboard *Strasbourg* had felt about Louise's involvement — not because of her inexperience, but simply because she was a woman. He wrote:

> It cannot be denied that we onboard *Strasbourg* were a bit worried about how the cooperation with the *Hobby* would

turn out. Admiral Herr was, from the very beginning, as expected, skeptical of the presence of women. We could not ignore the fact that the ship might end up in very critical situations in the ice, and if an accident would occur, those onboard might have to endure much hardship.[12]

In hindsight, it is evident that the dangers were real and that these men, familiar as they were with the treacherous Arctic waters, were only too aware of the potential challenges that lay ahead. Most of the men sailing on those mighty vessels were accustomed to extreme conditions and reacting quickly to unforeseen circumstances. The vast majority of those onboard were military men used to obeying orders, teamwork, and discipline. No woman had participated in such an endeavour before. Who could say what might happen or how Louise might behave in a crisis?

As they passed astern of the *Quest* sailing out of King's Bay, their Swedish "yollying" guests of the previous evening dipped their ship's flag to them and sent signals wishing them success in their mission and a safe return. It was what everyone hoped for.

Hobby sailed west from King's Bay toward Greenland. The commanding officers had determined that the Latham had likely been driven by

Louise and Hjalmar Riiser-Larsen onboard *Hobby* during the summer of 1928.

persistent winds to anywhere between the north coast of Svalbard and the coast of Greenland. Wireless communications between the ships was paramount to ensure that no potential zones were overlooked. Time was increasingly of the essence, so meticulous planning prevented any duplication of efforts. They passed their first ice early on. These were stray pieces splintered from icebergs rather than chunks broken from the outer edges of the heavy pack. As they adjusted course and proceeded northward, *Hobby*'s engines slowed as their route became more obstructed. Louise wrote:

> Butting the ice hard; hitting it with our bow; backing up and, with renewed force, butting it time and time again; heavy blocks of ice broken by the bow, scratching *Hobby*'s sides; bumps so hard the coffee and soup often left their cups and lodged on shirt or trousers; then out into a lake-like open area with still waters, here so walled in by miles of heavy ice to the south, the ocean swells and rough seas had no effect.[13]

Reaching the farthest edge of the pack ice, *Hobby* began its search at the designated coordinates, moving westward toward Greenland. They combined efforts with Jean-Baptiste Charcot and the *Pourquoi Pas?* so that no area of the vast cold region was left unexplored. Hour after hour, day after day they sailed on, scouring the territory around them. Four pairs of binoculars were trained on the ice or the horizon at any given time. Lützow-Holm and Captain Johannesen took turns scanning the horizon from the precarious crows nest. Radio communications were monitored around the clock so that all participating vessels stayed in contact.

As the days passed and a routine was established, their common purpose drew everyone together into what Louise called "the *Hobby* family." Despite the gravity of the situation, it is clear that Louise was in her element. She wrote: "Going to bed is easy. Two things come off: hat and boots, then I crawl in and call it an Arctic day; put on a fur wrapper, pile on the blankets and sleep like a rock!"[14]

Referring to Riiser-Larsen as "the salt of the earth" and marvelling at Lambrechts' "priceless dry wit," Louise came up with playful ways to tease the aviators. On most occasions, she and Julia dressed sensibly in high leather boots, wool riding britches, heavy jackets, and leather caps. Hilda, a young woman hired to assist with housekeeping and meals, chose to wear skirts. One day Louise overheard Hilda say to the steward, "Now I think I want to start dressing like the American women."[15] Riiser-Larsen and Lützow-Holm grimaced and asked Hilda to keep

Louise onboard *Hobby* during the summer of 1928.

wearing skirts, since they didn't want to lose the impression of having women onboard. Instantly, Louise knew what to do. A few hours later, Riiser-Larsen came down from the crow's nest and almost fell over from the strong scent of Chanel No. 5, which she had liberally daubed over a handkerchief and hung from a lamp in the mess room. There was no mistaking there were women onboard after that! Despite the solemn nature of their mission, Louise correctly surmised that tension on *Hobby* would be dispelled through humour.

By the third week of July, there was still no word of Amundsen. The stormy weather that plagued them during the early and most critical days had prevented many reconnaissance trips by air. Riiser-Larsen remained vigilant about the weather conditions and confided to Miss Boyd that the planes that had been assigned to them by the Norwegian government were ill-equipped and hardly suitable for such heavy use in the Arctic. Due to the harsh temperature, ice was continually collecting on the rigging and the crew was kept busy chopping it off with wooden scrapers. On more than one occasion ice came crashing down onto the deck, puncturing the airplanes' wings and causing serious damage to both planes. Polar aviation at this time was still in its infancy and flying airplanes under these adverse conditions was particularly risky. Riiser-Larsen, Lützow-Holm, and Lambrechts spent many hours maintaining the planes and preparing them for takeoff when they might be lucky enough to have a fair, sunny day. Finally, on a crisp, bright day in mid-July, both Lützow-Holm and Lambrechts were ready to take to the skies. Louise and the rest of *Hobby*'s passengers watched in amazement. She remarked: "Among the ice floes far in these Arctic waters, to see a hydroplane lowered off *Hobby* and go off gave me a real thrill ... it's a job getting the planes on and off."[16]

Whether the planes were in the air or anchored on the deck, everyone onboard was awestruck by the power and beauty of these mighty flying machines and what they could accomplish. Even the aviators were moved. Three years earlier, Lincoln Ellsworth had written of the Amundsen-Ellsworth Transpolar Expedition in a similar airplane:

> There we sat, he in the navigating cock-pit of one plane
> and I in the other, with nothing separating us from

Eternity, so it seemed, but the thin metal bow in front. Behind sat the pilot so far away as to give me a feeling of utter loneliness and I seemed to be floating alone through the void like a lost soul, beyond the confines of a three-dimensional world. The 640 H.P. Rolls Royce motors above us roared defiance to the mystery and desolation that surrounded us.[17]

Alarmingly, after flying over endless ice for three hours, both planes from the *Hobby* began experiencing technical problems. Just in time, open water appeared below, allowing the F36 and F38 to make emergency landings. With the gas levels running dangerously low, Lambrechts and Lützow-Holm conducted what repairs they could. Then, with a muttered prayer, they managed with difficulty to take off and return to *Hobby*. Louise and all onboard were most relieved when the planes landed in the water not far from the ship. The culprits turned out to be a broken water pipe and a faulty spark plug. Not life-threatening problems — unless one considers the extreme conditions they were flying in and the potentially fatal consequences.

Foggy weather continued to plague them. The pilots couldn't fly in poor weather, so Riiser-Larsen spent many hours aloft in the crow's nest searching out what lay ahead. Life onboard *Hobby* continued peaceably, with frequent radio contact and occasional visits with other vessels participating in the rescue mission. Louise's opinion of Riiser-Larsen, Lambrechts, and Lützow-Holm could not be higher:

> They are perfect corkers and the C's and I are crazy about them. Have already taken over 15,000 feet of film. Have to be careful now. But there has been so much of interest to take. Went on the *Braganza* and had an interesting time. Crocio, one of their fliers was a scream. Told me if I liked ice why didn't I buy a Frigidaire and sit in it at home! You will do better than come to this terrible Arctic, said he.[18]

After conducting thorough searches to the south and northwest of Svalbard, *Hobby* was directed toward Franz Josef Land. Louise was delighted to visit the location of her 1926 Expedition. On the way, *Hobby* returned to King's Bay to pick up airplane parts as well as to load up on supplies to replenish a hut on Cape Flora. *Hobby* was to travel to Cape Flora, find the derelict hut from the Jackson-Harmsworth Expedition of 1894–97 and rebuild it, as well as continuing to search around Franz Josef Land. It was still possible that Amundsen and his crew or even any still-missing survivors from the *Italia* might find and benefit from the hut.

Following the pack ice, *Hobby* encountered severe weather conditions and was unable to get close to land. A chance meeting with the Russian icebreaker *Sedov* allowed an opportunity to get together on *Hobby* and exchange valuable information about the rescue mission. Carrying on toward Victoria Island in the Franz Josef Land archipelago proved challenging. Louise reported:

> We rolled; we pitched; and things just catapulted about. The *Hobby* so covered in thick ice one plane got 37 holes put in it from falling ice; the other plane 27 holes. The wireless wires fell, also the heavy aerial. This smashed the tail of the plane. The *Veslekari* to the South of us and the *Braganza* to the West, had this weather to some bad degree too, we were all in it. But we reached Victoria Island to our great satisfaction. Too stormy to land, but sufficiently close to clearly see no life there. Such an Arctic Island. Solid ice, no land visible. Fascinating but awe-inspiring. As the French say, or have an expression "L'Enfaire Blanc" — White Hell surely![19]

In late August, Admiral Herr requested information about *Hobby*'s intentions to continue with the mission. They had been at sea for two and a half long months, hope dwindling with each passing day. But, while the journey had been challenging and, at times, frustrating, there was no question in Louise's mind. She replied to Admiral Herr that, as her crew were hoping for good results and were happy to continue searching for as long as possible, they should carry on. Admiral Herr replied:

> Please do not expose yourself to unnecessary risks in the present difficult circumstances. Leave the ice if you find it necessary to do so and under no circumstances stay any longer than September 10. You have richly accomplished the work you have taken on. Please keep me informed of your movements.[20]

Finally able to reach Cape Flora, *Hobby* dropped anchor under a turbulent sky. Later that day Captain Johannesen received a terse message from the Geophysical Institute in Tromsø that a torn-off seaplane rudder had been found floating off the coast of Norway. Louise and all onboard *Hobby* waited anxiously for it to be identified. Could it be from Amundsen's Latham 47? While they waited for news, *Hobby*'s crew began bringing supplies ashore for the hut. A sudden violent storm abruptly ended this undertaking and the remaining supplies and a food depot were hurriedly stored. All returned to the ship and *Hobby* set sail. Attempting to leave the area as quickly as possible because of the increasing storm conditions, *Hobby* suffered a near-failure in its engines. Riiser-Larsen stated that "the ship could still proceed slowly, but they risked that further damage could develop at any time and render the engine completely malfunctioning. Thereby *Hobby* would be left to fate until other boats could come to its rescue."[21] For this to occur in the seething, icy waters of Franz Josef Land was hazardous indeed. But the ship's travails were not yet over.

Making their way slowly through a minefield of pitching icebergs, *Hobby* managed to limp into Eira Harbour between Bell and Mabel Islands and drop anchor in the lee of some heavy ice. *Hobby*'s two machinists and the flight mechanics hoisted up and fixed the 2.8-ton engine in the cramped engine room, and it seemed that all would be well. But then, disaster struck again. An exhausted Riiser-Larsen was taking a nap in his cabin when he was suddenly woken by the smell of smoke. He confided in his diary:

I had my cabin beside the galley and there was smoke streaming out through its bulkhead. In the galley, I spotted a fire inside the bulkhead. Luckily mechanic Myhre was out on deck and I whispered to him: "Quickly, an extinguisher!" He got one out and I dashed into the galley and directed it at the bulkhead. In doing so, an enormous flame shot almost explosively up toward the bulkhead and the ceiling. There was gasoline in the extinguisher — a serious error by whoever filled it. Myhre stood behind me and saw this and immediately got another extinguisher. I tried it first with a small shower toward the wall. This extinguisher was filled with the right stuff. With a nearby axe, I created an opening between the two tables and then I emptied the extinguisher into the bulkhead where the fire had been fuelled and was burning with full flames. This extinguisher fortunately held enough to put out the fire. Otherwise, I do not know where we would have been. A wooden vessel, a room filled with gasoline barrels and in such waters.[22]

Riiser-Larsen does not mention the sticks of dynamite that were still stored in the clothes locker in Louise's cabin, so perhaps he was unaware of their existence. In any event, a catastrophe had been averted by the quick-wittedness of these two men. Everyone onboard soon learned what had happened. Fire was not something that sailors liked to talk about, let alone experience on a ship. Louise commented wryly: "Days on *Hobby* are never dull, I assure you."

With the engine fixed, it was only in the nick of time that *Hobby* weighed anchor and set sail before the ice locked them in for the winter with no way to escape.

On September 4, the floatplane rudder was confirmed as belonging to Amundsen's plane. There had been false sightings and identifications before, but radio messages confirming this news continued to arrive. Finally, all onboard *Hobby* accepted that the mission was over. Roald Amundsen, his crew, and the Latham 47 were never seen or heard from again. Louise received a last message from Admiral Herr:

> As of this moment, your involvement is terminated. I would like to express my respectful recognition and admiration for the eagerness, zeal, drive and generosity that you have shown the whole time since we demanded of the *Hobby* the hardest and most dangerous tasks. I wish to assure you once again of my gratitude and ask you to extend my warm thanks to your co-workers, passengers and *Hobby*'s crew.[23]

Louise replied immediately:

> I ask you to accept the warmest and frankest thank-you from me and all who are with me on *Hobby* for your very kind words. We ask you to accept our deepest sympathy

A recovered fuel tank from Amundsen's Latham 47, found in 1928.

in regards to the French nation's loss of Guilbaud and his companions and we only regret that fate has robbed us of the opportunity to fulfill our serious desire to be of assistance. Personally I feel deep gratitude to you for having given us the privilege to search areas where we could have been of most help. We ask you to accept our most respectful greetings.[24]

Hobby returned to Advent Bay in Spitsbergen, where the pilots and mechanics prepared to leave the ship and the two airplanes were unloaded. On their last evening together, the group gathered for a memorable occasion.

> It was a priceless party. 21 men and 6 women but Mrs C and I only ones who danced (Victrola on the floor). You would have died laughing had you seen me. Taken to dinner on the arm of the Director of the Coal Co., wearing my breeches I had slept in and worn for 2 ½ months, full of telltale spots where food and soup had missed my mouth in days when one did their best landing the food, sometimes in one's mouth. Dinner was at 11 p.m. We danced till nearly 4 a.m. I assure you the heat of two sets of woolen underwear and chamois lined pants outdid the best of Turkish baths! Back to *Hobby* where we sat in the tiny mess and chatted and it was 10 minutes to seven in the morning when the *Hobby* family broke up and we sailed soon afterwards. All so blue at parting. Not a throat among us without a hard lump.[25]

They had lived so closely together in tight quarters for almost three months, united by a common purpose out of respect for a great man. Despite the marked differences in their circumstances and backgrounds, they worked together as compatriots.

Hobby sailed from Spitsbergen on her return journey to Tromsø, where Louise bid farewell to the crew and ship. She and the Calhouns travelled from Tromsø to Oslo and then carried on to Paris, where they planned to spend some time getting back to their regular lives. But a few weeks later Louise received an official telegram from the Norwegian attaché in Paris informing her that a great honour would shortly be bestowed upon her. Louise had been awarded the Royal Norwegian Order of St. Olav by the Norwegian government because of her outstanding contributions to Norway and for exhibiting great bravery in a time of crisis. In mid-October of 1928, Julia Calhoun and Louise found themselves back in Oslo. Riiser-Larsen and Lützow-Holm met them at the station as they would also be taking part in the ceremony. Riiser-Larsen shared a journal entry from this time:

> Some time after our return home, Miss Boyd and Mr. and Mrs. Calhoun came to Oslo from Paris as Miss Boyd was to receive [the Order of] St. Olav from the hand of the King. Lützow-Holm and I were at the train station to meet them. Off the train came two entrancing young ladies in the latest Parisian fashions. Lützow-Holm and I looked at each other and thought the same thing: This is what we have sailed with for the last three months in the open northern ice???[26]

They had indeed returned to the "real world." It was a state she much preferred — at least when she wasn't exploring! Leaving the Grand Hotel in Oslo, Louise was driven to the Royal Palace for the luncheon. There, in the presence of Prime Minister Johan Mowinckel, Admiral of the Fleet Konrad Anders, the Minister of Defence, and the American ambassador, King Haakon VII of Norway bestowed the Order of St. Olav upon Louise Arner Boyd. It was only the fourth time that it had been given to a woman and the first time it had ever been given to a non-Norwegian woman. Riiser-Larsen had also received this award after his momentous 1925 flight with Amundsen.

After being wined and dined by the American ambassador, Louise received more exciting news. For her role in trying to locate Amundsen and his French compatriots onboard the Latham 47, the French minister conferred upon her the Ordre national de la Légion d'honneur. This honour was likely bestowed, at least in part, because of the high opinion of Louise held by Amundsen rescue mission coordinator Admiral Herr of the French vessel *Strasbourg*. Although he had been initially skeptical of her involvement, Herr had developed a warm respect for Louise by the conclusion of the endeavour:

> From the beginning of the rescue operations, forgetting your own personal projects, you have spontaneously offered the help of the ship you had boarded and you embarked on this journey with a drive and liveliness that sparked our admiration. Not only did you always answer the calls that were sent to you, but on many occasions you volunteered for the hardest and most dangerous cruises, showing devotion and courage that would

Louise proudly wearing the Ordre national de la Légion d'honneur. Photograph taken in Paris in 1928.

deserve the highest praises. Because of your actions, initiative and tenacity, we are honored to state that the *Hobby* has taken the lead in the search we initiated.[27]

To Louise's embarrassment, the French minister compared her actions with the heroic deeds of men at the front during the Great War, stating that in times of peace the Arctic was the most hazardous front. The next night, there was another dinner, given by the Italian minister, at which she had her first experience speaking Italian all evening. Each award and celebration was precious to her.

When *Hobby* had set out from Tromsø three months earlier, in June 1928, there was no telling what would happen or what the outcome would be. Louise had displayed zeal and commitment to the cause she had undertaken and won the respect of those heroic men whose lives were dedicated to exploring the polar world. With this trip, she had entered a perilous world of risk-taking and high adventure in a cold, frozen land that had completely won her heart. It was a world she would spend the rest of her life trying to return to.

Portrait of Louise Arner Boyd. Artist, date, and location unknown, but likely late 1920s.

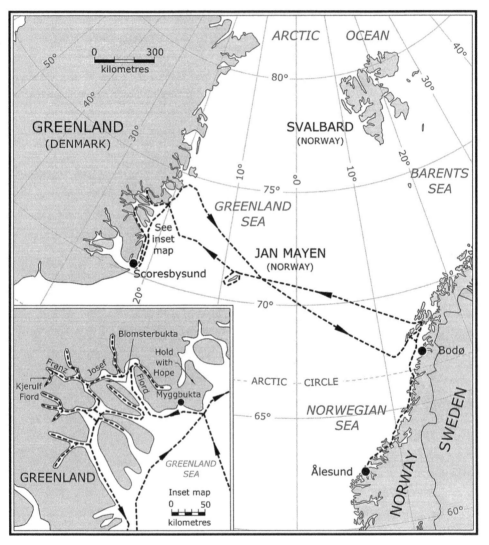

Route of Louise Arner Boyd 1931 Expedition.

CHAPTER FIVE

The Ice Queen Cometh

A lady an explorer? a traveller in skirts?
The notion's just a trifle too seraphic:
Let them stay and mind the babies, or hem our ragged shirts;
But they mustn't, can't, and shan't be geographic.
— *Punch Magazine*, 1893[1]

That was the trip that started it all. Where Louise found that place that fulfilled her completely, a place she had longed for but had never found.

The Arctic.

Her first short forays into northern waters in 1924 and 1926 to Svalbard and Franz Josef Land had introduced her to the travails of life onboard a polar vessel and offered her tantalizing glimpses of a life usually hidden from those in her sophisticated circle. But, by being in the right place at the right time, Louise was swept along by the tide of history to become an active participant in the 1928 Amundsen rescue mission. This was serious business. The approbation of notable individuals, including Hjalmar Riiser-Larsen and mission coordinator Admiral Herr of the *Strasbourg*, as well as the awards accorded her by the Norwegian and French governments, were testaments to her outstanding courage in the face of danger.

Louise returned to the United States with increased confidence in her abilities and a renewed purpose in life. Over the coming months, she was the talk of the town and everyone was excited by her flutter in the newspapers. Her friends and acquaintances believed that her Amundsen adventure had been a fine romp, and the stories that made the social rounds focused on the amusing anecdotes, harrowing incidents, and the famous people she had hobnobbed with. She was inundated with requests from strangers to be included on future expeditions. Most would-be crew members were woefully inexperienced with nary a pair of sea-legs amongst them. She heard from twenty-four-year-old New York City native Frank J. Rogers, who ardently declared: "If I were told that I could have any one wish I asked for, my one wish would be to tie up with you on all future adventures."[2] Radio telegrapher W.R. Bruce sent Louise a series of increasingly impassioned letters, finally ending with: "Gee, I wish I was going up there with you. Shall be with you in every dream. Be careful and hurry back. Perhaps I'll be able to pick up your radio."[3]

Louise also received letters from more promising individuals, including a Miss Balch, who was keen to join a future expedition in the role of geologist. This was Mary Balch Kennedy, who was the third woman ever to graduate from Stanford University with a major in geology. Dr. Bowman advised Louise: "Please don't bother to reply to this communication [about Miss Balch] ... I imagine a geologist on a boat would be about as useful as a fish out of water."[4] Ironically, Louise would indeed hire a geologist on future expeditions, although not the eminently qualified Miss Balch. The media coverage garnered her more than a few admirers, including one keen outdoorsman who boldly addressed his letter to "Miss Louise A. Boyd Arctic Bear Huntress, San Francisco, California," with a return address marked "Frederick Zorn Pioneer, Alaska Mineral Explorer, Anchorage, Alaska." Surprisingly, his eloquent letter exhorting Louise to visit him in the wilds of Alaska did reach her and remained permanently in her files.

While she did spend time answering her "fan mail," Louise also wrote to those seasoned explorers, military men, and scientists whom she had met in the Arctic. This enabled her to keep her memories of that fateful summer alive and strengthen her bond with that elite group of men who risked it all for the sake of their compatriot. And it nurtured the glow inside of her that had ignited at last. One of her correspondents was Captain Astrup Holm. In 1930, she wrote to him of an unexpected visit by some of her society friends to *Hobby*, docked in Tromsø harbour. She stated indignantly: "Most of them had seen my cinemas of our 1926 trip. Such insults as they hurl at our *Hobby* that we all love! There is nothing too awful they did not write me about her or now they say to my face. Poor 'Miss Hobbs' made a terrible impression on all of them."[5] In writing to Holm and other men she had met during her voyages, Louise discovered that these were the people with whom she could share her intense experiences of the desolate north — the warm camaraderie and common purpose onboard ship, the stormy crashing seas, the shifting pack ice.

Louise's social calendar was as busy as ever and guests passed in and out of Maple Lawn. The first of several renovation projects to her San Rafael home and property occurred during this period. It was likely that she then transformed a sitting room into what she nicknamed the "Arctic Command Centre." This housed her extensive library of travel and exploration books, in addition to those signed copies sent to her by the authors themselves. It also included those worn, cherished books by explorers including Amundsen, Nansen, Byrd, and Cook that had helped to nudge her on her own northward path. "The Arctic Command Centre" also displayed the many maps she had acquired, with a special emphasis on Scandinavia and the Arctic Ocean. Maps created for her that charted *Hobby*'s course during the Amundsen rescue mission, as well as her earlier Franz Josef Land voyage, were framed and hung proudly on the walls, as were her own black-and-white photographs. She also had a 180-square-foot vault constructed in a separate outbuilding to properly store her burgeoning collection of cinematic films. The more Louise researched, the more fascinated she became by the geography of Greenland, Franz Josef Land, and Svalbard. Certainly, it had become clear to her that this area was a largely unknown region with outstanding mapping opportunities.

Louise's vivid memories of sailing on the *Hobby* and the fierce joy she had experienced remained undimmed. By the summer of 1930, she was back in Scandinavia with plans to travel overland throughout Swedish Lapland. Not long after she had arrived in Sweden, the country was electrified by the discovery of the remains of S.A. Andrée's 1897 Arctic balloon expedition, which had vanished mysteriously. On July 11, 1897, Swedish engineers S.A. Andrée and Knut Frænkel and photographer Nils Strindberg had launched their hydrogen balloon ship *Örnen* ("The Eagle") from Danskøya in Svalbard in a bid to fly over the North Pole. They were never heard from again and their disappearance remained one of the greatest polar mysteries of all time. The discovery of the remains of Andrée and his ill-fated companions was made by the Norwegian sealer *Bratvaag* on an unexpected stop on Kvitøya in the Svalbard archipelago. Louise had encountered the *Bratvaag* during her 1926 expedition and had met its captain, Peder Eliassen. A state funeral in Stockholm was planned for Andrée, and Louise received a personal invitation — yet another indication of acceptance by her peers in the polar world. Historian Sverker Sörlin has reported that the public outpouring of grief was "one of the most solemn and grandiose manifestations of national mourning that has ever occurred in Sweden."[6] Louise remarked that it was the most impressive funeral she had ever attended. Her travel diary states that Captain and Mrs. Eliassen and Harald Leite and his wife (owners of the *Bratvaag*) regularly visited her Stockholm apartment. This provided her with more opportunities to socialize with like-minded colleagues, as well as nurture her professional network.

By the time she returned to California, plans for her next adventure to Greenland and Jan Mayen during the summer of 1931 were beginning to crystallize. This would be a photographic reconnaissance mission and a precursor to a scientific expedition two years later. It would also enable her to gain an overall familiarity with the coastal areas of East Greenland.

Louise made an early and critical decision to solicit the support of the American Geographical Society for her work. Created in 1851 to promote geographical understanding, this scientific organization had been an enthusiastic supporter of polar explorers, including fellow Americans Robert Peary and Richard Byrd. Louise had been in contact with AGS director Isaiah Bowman and his staff for several years as they had supplied her with maps and technical information for her previous voyages. She was deeply honoured when elected a Fellow of the American Geographical Society.

It is likely that Bowman met Louise for the first time in late 1930 at the AGS offices in New York. When the day for their first meeting arrived, Louise likely felt some trepidation. Educated as a geographer and mapper at Michigan State, Harvard, and Yale universities, Isaiah Bowman had participated in several high-profile expeditions in South America, including the celebrated 1911 discovery of Machu Picchu in Peru with Hiram Bingham. He advised President Woodrow Wilson at the Versailles Conference in 1919 and was elected director of the prestigious American Geographical Society that same year. Despite his impressive credentials and Louise's comparative inexperience, he was always gracious and respectful to her over the course of their long correspondence.[7]

Louise enjoyed her tour of the building and the chance to meet AGS staffers Miss Platt and Miss Belden, who had assisted her many times. In the early 1930s the AGS, like most Western geographical societies, was a male

Isaiah Bowman, likely in the 1930s.

bastion of privilege. Although there were many women who worked tirelessly as staff members, there were few if any women in senior positions, and even fewer women explorers. Louise would have been shown the great library and archives where precious documents, maps, and artifacts pertaining to the world's leading explorers were conserved. As she gazed around her at shelf after shelf of massive tomes by intrepid explorers, it would have taken her breath away. Privately, she likely thought to herself what a fine repository it would be for her own Arctic maps, diaries, and photographs.

As Louise outlined her plans for her upcoming Greenland expedition and asked for AGS support, Bowman would have questioned her regarding her past experience as well as her objectives for the next voyage. He would have tactfully inquired about her academic credentials and learned that Louise had none whatsoever beyond the education she received at Miss Murison's School for Girls in San Francisco years earlier. He implied that AGS support was virtually assured and that his organization could assume a leading role in hiring appropriate scientists for the job. In addition, Bowman would approach other scientific organizations to determine their interest in joint sponsorship. Louise was delighted to learn that she would be able to use the American Geographical Society name in connection with the expedition. Bowman proposed contacting the Woods Hole Oceanographic Institution, the American Museum of Natural History, and Yale University to secure their additional support and assistance in finding scientists for the expedition. Louise wrote to him:

> I want the scientific personnel selected for the work by your Society, as well as the other institutions to consist of outstanding men in their respective line. I think you heartily agree with me that, entirely aside from my expense in the matter, the nature of the expedition and the fact that it is under the auspices of your splendid Society makes it essential that nothing less than the very finest in the way of scientific personnel should be selected to make the expedition.[8]

Additionally, she was thrilled to learn that Dr. Bowman wished her to submit her extensive collection of still pictures and cinema reels and maps relating to her 1926 and 1928 expeditions to the Arctic to the Society for the use of their organization. Sadly, a few weeks later, she came down to earth with a bump. A cablegram from Dr. Bowman on February 23, 1931, stated tersely:

> All three other institutions regret lack of trained personnel to accompany your expedition owing demands [to] other expeditions under scientific leadership.... Kind of expedition we had discussed proves not feasible unless a scientific director gives whole time to it and itinerary is planned to attain scientific objectives that will attract first rate men. My following letter sets up a program for another year which I believe will interest you.[9]

Overnight he must have had further misgivings as he backpedalled once again in a letter sent one day later:

> My telegram referred to a "program for another year." Repeated consideration of the cruise, the program, and your letter of February 6 makes it clear that an expedition of this sort really requires a scientific director who can give his whole time to it or a very substantial portion of it. There is a large amount of work to do.... We are not prepared to do these things here.[10]

It is easy to imagine how disappointed Louise must have been and rather ticked off, as well, since months earlier Bowman had been nothing but encouraging. He advised her to scale back her plans and to adopt a limited program for the 1931 expedition. Dr. Bowman thought that there would not be enough time to secure the services of qualified scientific men, although there was an implicit message that she was not capable of choosing such individuals herself. However, Louise was pleased to see that he referred to her "future expeditions" and that he had mentioned her plans to other explorers. This included discussions with noted Australian explorer Sir Hubert Wilkins, who had served with Shackleton, made a trans-Arctic crossing by air from

Alaska to Spitsbergen, and who was currently contemplating an ambitious transatlantic voyage by submarine:

> I was talking with Sir Hubert Wilkins the other day about your proposed cruise and he was tremendously interested to know that you were to be in Arctic waters at the time he proposes to conduct his submarine cruise. When his preliminary trials have been completed and his route more precisely determined it will be possible to give you locations and dates. Of course these are only expectations. One can imagine circumstances under which your journey in the same waters might be of the greatest value to him.[11]

Louise responded prudently:

> I have concluded to undertake this trip as originally planned by me, and shall have with me friends from America and from abroad. We shall endeavour to develop from the present situation a voyage that undoubtedly will be productive of results of great interest to all and which may possibly be of some value from a scientific standpoint.[12]

Despite her disappointment, Louise's diplomacy enabled her to stay in the good graces of the American Geographical Society and its director. Regardless of this setback, Louise continued to organize a Greenland expedition for the summer of 1931.

Unlike the majority of other contemporary explorers, who had to scrabble for funding, Louise's expeditions were entirely self-financed. As a result, she was free to concentrate on the details of her mission — researching her scientific objectives and destination, finding her ship and crew, and deciding on the expedition participants.

She was saddened to learn that *Hobby* was not available and that both Captain Johannesen and Astrup Holm were busy. Louise would be sailing in uncharted waters in more ways than one. Holm's suggestion that she charter the *Veslekari* was met with immediate approval. Like *Hobby*, the *Veslekari*

The *Veslekari*. Unknown location and date.

had impeccable credentials as an Arctic expeditionary vessel. Louise was somewhat familiar with the ship already, as it had been part of the Amundsen rescue expedition. There were other connections with Amundsen as well. Built by Christian Jensen, the *Veslekari's* sister ship was the *Maud*, which had sailed with Amundsen on his 1918 attempt to traverse the Northeast Passage. The *Veslekari* was constructed of solid oak, pine, and greenheart, and other materials left over from the *Maud*. Considered one of the strongest of all Norwegian wooden sealers, *Veslekari* was 134 feet in length, 27 feet in breadth, with a gross tonnage of 285 — almost the exact same dimensions as *Hobby*. The connections between Louise's upcoming expedition and Amundsen would have been powerful indicators to Louise that the great explorer himself had given his blessing.

Her captain on this expedition was Paul Lillenes (known as Lisjenes-Pål in Norway). Born in rural Tjørvåg where his family had lived for generations, Captain Lillenes was a legendary sea captain in northern Norway. He had been awarded a gold watch from the Danish government in 1908 when he brought mail and supplies to a Danish expedition that had received none for two years. In 1912, as captain of the *Sjøblomsten*, Lillenes had rescued Danish explorers Ejnar Mikkelsen and Iver P. Iversen of the *Alabama* Expedition, who had been stranded on Greenland with no outside contact for three years. For his bravery, Lillenes received a medal from King Christian X of Denmark. Although known as a formidable master with a fiery temper, he was nevertheless in great demand as a sealing captain since he always got a good catch, resulting in higher pay for his men. Louise heard that once, while commanding from the crow's nest, he became so furious and stamped so hard that he kicked the bottom out of the platform, but was so fat that he did not fall through. Louise was assured that Paul Lillenes was her man and she never regretted the choice.

As was customary, the captain was responsible for securing crew services and, with the exception of reliable Francis Gisbert, Louise would not be meeting them until she reached Norway. However, she was solely responsible for hiring the scientists since the American Geographical Society was not willing to do so. Louise had to act quickly to locate individuals who were available. Louise's close friend Robert Hewett Menzies readily accepted her invitation to join the upcoming expedition. Tall and lanky, Robert was a

San Rafael neighbour as well as a noted botanist and horticulturist. He was also a good friend of botanist Alice Eastwood who acted as Louise's mentor. Robert was the son of Scotsman Thomas Menzies, who had travelled to the American West in the 1870s. There was a hint of mystery about Robert due to a distant connection to celebrated surgeon and botanist Archibald Menzies, who sailed with explorer George Vancouver. Once Robert had accepted, his wife Winnifred was keen to accompany him and Louise was happy to accept another expedition member. Later, Winnifred wrote about her feelings prior to the expedition.

> Not being photographer, botanist or scientist, many of my friends asked me, when they heard that my husband and I had had the very good fortune to be invited to join the Louise A. Boyd Expedition of 1931 to Northeast Greenland, this question, "Why are you (with the emphasis on that useless YOU) going on a Scientific Expedition?" I hung my head, thinking of how much this wonderful opportunity would mean to many eager students — and

Captain Paul Lillenes being painted by artist Dagfin Werenskiold onboard the *Veslekari* in 1930.

felt very apologetic until an old friend replied for me to these candid inquirers, "Well, at any rate, I'll wager she will see more than any of your scientists with their noses to the ground." Feeling immeasurably cheered, I vowed that I would try not only to see, but to record my impressions of what I saw.[13]

Louise also contacted Carl-Julius Anrick, a Swedish cartographer whom she had met the previous year while touring Scandinavia. Recently married, he also requested that his wife be allowed to accompany him. Though somewhat discomfited by this suggestion, since she had never met the woman, Louise nonetheless agreed. Widely published in his field, she thought Anrick would make a positive contribution to the team. Another member of the group was Harry Whitney, an avid American sportsman and big game hunter from a wealthy American family. Though not a scientist, he was an experienced explorer who had travelled to eastern Greenland the year before. In 1908, Whitney had travelled on the *Roosevelt* with Robert Peary and gained fame as the man to whom Dr. Frederick A. Cook had reportedly consigned his data and instruments upon his return to civilization — proof that he had conquered the North Pole. As reported in the *New York Times*, Whitney figured prominently in the Peary-Cook North Pole controversy. Louise was keen to learn more about his Greenland experience, as well as about the *Effie M. Morrissey*, on which he had sailed. The *Morrissey* was another valiant Arctic ship with which Louise would become better acquainted in the future.

The *Veslekari*, owned by Elling Aarseth of Vartdal, had its home port in the northern fishing town of Ålesund. The small community was abuzz with news of the upcoming expedition. The days leading up to their departure were hectic. Anrick reported: "With polar trips you cannot just walk up the gangplank and sail off; there is equipment to replenish; there is hammering and building, painting and loading coal; the newly installed electrical light has to be tested, the compasses have to be tested during a trial run. And since we are leaving for Greenland, both passengers and the crew must be examined by an approved doctor, otherwise you cannot enter the Danish colonies."[14]

But *Veslekari* was not the only excitement in town. On June 27, the *Aftenpost* newspaper had published a bold political manifesto from Norwegian Hallvard Devold:

> In the presence of Eiliv Herdal, Tor Halle, Ingvald Strøm
> and Søren Richter, the Norwegian flag has been hoisted
> today in Myggbukta. And the land between Carlsbergfjord
> to the south and Besselfjord to the north occupied in His
> Majesty King Haakon's name. We have named the country
> Eirik Raudes Land.[15]

In formally claiming a vast area of East Greenland for Norway, Devold and his colleagues directly challenged Danish sovereignty. Although Norway and Denmark had disputed ownership of Scandinavian lands and waters in the past, in the 1930s, East Greenland was under Danish rule. Commercial interests and Norwegian nationalist fervour sparked a movement opposing Danish control of East Greenland. Explorer and geologist Dr. Adolf Hoel, head of Norway's Svalbard and Arctic Ocean Survey (later the Norwegian Polar Institute), and lawyer Gustav Smedal spearheaded this movement and masterminded Devold's plan to raise the Norwegian flag at Myggbukta. People living in small northern Norwegian communities such as Ålesund were fiercely patriotic and independent. The "Myggbukta situation" was the talk of the town, with the majority of townspeople favouring Devold's action. Departing Ålesund only a few days after this manifesto was published, many wondered if the Louise A. Boyd 1931 Greenland Expedition, which was due to visit Myggbukta, had a political agenda.

On July 1, huge crowds gathered along the quay and the hills around it. As expedition members stood onshore making their final farewells, a murmuring noise from the swelling crowds could be heard. Fingers pointed to the ship and everyone turned toward it. Erik Bratseth, Louise's new young assistant with a wry sense of humour, relayed what happened next:

> Just before we set out, an incident occurred which partly
> helped to dispel the tension our departure seemed to have

created amongst the expectant spectators. An Ålesund man named Kallemalukken had taken part in the festivities rather too liberally. He was, in fact, completely drunk. In his inebriated state, he realized that a ship's mast is there to be used. And what lies closer to the heart of a clever fellow such as he [than] to use the mast as a springboard into the salty waves? With greedy eyes, the gaping, sensation-seeking spectators of this free entertainment followed his staggering climb up the 75 feet mast. With rising expectations, they also followed the complicated "dive" from the top of the mast. But no, unfortunately, there was no splashing of spinal marrow and grey matter on the not yet swabbed deck. Instead, there was a huge splash in the debatably clean water alongside the boat. A couple of swimming strokes, a rusty hook tangled in a moments ago, well-pressed suit, a few hauls and an overflowing, human shape rescued by helping hands landed on the pier. Shortly after this, the boat set forth. Later, Mr. Gisbert kept a watchful eye on me and warned me several times about jumping from the top of the mast in the same way. I guess I give the impression of wanting to amuse the group in such a way. I am, however, not so inclined and the worry is unfounded.[16]

As *Veslekari* left Ålesund harbour, Louise was looking forward with great anticipation to visiting East Greenland. Her plan was to explore every inlet and sound in the Franz Josef and King Oscar Fjord areas. She also hoped to travel south to Scoresbysund and visit the fjords there.

Veslekari travelled north along the Norwegian coast en route to the Lofoten Islands. Captain Lillenes then set a westerly course through the choppy Norwegian Sea to the island of Jan Mayen, located halfway between Norway and Greenland. The pitching and rolling of the ship felled one expedition participant after another with the exception of Louise. Bratseth commented that "our Miss is admired among the people here for her sailor-like gait and decent behavior. On the other hand, several of the other expedition members cannot consider themselves sailors."[17]

The Swedish geographer Anrick had a particularly violent bout of sea-sickness and remained confined to quarters. His worst fears about the *Veslekari* had come true. Prior to boarding, he had asked about her and was dismayed to hear: "*Veslekari*! God help us all! First she rolls like an ordinary boat, then she rolls some more, and then you think that she will go all the way around."[18] Anrick's duties of collecting temperature readings fell to others.

Day after day, *Veslekari* sailed on without misadventure. All eyes strained forward searching for a glimpse of Jan Mayen. Then, without warning, dense fog fell like a curtain before them, making a sighting even more challenging. At last, the fog lifted and all onboard were rewarded with a glimpse of the snow-covered peak of Beerenberg. After *Veslekari* dropped anchor, her rowboat was lowered to the water. On Jan Mayen, three eager station personnel were waving from the rocky shore. *Veslekari* was bringing mail from loved ones and much-needed supplies, so the visit was particularly welcome.

Jan Mayen was a barren volcanic island composed of two mountainous sections connected by an isthmus. Partly covered by glaciers, the highest summit was the extinct volcano Beerenberg, in the north. Jan Mayen had previously been the site of a Dutch whaling station; it had been abandoned, and since then had been visited only by hunters. It had been the site of previous expeditions, including the Austro-Hungarian North Pole Expedition in 1882–83 under the command of Emil von Wohlgemuth.

On their second day, Louise and others rose at 6:00 a.m. to hike around the island in the company of station chief Olonkin. Bratseth reported:

> Around the station there were a lot of pictures and meters of film taken in the sunshine. Some of our party preferred to take it easy, wherever they were — they had for a long time had more motion than they frankly could say they liked — and I hiked across the island with Miss Boyd and Mr Gisbert.... After a fairly strenuous march across soft sand and hard rocks, we finally reached the top of a ridge from where there was a pleasant descent to the north lagoon. This is no doubt the first photography expedition

that has visited the island, so we have to be ambitious while the weather is good.[19]

The group only returned to the ship at 10:00 p.m., given Louise's enthusiasm to capture everything she saw. Several days were spent on the island taking advantage of the fine weather. Each clear morning, Louise would be rowed across the water wondering which new vista she could capture on film. With Erik struggling behind with her cameras and photographic equipment, Louise strode confidently across the rough, rocky terrain, passing raucous bird rookeries and rusting fox traps. This was the first time that Louise used the camera both to obtain photographic records and as a mapping instrument. This dual role of photographer and leader would be continued on future expeditions. She stated:

> My photography of coastal features, in panorama and in detail, as well as of ice conditions, was an almost continuous process from either ship or motor dory; and while on shore I took every opportunity to take my cameras up on to high ground from which I could get wide and distant views that often afforded an understanding of the topography in no other way so easily obtained.[20]

Louise's time on Jan Mayen drew to a close. As *Veslekari* headed out on a westerly course toward Greenland, all onboard could see the white peak of Beerenberg for miles. Although the weather was calm when they left, as the hours passed, the sea grew choppier and the wind began to howl. Louise remained on deck with the crew as long as she dared. About 150 miles northwest of Jan Mayen, they encountered their first iceberg, surrounded by dozens of ice floes. It was a substantial size with a large flock of noisy kittiwakes perched on its long, flat surface. *Veslekari* pushed forward with caution. These were ice conditions unlike anything Louise had encountered before. There were to be no easy hours of slush ice and long passages of open water.

Anrick stated:

It is a strange sight to meet the ice. The sea was rough, it looked cold and gloomy and the flat iceberg we met drifted mighty and majestically, unruffled by wind and sea, on its way south. At about seven in the morning, we met the ice zone. It is like gliding into an archipelago where the blocks of ice represent islands and skerries. Here and there they have capsized and you can see side-turned ice blocks protrude from the water. Our horizon is rough but wide and the sight large. The boat turns and circles the blocks while the engine is going full blast. A couple of hours pass.[21]

This area was notorious for the ice belt that bordered Greenland's eastern coastline. Louise and her fellow passengers watched in fascination as *Veslekari* battered her way relentlessly through the ice. Bratseth said admiringly that, although the crashing of the ship through the ice was accompanied by the howling of the female passengers, Louise herself was having a marvellous time. For hours on end, Captain Lillenes barked orders to the

Veslekari moored in Blomsterbukta, East Greenland. Photograph taken by Louise in 1931.

crew from the precipitous crow's nest. At times, the ice around the ship towered eight feet above the stern railings, and for a few hours they were beset. Due to the crew's resourcefulness and skill in setting dynamite to blast their way through the most impenetrable areas, they were not locked in for more than a few hours. Other ships were not as lucky.

Veslekari was in radio contact with two other vessels trying to reach the coast of Greenland. Renowned explorers Dr. Adolf Hoel on the *Polarbjørn* and Lauge Koch on the *Godthaab* were experiencing equally challenging ice conditions. The three ships shared as much information

Sculpture of Adolf Hoel.

as they could. Norwegian Adolf Hoel was one of the instigators of the plan to claim Myggbukta for Norway, while Danish scientist Lauge Koch had been appointed the Danish police authority there. Both Hoel and Koch promoted northern territorial expansionism through conducting scientific activities. The potential for open conflict could not have been greater. Telegrams sent by Louise to both the Norwegian and Danish ships displayed her diplomatic skills. Koch and Hoel would both become good friends and advisors of Louise.

On July 15, they could clearly see the Greenland coast and the peninsula of Hold-with-Hope that was their goal. After four difficult days in the ice, *Veslekari* reached a safe haven and dropped anchor. Large floes were piled up against the land and blocked their passage, so it took their launch half an hour to wind its way to the shore. *Veslekari* was the first ship to reach the east coast of Greenland that summer and Winnifred Menzies commented that this was due to the Captain's "almost uncanny knowledge of ice conditions" and that "he never left the crow's nest for more than the briefest rest, or a cup of coffee, while we were in the ice."[22]

Captain Lillenes told Louise that this had been one of his most difficult voyages to that coast. Later, Louise would be thrilled with a *New York Times* headline: "Three Greenland Groups Held by Ice Barrier; Bartlett Caught, but Miss Boyd Gets Through."

They had reached Greenland at last. Louise wrote to botanist Alice Eastwood at the California Academy of Sciences that "the east coast of

Hold-with-Hope, East Greenland. Photograph taken by Louise in 1931.

Greenland is the most fascinating place I have ever been!" A day was spent hiking around the uninhabited headland where Louise filmed and she and Menzies collected botanical specimens. Later, Alice Eastwood confirmed that they had collected seventy-five of the eighty-nine flowering species known to occur in East Greenland, as well as three not previously recorded. On Jan Mayen, they had collected twenty-two species, including a new species of *taraxacum*. Menzies's botanical report on the expedition states that he was "incapacitated" on most field visits, so all collecting was left to Louise. Although the specimens were fragmentary and only basic data about where the specimens were collected was noted, her skills as a botanist were improving.

As *Veslekari* continued, everyone onboard ship was anticipating the arrival at Myggbukta. The Captain and the stalwart crew were immensely

Hallvard Devold in the early 1930s. Unknown location.

proud of their Norwegian colleagues and Lillenes referred to Devold as "the young Norwegian Earl of Eirik Raudes Land."[23] Bratseth said, "At the moment, Myggbukta was in the middle of world politics and to patriotic Norwegians it felt as if they were standing on the mountains of Sinai with the earth trembling below."[24]

As they approached the community, the men from the station lit a fire on shore to guide them in and *Veslekari* anchored just before midnight. The Norwegian flag waved defiantly from the flagpole outside the station. *Veslekari* was the first ship to visit Hallvard Devold and his men since the occupation began. Devold had been given authority as a police officer, and his first role in this capacity was granting Louise her visa. Either because she was a woman or an American (or both), it is likely that the political intrigue was barely spoken of in Louise's presence. Devold and his men were over-joyed to have provisions dropped off and to converse with outsiders. In his autobiography, Devold's pleasure in Louise's visit related more to the goods she offered than to any political ramifications:

> We were invited for a "midnight lunch" onboard *Veslekari* and were given mutton cutlets in addition to a variety of fresh and canned fruits. We drank port wine with the des-sert. It had been a long time since we had seen this kind of food and drink and it tasted excellently. A few hours after midnight, we said goodbye and Miss Boyd and her guests collected their warm water bottles from the steward and went to bed. "No, are you leaving already, Devold?" Lillenes said to me as we were getting up from the table.... You don't have to go to bed right away. I'll be back in a short while." An hour later, Lillenes returned with a quan-tity of whisky and soda and we all had a fine chat with a compatriot who knew something about the situation. "You should be thanked for what you did, boys," Lillenes said as he glanced toward the flag which flew from the pole. "There's great enthusiasm at home so something will come of it, I hope."[25]

But it was unusual for Louise to retire early from any party. It is possible that she wished to allow Captain Lillenes, a keen Norwegian nationalist who had had his own skirmishes with the Danish authorities, an opportunity to celebrate the occupation with his kinsmen. By withdrawing early, presumably before the conversation became less inhibited, she was also preserving her neutrality as an American citizen.

Hiking and photography on Myggbukta proved to be a thoroughly troublesome affair and Louise soon learned that the name of the community (translated as "Mosquito Bay") was well-deserved. For once, Erik Bratseth did not display his usual eagerness to accompany her on inland trips. He later told Louise that what he remembered most of this period was: "The same hopeless dance keeping the beasts away from you. It seemed like a fight for life. A hike in deepest Africa would be preferred to an excursion in Myggbukta."[26] Despite these challenges, thankfully, their visit to the occupied territory at Eirik Raudes Land proceeded without a hitch and no diplomatic incident occurred.

Winnifred Menzies, Louise, and Robert Menzies at Myggbukta, Greenland, during the summer of 1931.

After sailing south from Myggbukta, *Veslekari* made several stops along the north shore of the Franz Josef Fjord before anchoring off the coast of Hoelsbu in Musk-Ox Fjord, where they spent a few days. Louise met up with John Giæver and Otto Jonson, two seasoned Norwegian trappers who manned the wireless and meteorological station there. Giæver was a passionate nationalist, eager to have news of the flag-raising by Devold. Two years later, the International Court at The Hague would rule against Norway's claim to territory in Greenland and Giæver would confide to his diary: "It feels like the bottom has fallen out of our existence here. Nothing seems to matter anymore. We are in Danish land."[27] Like Devold, Giæver and Jonson were happy for the diversion provided by *Veslekari*'s visit and accompanied Louise on her hike to the fjord. As requested by the American Geographical Society, Louise collected data on the status of muskoxen in the Franz Josef and Oscar Fjords and submitted a report upon her return. Giæver had managed to tame two young muskoxen calves, which followed Jonson and him everywhere with doglike devotion. Giæver reported:

> Among Miss Boyd's companions were a very newly-wed couple, Swedes…. The turtle doves, each with an apple, went off into the hills on a walking tour. All at once the charmingly pastoral idyll was shattered by terrified screams and shouts issuing from the hills. It was our turtle-doves who came flapping in fright from out of the wilds, soaked in sweat and jabbering confusedly in two different languages at once. From the Babel it emerged that the two dears had been attacked by a couple of monsters…. They had come running for dear life, leaving a trail of binoculars, cameras, apples and walking sticks…. "Thank God we're safe and oh God here they come, run for your lives." On the top of the hillock stood the 'monsters,' Lita and Lensman [the two tame muskox calves]…. After the first surprised sight of these two, Otto and I started to shake with mirth. Soon the company began to titter, then to laugh and finally everyone including the turtle doves were almost hysterical with merriment.[28]

After leaving Hoelsbu, *Veslekari* proceeded to Waltershausen Glacier at the head of the North Fjord, then on to Geologist Fjord, which lay between Strindberg Peninsula on the east and Andrée Land on the west. These land features were named by Swedish explorer A.G. Nathorst for the two Arctic balloonists who had perished during the Andrée Expedition. Louise was moved to see the locations named for these heroic men. She was photographing and filming geographic features at every opportunity. Carl-Julius Anrick reported: "Our motto during the trip was 'in and out of every fiord arm.' We wanted to see if we could get in everywhere ... Miss Boyd wanted photos of every fiord."[29]

Travelling on, *Veslekari* continued up the Franz Josef Fjord and finally entered the Kjerulf Fjord. Fieldwork conducted in this region led to the most significant discoveries of the expedition. Louise commented:

> I discovered a previously unsuspected connection between Kjerulf Fiord at the head of Franz Josef Fiord and Dickson Fiord at the head of the King Oscar Fiord. As we had no topographer with us that year, to make a map of this interesting area, I took upon myself the task of making a complete photographic record of it, taking over 200 photographs from 50 carefully selected stations. From these photographs the American Geographical Society was able to construct a topographical map.[30]

Louise was buoyed by further discoveries and relentless in her pursuit of photographs documenting this area. *Veslekari* had previously been unable to penetrate the entrance of the nearby Ice Fjord — the narrowest of all the tributaries of Franz Josef Fjord. Louise displayed what Anrick referred to as "the untiring energy of the Americans and unconditionally wanted to attempt the Ice Fiord again."[31] Against all advice, Louise directed Captain Lillenes to try again. On the second attempt, *Veslekari* successfully entered the fjord, which had never before been visited by a ship. On the basis of this visit and Louise's photographic evidence, inaccuracies in maps of this area would be corrected. Additionally, although the existence of the Jaette Glacier at the inner end of the fjord was known, Louise and her team discovered a second glacier. Anrick described the scene:

> We got another unexpected picture. The ice streams did not go together. To the left, the somewhat steeper Giant [Jaette] Glacier came from the west, and then, on the eastern side of Mittlandet, the north glacier came with its even longer break. We got the impression that this is where the largest icebergs could originate. Furthermore, the Giant Glacier did have a worthy companion. When it was to be named, Miss Boyd and I agreed on a Swedish name for this big glacier in this area mapped by Swedes. From Miss Boyd's side, this name was in honor of a man whose research has tied together Europe's and America's geological eras and I myself dare humbly to say thank you to my old teacher, Gerald De Geer.[32]

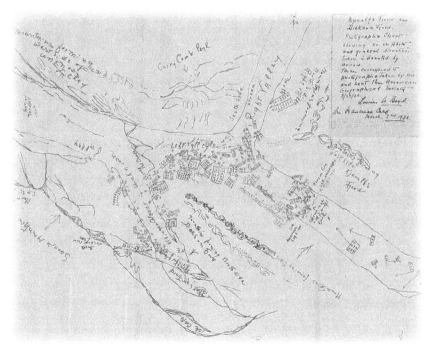

Louise's hand-drawn map of Kjerulf Fjord, Greenland, showing camera locations for her photographic work.

It was a thrilling discovery. Two years later, Louise was humbled to learn that the area between the Jaette and De Geer Glaciers was officially named "Miss Boyd Land" in her honour. Instigated by Lauge Koch, this naming of a landform emphasized acceptance by her peers in the polar world.

In mid-August, *Veslekari* arrived at the Danish settlement of Scoresbysund. Named after the British explorer and whaling captain, the community consisted of the governor's house, a church, warehouses, a store, a few European homes, and several Greenlandic dwellings. Upon their approach, Danish flags could be seen waving from every flagpole. There was some murmuring and a decided sense of discomfort amongst the crew, since the *Veslekari* flew the Norwegian flag and the Stars and Stripes. Winnifred Menzies, wife of Robert Menzies, their botanist, commented:

> After some delay, we began to wonder if we were going to be allowed to land, for although our Danish permits were all in order, we were sailing in a Norwegian ship with a Norwegian captain and crew and flying the very flag that had given the Danes much concern when flown over more northern territory as a sign of the occupation. However, a launch set out from shore, the delay having been caused by the engine refusing to start, not politics, and the Danish Governor came aboard.[33]

Many local people paddled out to the *Veslekari* in their kayaks. Although vessels visited Scoresbysund each season, few women had ever visited the colony, so Louise and the other ladies onboard received much attention. They landed at the small wooden dock and then all went ashore. They were curious about the huge seaplane moored there. Louise was particularly delighted, since polar aviation was a passion of hers. It turned out to be the *Grønland Wal*, D-2053, from Hamburg, Germany. Captain Wolfgang von Gronau and three colleagues were en route from Germany to the United States via Iceland and Greenland. This was the second flight for Gronau, who wanted to prove that transatlantic flights from Germany to the United States were commercially viable. This stop in Scoresbysund was near the beginning of his route, so he and his companions did not have a lot of time to spend with Louise's party. However, an invitation to dine aboard *Veslekari* was accepted immediately.

Gronau and his crew were busy during the day but arrived punctually at the gangplank at 7:00 sharp. Bitter was their disappointment when they learned that *Veslekari* kept Norwegian time, so Louise and her party were already in bed. Gronau and his crew observed local time!

As the weather improved, *Veslekari* began preparing for their departure. Louise asked Gronau to take some mail for her. He bowed and said magnanimously, "It will be the greatest pleasure, but we may never reach our destination."

The first clear day for flying saw the *Grønland Wal* take to the air. *Veslekari* sailed to a larger settlement located at Cape Hope. While there, the *Grønland Wal* flew over their heads and Captain Gronau saluted them. All onboard *Veslekari* waved furiously in response and the local people ran to the flagpole to dip the Danish flag. Happily, Gronau's flight was successful and the letters from the *Veslekari* may have been the first airmail from Europe to America by way of the Greenland air route.

In Cape Hope, Louise and *Veslekari*'s passengers met the local Greenlandic people, who were equally curious about them. Winnifred Menzies wrote:

> They stood grouped around the doors smiling a welcome and eager to have us come in and visit them. Their picturesque, colorful costumes fascinated us and I fear we forgot our manners and stared. However, the women seemed pleased when we admired their beautifully embroidered trousers and boots and the fine beadwork on collars and wristbands.... We had to visit each house in turn, giving the inevitable handshake, some trifling present and sweet chocolate to the children. In each instance, a generous return was made in spite of our remonstrances. A cheap bead necklace was returned by a beautifully made knife with walrus handle. Pretty bead necklaces were sewed onto our wrists with fine sinew, which was greased by being rubbed briskly against the cheek of the seamstress.

Louise returning home. Photograph likely taken in New York in 1931.

An old pair of knickerbockers and plaid waistcoat of my husband's made such a hit that the whole colony had to come and admire.[34]

After their visit, they made their way back to the ship. Half the colony returned with them as *Veslekari* was taking them back to Scoresbysund for the church service. They were told that women were not able to attend church services in the summer since women do not travel in kayaks, but had to wait until winter so they could travel by sledge. Wide-eyed women and children clambered aboard the ship. Winnifred Menzies remarked: "Such a sight was our ship — Eskimos all over it, their bundles stacked against the engine room, mothers nursing their babies on the deck, men whittling out souvenirs for us, seven kayaks safely stored on the fore deck. There was the happy atmosphere of a lot of enthusiastic children having a glorious adventure."[35]

After the service, they returned with their charges to Cape Hope. After the local people reached shore safely and *Veslekari*'s launch began motoring away, they heard rifles firing in salute and they blew *Veslekari*'s whistle in acknowledgement. With that, they left Greenland in September 1931 and set a course back to *Veslekari*'s home port of Ålesund, Norway.

Upon Louise's return to the United States, *The Christian Science Monitor* noted admiringly:

> Women, women everywhere — and four conquer Greenland's icy mountains. Of course, there were men along; they were needed, but Louise A. Boyd led that expedition.... Just when the Danish-Norwegian dispute makes real Greenland information all important, the women produce it. These mappers of desperate geography minimize their big accomplishments — *all in a day's work*, say they.[36]

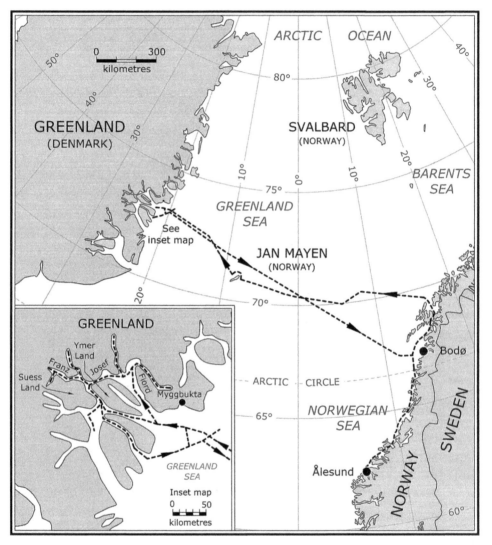

Route of Louise Arner Boyd 1933 Expedition.

CHAPTER SIX

GREENLAND BECKONS

*A land remarkable for the splendid dignity of its scenery and possessed
of a subtle power of inspiring affection tempered by a sense of awe.*
— A.C. SEWARD

After returning to the United States, Louise travelled to New York
to review expedition results with Dr. Bowman at the American
Geographical Society offices. Her Greenland trip had been planned only
as a reconnaissance mission, but still, the results of the 1931 Louise A.
Boyd Expedition were impressive: extensive photographic documentation
of the coastal areas of East Greenland in the region of the Franz Josef and
King Oscar Fjords; the discovery of a second glacier next to the Jaette
Glacier and a previously unknown land area between the two; first entry,
by *Veslekari*, into the supposedly impenetrable Ice Fjord; the discovery
of a geographic connection between the Kjerulf and the Dickson Fjords;
detailed documentation on the state of muskoxen on East Greenland and
Jan Mayen; and the discovery of botanical species previously unknown to
science. Bowman was pleased, and likely surprised, with what Louise had
accomplished. He was particularly complimentary about her improved

photographic skills. Louise had benefitted from Bowman's advice as well as that from the Scott Polar Research Institute and the Royal Geographical Society. She said gleefully: "Regarding what you say about it being hard for you to believe these photographs were taken by the same woman, I don't blame you for feeling as you do. They were! I have ample proof of these facts, also that I had no assistance from any man or woman other than a man to carry my equipment!!"[1] Under Louise's leadership, the 1931 Expedition contributed to the annals of American polar exploration and geographic science.

Although he never visited either polar region, Bowman was a good friend to polar explorers and was close to many, including Stefansson, Byrd, Wilkins, and Bartlett. While in New York, Louise spent happy times organizing her expeditionary data, reviewing her photographs, sorting out the botanical specimens, and beginning to write up her results. She was delighted when Bowman invited her to dine with him and Vilhjalmur Stefansson. Stefansson was one of the best-known American polar explorers of his time. Their luncheon was cordial and marked the beginning of a long friendship. Louise was pleased to receive a letter from him in which he treated her as a colleague on an equal footing:

> I am hoping you will want to come down and see my library. Of course, it is not larger than Bowman's but it is better arranged for examination since it is all within arm's reach. I was hoping to have it straightened out in time for your inspection but shall perhaps not be able to manage that ... I am also most anxious to talk further with you about your plans.[2]

News of the scientific discoveries of this most unusual American female polar explorer was spreading, and recognition of her work followed. In early 1932, the Swedish Society for Anthropology and Geography awarded her the Andrée Plaque for her contributions to Arctic exploration and her collegiality with Swedish scientists. Louise was flattered by Bowman's request to submit a scholarly article to a pre-eminent scientific journal. Initial planning for her next Greenland expedition was

The Andrée Plaque was awarded to Louise on February 13, 1932, in Stockholm, Sweden.

already under way by the time "Fiords of East Greenland: A Photographic Reconnaissance throughout the Franz Josef and King Oscar Fiords" was published in *The Geographical Review* in late 1932.

The SS *Veslekari* was hired, but Louise was faced with working with another unfamiliar captain. Captain Johan Olsen was a highly respected and skilled navigator and sealing master from Ålesund. He was one of only three ice-masters from northern Norway who had been awarded the Royal Norwegian Order of St. Olav. Unlike the temperamental Paul Lillenes, Johan Olsen was courteous and gentlemanly. On the upcoming 1933 voyage, Louise learned to trust his judgement implicitly, and Olsen would work with Louise on three polar expeditions.

Captain Johan Olsen onboard the *Veslekari*. Unknown date.

From the outset, the 1933 Louise A. Boyd Expedition was planned as a scientific mission that extended the objectives of the 1931 trip. Danish explorer Lauge Koch provided Louise with invaluable scientific advice. Koch had been active in East Greenland since the late 1920s and was currently engaged in an ambitious long-term expedition over four summers and three winters. The goal of her next expedition was clear. Louise wrote: "As the Danes and Norwegians had completed the exploratory survey of the region, it was felt that the most useful work we could accomplish would be the intensive investigation and mapping of small critical areas with a view to obtaining a true picture of the typical physiographic features of the region."[3] The plan was to work extensively in the Franz Josef and King Oscar Fjord areas of East Greenland and "to make mapping by photogrammetrical methods the major features of our work partly to supplement the investigations of the physiographer of the expedition and partly to try out new methods of field survey which had been developed.... This was the first time that any American expedition was equipped for ground photogrammetry."[4]

With input from the American Geographical Society, Louise chose the members of her scientific team with care — a surveyor, a geologist, a physiographer, and a botanist. For the first time, Louise allowed no personal friends on this trip. Bowman assisted Louise in locating a physiographer for their expedition. He proposed Harlen Bretz of the Department of Geology at the University of Chicago. At fifty-one, Bretz was the oldest member of the team and only five years older than Louise. Throughout the 1920s, he had conducted extensive research into the origins of the Channeled Scablands region of eastern Washington. His contention that the Scablands were the result of catastrophic flooding sparked what became a major controversy in American geology. After urging Bretz to apply for the position, Bowman received a worried letter from him:

> I have long been interested in the geology of Greenland and the opportunity your letter outlines makes a distinct appeal to me. I am in excellent physical condition for such a trip and I believe family arrangements for a summer's absence can readily be made. Before you advise

the leader of the expedition of my interest, however, I should like to ask you in confidence if you know of any unhappy restrictions, inconsiderations or interferences by this leader in special work on previous similar expeditions. I am slow to take offence and clearly recognize the need of cooperation with the leader's plans on such a trip. I ask chiefly because I anticipate a woman leader, know something of feminine psychology but do not know this particular person. Furthermore, I should not care to go unless there will be opportunity to do a bit of good work and to publish my ideas. My queries sound superfluous and ill-mannered but if you can forgive their crudeness and can assure me that there are no grounds for my fears, I should be glad to have you suggest me for the physiographic work.[5]

Bowman responded positively to this letter, the contents of which Louise was not aware. Had Louise known that Bretz had negative preconceptions about her as leader solely on the basis that she was a woman, she might have thought twice about taking him on.

A few of the men she chose were experienced explorers as well as experts in their respective fields. Louise picked several men from a desire to assist them in their scientific careers. In a letter to Lauge Koch, she wrote: "I do not wish to serve personal interests alone and therefore plan to take along a few young scientists who will benefit both themselves and science from a summer's experience in the fascinating region of East Greenland."[6]

Thirty-six-year-old Osborn Maitland "Mait" Miller was a decorated war veteran and old-school Scot with an inventive mind. Trained at the Royal Geographical Society in England and one of the founders of the School of Surveying at the American Geographical Society, he had several dramatic treks under his belt, including an AGS survey expedition to the headwaters of the Marañon River in Peru in the late 1920s and the 1931 Grenfell-Forbes Expedition to Northern Labrador. During this latter trip, Miller had developed an approach for using aerial photography to create maps.

Lively and energetic, twenty-six-year-old Walter Abbott Wood III from Hoosick Falls, New York, was hired as assistant surveyor working alongside Miller. Wood's first expedition was a 1929 mapping mission in the Himalayas near the Kashmir-Tibet border. He had also participated in treks to the Yukon Territory in Canada, and to Guatemala and Panama. A graduate of the newly anointed American Geographical Society's School of Surveying who had also studied photogrammetry in Zurich, Wood was a promising surveyor.

British geologist Noel Ewart Odell was another of Miller's colleagues, as they had been teammates on the Grenfell-Forbes Labrador Expedition two years previously. While a world-class geologist working at Cambridge University, Odell was famous as a mountaineer with several first ascents under his belt. He had been a member of the ill-fated 1924 attempt on Mount Everest, and was the last person to see George Mallory and Andrew Irvine alive. Forty-three-year-old Odell was also quite a character:

> Odell, a wonder on the mountain, is quite useless in the ordinary affairs of life. But his great quality was his refusal to worry about anything. In an emergency, and we had plenty of emergencies on our trip, he never offered fatuous advice. Instead he would sit placidly on a rock and read the *Times Literary Supplement*, a copy of which, by that time many months old, he always carried in his rucksack, and so he would wait for the situation to clear. It made you ashamed to worry and at the same time heartened you to get something done to justify such implicit confidence.[7]

Louise's early communications with Odell proved satisfactory, although she was perturbed by his questioning about mountaineering opportunities in Greenland. She attempted to quash all talk of this since mountaineering was not part of her agenda. She was also upset by his insistence on bringing his wife.

Gwladys "Mona" Odell had been one of the earliest members of the Ladies Alpine Club and had climbed in the Chamonix and Zermatt areas in Switzerland and the Canadian Rockies. She had also accompanied her husband to Labrador in 1931 during the Grenfell-Forbes Labrador Expedition. Louise knew neither of the Odells but she did want him. Despite misgivings, Louise agreed to his wife joining the group. She would later regret inviting both.

The youngest member of the team was twenty-four-year-old botanist William Drew of the Gray Herbarium at Harvard University. Louise wrote to him:

> I have a letter from Professor Fermald proposing you as a member of my next expedition to East Greenland. Your qualifications seem acceptable but the question of remuneration having been raised, I am bound to say that no member of the scientific staff will receive a salary, nor will anyone receive compensation afterward for working up the results for publication. Expenses will be paid from New York to New York (or Boston, if you prefer). Will you let me know if there is any further information that you desire and if there is a likelihood that you will wish to join the expedition?[8]

Louise was dismayed by his query about remuneration. It seemed that the opportunity to participate in a historic expedition that would benefit science as well as an all-expenses-paid trip to Greenland was not sufficient. He later wrote about their first meeting in New York:

> Miss Boyd could be very generous, like sending me a check to pay for coming to NYC for an interview at the suite she rented at the Waldorf-Astoria. It was large enough for both my wife and I to go. We embarked at Boston on an Eastern Steamship vessel for the overnight trip to N.Y. where we landed near the present aquarium and Battery Park. It was a neat means of transport which failed to survive the Depression. We reached her apartment and then went to the American Geographical

Society offices, returning to her suite at noon for lunch
— preceded by numerous cocktails with which my wife
and I had had no previous experience![9]

During this meeting in New York, Louise sized him up accurately. He
was rather inexperienced in the ways of the world but he knew his plants.
Shortly thereafter, young Mr. Drew signed on the dotted line as the expedition botanist.

After months of preparation, the team gathered in Ålesund, Norway, in
late June 1933. Given that this was a scientific expedition, Louise ensured
that team members had their own professional library provided for them,
and all necessary equipment at their disposal:

Compared to most Arctic expeditions, mine were small
in size both as to personnel and ship. Being a firm
believer that geography, certainly that of the polar

The community of Ålesund, Norway. Photograph taken in 2015.

regions, can best be studied by explorers and scientists equipped with the most precise and practical instruments that modern times have developed, and which would enable them to obtain the most thorough and detailed knowledge of areas not easy of access and where time plays an all-important factor, I spared no efforts of expense in order to equip every branch of our work along those lines.[10]

With no formal scientific training to guide her, Louise relied heavily on American Geographical Society staff and her growing network of colleagues in the polar world. Although advice was offered by others, Louise was the one who ultimately decided what equipment to take and for what purpose. In this, she did not take a wrong step. After hiring *Veslekari* again from Elling Aarseth of Vartdal, she arranged for a self-recording echo-sounder or sonic depth-finder to be installed onboard

Elling Aarseth & Co. shipping crate.

and adapted to enable the surveyors to measure ocean depths to at least 1,800 metres. Louise stated that "the purpose of the soundings was to determine the character of the fiord bottom rather than to make an accurate hydrographic study."[11] Loaned by the United States Coast and Geodetic Survey, two portable automatic tidal gauges were taken onboard and would enable the expedition to gather tidal information. A new Wild phototheodolite and a Wild Universal theodolite would assist Miller and Wood in their surveying work.

In Ålesund, *Veslekari* was just out of dry dock and had been repainted and scrubbed to within an inch of her life. Louise had been there for several weeks already making final preparations. But for Louise, it wasn't all work. The *Sunnmørposten* newspaper noted the excitement of over three hundred local children attending a festive ice cream party she hosted for the town. Over 1,500 ice creams were handed out during the noisy event, which lasted for several hours. A journalist noted that "hurrahs were rung for the happy giver who looked quite pleased at having been able to create as much immediate joy around her."[12] Decades later, these children's parties, which she hosted for many years, are still remembered in Ålesund.

Eventually, all expedition team members gathered in the town and were preparing to leave. Bretz described the hectic scene:

> Miss Boyd met the *Iris* and took us to the *Veslekari* at once. Here we plunged into a hundred interesting details for half an hour, then the taxi she keeps constantly on the job between hotel and pier lifted us up the hill and through the maze of narrow crooked streets to the Hotel Scandinavie. Here a "skoal!" round before a 3:00 dinner; whisky and soda at which Mrs. Odell was hostess. Everybody takes it, Drew is as diffident as I; we stop before the others do. Back to the ship and more fussing around while a small army of porters is loading under the supervision of the Captain and the general manager, Mr. Jurgens of Elling Arseth and Co., the owners. Truck loads of rum, whisky, gin, vermouth, brandy, wine and

Ålesund's maritime heritage. Photograph taken in 2015.

beer (39 cases of wine alone), 80 cases all told. It doesn't look like a Greenland voyage so much as Bill Thompson's search for the tree-climbing fish.[13]

Sir Hubert Wilkins' ship, the *Wyatt Earp*, was docked only yards from *Veslekari*. Wilkins would sail south to New Zealand later that week and then on to the Ross Barrier, Antarctica, where he and his team planned to establish their base. This would provide the launch point for their flight across the Antarctic continent. Sir Hubert proved to be quite delightful. Louise and a few of the scientists toured the impressive *Wyatt Earp* and then Wilkins and his wife dined onboard *Veslekari*. During that auspicious meal, he regaled the group with his Arctic tales. They shared stories about Stefansson, since Wilkins had sailed with him as photographer on the Canadian Arctic Expedition 1913–18.

Also present at the meal was famed Norwegian aviator Bernt Balchen. Balchen had been the chief pilot for the Ellsworth-Wilkins Trans-Antarctica Expedition, and in 1929 he and Richard Byrd had been the first to fly over the South Pole. Aside from other accomplishments, he had been Amelia Earhart's technical advisor. Balchen had also been a close friend of Roald Amundsen. He and Louise had much to talk about.

The last dinner guest was Norwegian scientist and nationalist Adolf Hoel. Although Louise continued to be on the best of terms with him and referred to him in her writing as her "good friend," Louise's true feelings were conflicted. He had been courteous to her during previous meetings but was known to be rather unprincipled, with few qualms about stealing other people's ideas. Louise warned the scientists onboard about Hoel and cautioned them to be as discreet as possible about their specific objectives. Odell told the group that Hoel had a similar reputation in England.

Finally, *Veslekari* slipped away from the dock at 11:00 p.m. with half of Ålesund's population there to see them off. As they sailed, Louise caught sight of Sir Hubert on the wharf furiously waving his hat and cane. Miller, Bretz, Wood, Drew, and Odell stood next to Louise on the bridge. Slowly, that sea of faces, the dramatic outline of the masts and sails of other ships moored in the harbour blurred. Louise must have felt the burden of responsibility that was hers as expedition leader as she pondered the dangerous path ahead.

Initially mirroring the 1931 route, *Veslekari* travelled northward to the Lofoten Islands, where the new self-recording echo-sounding equipment was tested. This technology represented the most advanced and up-to-date methods in measuring the ocean depths. Two representatives from the British manufacturers Henry Hughes and Son accompanied them on this leg of the journey to ensure that everything was in tip-top shape. Prior to this expedition, no other vessel of a similar size had been able to measure at a depth greater than 1,370 metres. Louise was fascinated by what she could learn from this equipment. She stated: "While these tests were being made, those of us in the chart room felt as if we were in a ship with a glass bottom as we watched the instrument tracing the profile of the continental shelf and slope to more than 1,800 metres below us."[14]

With the tests successfully completed, the Henry Hughes representatives departed. *Veslekari* loaded up on coal, drinking water, and ice, and set sail for Jan Mayen. Four stormy days followed. Heavy seas washed up and over *Veslekari*'s railings and water poured into the galley, but Louise was in her element. Finally arriving at Jan Mayen, *Veslekari* anchored at Jameson Bay on the south side of the island. As in 1931, the ship brought mail and provisions for those staying at the two stations. The men there were overcome with joy at the sight of *Veslekari* and the first mail they had received in ten months. All aboard spent a day visiting with the men at these stations.

Two years to the day after she had visited in 1931, Louise, Drew, Miller, and several crewmen travelled by motorboat about five miles east of Jameson Bay. This was to be the first of two days of botanizing. Drew and Louise gathered specimens at the base of the bird cliffs and they had a fine view of Beerenberg as they worked. They collected twenty-eight vascular plants (of which two were unknown to science) and three lichens at five different locations. Louise enjoyed the camaraderie of working with Drew, whom she found to be knowledgeable, deferential, and an agreeable companion.

At the same time, Odell and Wood with two porters had left the *Veslekari* to begin work on their own project. Odell wrote:

> At least two of our party, with the mountain fever strong upon us after four days' imprisonment in a rolling sloop, were anxious to view and photograph this summit scene, as well as ascertain the actual size of the crater, and the writer had designs on a collection of volcanic rocks to supplement that made by Wordie from the upper parts of the mountain ... Walter A. Wood and I made our way up vast névé slopes, in thick mist, to an altitude of 5,300 feet by aneroid. A circuitous route amongst vast crevasses followed, and at 6,000 feet a sudden and short-lived clearing of the atmosphere revealed an astonishing view of the glacier we had come up, and the barren lava fields beyond to the ocean.... We struck across the couloir to its northern confining buttress which gave a mostly steep ice-climb to the top.... We climbed along the crater rim in a northerly direction over several ice-towers, and just as we decided to retreat, owing to driving hail, a startlingly close lightning flash and simultaneous peal of thunder drove us precipitately off the exposed summit.[15]

The climb to the summit had taken seven hours, but the descent took only two. This was only the second ascent of Beerenberg. Despite Odell and Wood's keen desire to continue climbing in other areas, Louise was not supportive. It would prove to be an ongoing source of strife between her and Odell.

By this time, the scientists had begun settling into life onboard *Veslekari*. Seasickness would be ever-present because of the constant, often violent, up-and-down motion of the ship and the vibrations of the engine. Louise also heard complaints about *Veslekari*'s atmospheric aroma, especially from Bretz, who found it offensive:

Ready to admit now that the *Veslekari* has recently been sealing. Since the fires have warmed up her vitals, she exudes a smell that penetrates the cabins and the dining salon, like nothing I ever smelled before. Not carrion, not recently dead; a kind of nauseous aromatic oily redolence. Every ship has her smell, say my companions. My opinion is that Miss *Veslekari* has a dozen all packed into one.[16]

Young Mr. Drew was doing particularly poorly. After several days of discomfort and cramping, radio communication with a Norwegian doctor confirmed that Drew had appendicitis. Everyone was thunderstruck about the potential medical emergency. Drew's predicament was a significant blow to the expedition, since he could not be replaced at that stage. Louise's botanical training by Alice Eastwood of the California Academy of Sciences would come in handy once again. As quickly as possible, *Veslekari* sailed to Mary Muss Bay on the eastern side of Jan Mayen, where a Norwegian whaling ship was anchored. Although it had no passenger accommodations, the captain graciously agreed to give up his own cabin for Drew and transport him back to Norway. The meeting with the captain and crew was one that those onboard *Veslekari* would not soon forget. Louise confided:

Between the [whaling] ships, acting as a bumper was the slimy, decomposing body of a large whale, so decomposed, its odor was something awful. Connecting the two ships was a long, narrow, old and patched wooden ladder with several missing rungs, which served as a gangplank, passing directly over the whale. Due to a big ground swell and the high wind of the night before, both ships were rolling hard and their rolls did not coordinate. The deck of the *Pioner* was much higher than that of the *Sylvia* and an invitation to come on the *Pioner* and see the factory ship boil down the whale blubber into oil meant daring the ladder. These under best conditions, are not my strong point, nor am I good on them. My destination, as I looked up, was at an angle of 45°. So, with a forced smile, I accepted with gusto before mind over matter could change the situation. Firmly gripping each cross piece on the upward climb, I slowly advanced. Even the whale did not let me forget him. A strong off wind gave stifling reminder of his presence below me. Later, the skippers tactfully let me get off the *Pioner* down the pilot's ladder, a feat I was thoroughly accustomed to and which held no qualms … Later that day, the other members of the expedition accompanied the departing botanist to the *Sylvia*. The skipper of the *Sylvia* took the lead over the ladder and before all, lost his balance and fell onto the slimy, rotting whale from which his crew unceremoniously rescued him by aid of a boat hook firmly hooked in the seat of his pants. His wet, slimy legs refused to function on the iron decks and the last sight of him was with the crew gripping his pants and shoulders as he passed out of sight. And no one had a camera![17]

Leaving Jan Mayen and a pained Drew behind, *Veslekari* turned her prow toward Greenland. Usually the pack ice in the Greenland Sea was heavy, thick, and difficult to traverse. During her 1931 Expedition, the ship had been beset on several occasions and met with ice piled high above the railings. The conditions they encountered when they set sail for East Greenland this time were quite different. It was July 11, and while there was some drifting ice and thick fog, for the most part *Veslekari* encountered a calm open sea with no large fields of ice. Lady Luck was on their side. Passing Hold-with-Hope a mere thirty-six hours after leaving Jan Mayen, they continued to Myggbukta in Mackenzie Bay, where they dropped anchor. Louise was overjoyed:

Our goal was now before us — the fiord region of East Greenland — a land where deep inlets cleave the coast and run back among the mountains as far as 120 miles from the outer skerries; where walls of rock, bizarre in form and brilliant in color, rise to heights of more than a mile above the calm waters of the fiords; where mighty glaciers come down from the inland ice cap to the fiord heads and spill over the valley walls.[18]

Many of the scientific team dreaded their visit to Myggbukta, where the mosquitoes were fiercer than anywhere Louise had ever travelled before. The team's goal here was to erect one of two tidal gauges on behalf of the U.S. Coastal and Geodetic Survey. Louise, Miller, and Wood went on a reconnaissance mission and set the gauge up on tiny Tern Island. Returning to the ship, Louise was surprised to see an airplane parked next to *Veslekari*. In their absence, Lauge Koch had spied *Veslekari* and had come to pay his respects. Koch was ebullient with the results of the recent Hague decision that called for Norway to withdraw from East Greenland. As Adolf Hoel had keenly supported the Norwegian side, Lauge Koch had adamantly upheld the Danish position. Dining onboard *Veslekari*, Bretz, Miller, and Odell peppered him for details about this controversial

Louise and Captain Johan Olsen in Greenland in the late 1930s.

issue and ruling, but Louise kept quiet. Finally, the discussion turned to expeditionary matters. Koch was happy to share information regarding pack ice conditions he had viewed from the sky. Entrances to all fjords in the area were blocked with heavy ice. This was vital information, since Louise's team had planned to take echo soundings off the coast at the fjord entrances. Koch and his team stayed a few hours and then flew off. Captain Olsen had been strangely absent during this visit. When she later asked why he did not come to the cabin, he replied stiffly that it was up to Koch to go and find the captain. Louise realized then that, like most Norwegians, Captain Olsen and his crew proudly supported the Norwegian position regarding the occupation of East Greenland and had resented Koch's crowing about the Danish victory. Louise said no more about it.

Veslekari sailed along the coast for the next few days, stopping at locations of interest to the scientific team. Although Captain Olsen had responsibility for the ship and all nautical issues, there was no doubt that Louise was in command of the expedition. Onboard they read, played bridge, transcribed notes, and wrote letters. The shipboard routines continued with occasional diversions. Mait Miller's birthday provided an excellent opportunity for celebrating. They had toasts all round, then a round of singing in various languages. This was followed by amusing gifts from his colleagues: a used pipe cleaner; two days' collection of cigarette butts from ashtrays, carefully packaged; an old safety razor with a dull blade; and a box of burnt matches. Each of these gifts was solemnly presented so as to elicit the best reaction from unsuspecting Miller. But the pièce de resistance was yet to come. When it came time to cut the beautifully decorated cake, he was charmingly touched. Bretz related:

> Miller blew out all candles at one breath then grasped knife and fork to cut the lovely thing into seven pieces. We all held our breath. The frosting cut beautifully but the cake was tough… Standing above it, goaded by laughter and ribald comments, he poised and sliced very delicately. But what a funny cake! It yielded to pressure but it wouldn't cut. Still sincere about doing a good job, he tried prodding

Lauge Koch in Greenland. Unknown date and location.

here and there. Laughter raised the saloon roof and burst open all the windows. I simply gasped at last because the dear man was so innocent. Wood reached over and turned the cake upside down. "Try from that side" he cried. That side wasn't frosted and the genuine bath sponge texture was obvious to all. "An Arctic sponge cake." Miss Boyd informed Miller and somebody added "Doc's bath sponge, Miller." He plunged the fork down with strength enough to go through the plate below and he sawed as one saws to cut off a musk ox bull's head. I stopped him forcibly and the cake rose serenely and stood before him again, waiting to be carved. "Just you wait," he warned me. "You've got a birthday coming before we get back!"[19]

The shared laughter and warm feelings expressed during the party did everyone a world of good. The next day Adolf Hoel arrived unexpectedly on the *Polarbjørn*. At dinner, Hoel told them about running aground on submerged rocks off of Clavering Island three days earlier. They were able to escape only by shifting twenty tons of load by motor boat, pumping the bow tank of water ballast, and praying that the next high tide would lift them off. Bretz remarked after Hoel departed: "The old fellow isn't so bad in some ways. I'm sorry for him, for he is a thwarted man, all his ambitions unrealized and unrealizable. What a world of difference between his diffidence and Koch's magnificent assurance. Koch in his Arctic parka was the perfect picture of the successful intrepid explorer of the frozen North."[20]

After a few days, *Veslekari* arrived at Ymer Island, where the second tidal gauge was erected. With the ship anchored, the scientific team was rowed to shore, eager to continue their respective tasks. Hours later, Louise set up her photographic equipment near the west side of the bay and began shooting a series of photographs of rock formations. Suddenly, sharp, repeated blasts of *Veslekari*'s whistle pierced the air. *What could it mean?* Louise's first thought was fire onboard. She needed to return to the ship as quickly as possible. This was not easy, given their heavy tools and unwieldy equipment, and they were unable to reach the rendezvous point with

Adolf Hoel. Photograph taken in Svalbard, Norway, in 1936.

the ship for several hours. Louise learned that an urgent distress call had been sent by Adolf Hoel. The sturdy *Polarbjørn* had run aground about eighty miles to the south. *Polarbjørn* was listing dangerously and needed immediate assistance. Louise outlined the significance of the Arctic SOS: "It becomes a direct command, a personal one, and a responsibility to you regardless of your own condition, be it scarcity or meager fuel supply, or working plans of members of your expedition in an area in which, at best, you have a bare five or six weeks before the winter closing of the coast, when you have to be safely out."[21]

When all team members were onboard, *Veslekari* lifted anchor and steamed full speed through Antarctic Sound and King Oscar Fjord. Sailing through the night, they were fortunate not to encounter much pack ice, which would have impeded their progress. Ten and a half hours later, they received another message that *Polarbjørn* was free and their services were no longer required. Their relief was great and the tension onboard dissipated. Their engines had been taxed to the limit so maintenance had to be undertaken before they could be under way once more. As they were committed to a program of work in the Franz Josef Fjord region, they set a course back to their original position. When they entered Antarctic Sound, Captain Olsen called out that he had seen something unusual. Upon investigation, they discovered a sharp narrow reef about thirty feet in length below the water that did not appear on the charts. They notified Koch and Hoel of its precise location, since it posed a hazard to navigation. If they had hit it on their way to assist the *Polarbjørn* the night previously, they surely would have been wrecked.

Veslekari then entered the north side of Franz Josef Fjord. The *Polarbjørn* sailed into view and Louise and her team went onboard to find Hoel. He was gracious in acknowledging their assistance but explained that he had called *Veslekari* immediately without waiting to see if the next high tide would lift them off the rocks. To make matters worse, Lauge Koch had picked up the radio messages between *Polarbjørn* and *Veslekari* and had flown to offer assistance to Hoel. This assistance had been flatly refused. It seemed that Hoel would prefer to put his ship and crew at risk and disrupt the progress of another vessel rather than accept Danish help.

Four weeks into the expedition, some members of the scientific team were growing restless. The Odells, Wood, and Miller had undergone the challenges of expedition life before including living in cramped quarters under difficult circumstances. However, Harlen Bretz had never taken part in an arduous expedition. His diary reflects his discomfort in taking orders from a woman, as well as increasing homesickness. His moodiness infected others onboard. It became evident to Louise that Bretz was far outside his comfort zone. He confided in his journal:

> In the midst of this riot of Nature untamed, we sup in royal fashion, a highball for aperitif, port with the last of the meal. But oh, times come when I'd ditch all this hectic little social and hectic big physical world of East Greenland for a back porch supper of simple fare, with Rhoda's chatter, Rudolf's latest-and-soon-to-be-forgotten song roaring and Mother's quiet smile at those wonderful kids. I know — I know — but can't a feller feel a little homesick now and then?[22]

Dissatisfied rumblings came from Bretz and Odell. Delays in the ship's progress occurred because of stormy weather, dense fog, heavy pack ice, icebergs, underwater reefs, equipment failure, distress calls, seasickness, polar bears, tardiness of team members returning to the *Veslekari*, rendezvous with other vessels, and myriad other factors. A reminder from Captain Olsen about the unpredictable weather in East Greenland sent the scientists into a panic with each one jostling to ensure that his own project assumed priority. Louise was unfamiliar with and unprepared for the academic ego. For her, the success of the expedition would be measured by the collective output of the team. But for scholars Bretz and Odell, their own individual projects were of greater significance and they fought to protect them. Each argued vigorously that his scientific work was being unnecessarily curtailed. There was an unpleasant inference that Louise did not understand how scientific fieldwork was done. Polite and friendly to her face, privately Bretz held her in contempt. He wrote scathingly in his diary:

Really and truly, I think this woman is far out beyond the end of the limit. My confreres are instructed to go into my papers for this letter diary if anything untoward should happen to me, and to send it on before it might wreck everybody. For everybody thinks as I do. I need rest and recuperation from her awful irrelevance, her terrible clack, her frightful sentences, her selfishness, her incompetence to lead a scientific expedition. God what an arraignment this party could make of its grievances. We laughed at first and I thought we could continue to laugh, for the humor was rich. But we didn't reckon on the irritation of her interference, her inability to learn some of the geological concepts and her greed for being in the center of everything going on. Yet I must say that once she has what she wants and once you can endure the narratives, she is generous and thoughtful in little things.[23]

A close reading of Bretz's diary and his correspondence both during and after the expedition emphasizes his discomfort with nontraditional gender roles. From the start, he questioned Louise's ability to lead the expedition on the basis of her being a woman. He criticized her heavy drinking despite the fact that he did so himself. His conservative views extended to Noel Odell's wife, Mona, as well. As long as she was "sew[ing] on men's buttons, mended rents, offered to darn socks, cared for those with minor injuries … we have respected and prized her."[24] But as soon as she stepped outside that role, he portrayed her much less sympathetically. Bretz's patronizing attitude toward Louise was transmitted to Odell and to the other more junior members, Miller and Wood. In doing so, Bretz successfully undermined Louise's authority as expedition leader. Each scientist ignored the fact that Louise was providing each of them with a free fieldwork season in an inaccessible region of the world. It was a unique opportunity for them all. There was no scrabbling for funding dollars, no competing with other scholars for the chance to work in Greenland. It had literally fallen into their laps. Louise was oblivious to the fact that Bretz disliked her. The extensive later correspondence between Bretz and

Louise reveals only positive feelings on Louise's part. She commented to Miller that she would be pleased to sail with Bretz on another expedition, stating that "he [Bretz] isn't under-handed, he says just what he thinks, he strikes out from the shoulder."[25] When Bretz heard this, he responded privately: "God, she little knows what thoughts we all have of her, what blows I haven't hit that I ached to deliver."[26]

They had been working and living together in close quarters for many weeks. As leader, Louise worked hard to present a confident front to the others. Mistakenly believing Bretz was her ally, she confided to him that she had suffered from timidity before her polar work and that she had had to force herself to appear assertive. In an unguarded moment, Mona Odell told Louise about the so-called "Raspberry Club." Instigated by Odell and Bretz, they, with Wood and Miller, would get together on the deck or out in the field and "razz" each other about personal idiosyncrasies. According to Bretz, Louise was a favourite target and her "shrill" voice and habit of speaking volubly when excited had already been mimicked during "Club" meetings. After learning about the "Raspberry Club," Louise admitted to being a little overly sensitive. She likely wondered if she was the subject of merriment when she saw Bretz, Odell, Miller, and Wood laughing together. In his expedition diary, Bretz refers to the "ribald mimicry, bitter denunciations and sarcastic laughter"[27] whenever the four of them met. Ill will also developed between the Odells and Louise. It is clear from several expedition diaries that Mona and Louise clashed on several occasions. Bretz's diary suggests that, for whatever reason, Mona suffered a nervous collapse in the final weeks of the expedition.

Once their work in the Ice Fjord was complete, *Veslekari* sailed for the inner end of Franz Josef Fjord. As they sailed, the waterway narrowed and it was as if they were travelling through a majestic canyon. Finally, they arrived at the head of the fjord with mighty Riddarborgen rising 6,161 feet on their left and the Nordenskiöld Glacier due west. Some group members went north to conduct research at Frænkel Land while Captain Olsen and Louise went to the Kjerulf Fjord, which branched out from the Franz Josef Fjord in a southerly direction; on her 1931 trip, Louise had been unable to take the ship beyond the entrance to Kjerulf Fjord because of icebergs. After a hard day of fieldwork, they were returning to the *Veslekari* when one of the crew unexpectedly found a sealed bottle close to the water's edge. In the bottle was a note in Swedish and English written by Dr. Josef Hammar, chief surgeon to Nathorst's Swedish Expedition of 1899, which had attempted to locate members of the Andrée Expedition. The note read: "This point, the inmost of Frans Josefs Inlet I have reached at the 12 Aug. 1899 alone on a canoe: Dr Josef Hammar. The Swedish Greenlands expedition 1899. Surgeon on Antarctic."[28] Louise noted:

> Our finding of this note was a queer turn of fate. It marked the third time in as many years that these valiant balloonists, whom I had never known in life, had crossed my path. During our search for Amundsen in 1928 we had met Captain Eliassen on the Norwegian sealer *Bratvaag*. While at White Island in 1930, Eliassen had found Andrée, chopped the ice from his body, recovered his diary and photographs and had also found Frænkel. Strindberg's body was recovered later; and thus was solved a mystery of thirty-three years' standing. By chance that same autumn I was in Stockholm and with Captain Eliassen and Docent Hoel I attended the funeral services of the three balloonists. In the spring of 1932 the Swedish Anthropological and Geographical Society conferred on me their Andrée Plaque.[29]

Following the scientific team's reconnaissance mission, they decided that a prolonged trip to Frænkel Land was in order. Accordingly, preparations were made for a stay of three to four weeks, which satisfied all the scientists. In recent weeks, onboard squabbling had become more pronounced. The objectives of one scientist would conflict with those of another, so someone was always dissatisfied. Few seemed willing to compromise. Finally, a meeting was called to clear the air. Bretz commented:

> The upshot of tonight's conference was that the party could be landed with supplies for two weeks and that I

then could take command of it for my unfinished fiord work, the party (minus me) going up into Goodenough Land for Odell's work and Miller's and Wood's mapping. The conclusion reached heartens me wonderfully. I didn't know I was feeling so blue. I can do a lot if there are no delays or late startings, photographic expeditions and other geologizing. Of course I have had the advantage of Odell so far in our waiting to get in, our visiting Eskimo ruins, our visiting with Koch, Hoel, our rescue (?) of Hoel, etc. I have been seeing a great deal of meat for my pot and Odell, whose field lies in the interior, hasn't. I feel sure now, with a definite schedule and sequences and overlap, that my work will get done in time. The whole summer would be largely a futility if this failed to materialize.[30]

Their plans to conduct extensive fieldwork at Frænkel Land were welcomed by the scientific team, although it proved more challenging than expected for some. According to Olds:

With the return of the reconnoitering parties to the *Veslekari*, the scholars so pampered aboard the vessel now were to face a more rugged test of mettle…. This would be no minor excursion. Elaborate preparations were required for the extended journey on foot across trackless stretches of rock-ribbed mountains, boulder-filled terraces, slippery glaciers and icy streams. To transport all their gear and scientific equipment from the ship to the base camps and from one camp to the next, the party would have to carry everything on their backs. No native porters, pack animals or vehicles were available in this uninhabited world, no trails to follow, no friendly villagers, no sources of food along the way, not even sledges and dogs.[31]

They made their first camp at an elevation of 1,991 feet near Arch Glacier in the upper Gregory Valley. Camp Two was established four and a half miles west. At an elevation of 2,188 feet, it was situated on a sandy terrace with avalanche boulders. Sunless and brisk during the day and distinctly chilly at night, this location nevertheless provided endless fascination for the team. Louise remarked ecstatically:

> Inanimate nature seemed almost alive in these valleys. Changes were continually taking place in the topography: rocks, large and small, single and in groups, constantly ripped down the steep mountainsides, forming deep troughs and rolling out on the valley floor. On the south wall, ice calved off from hanging glaciers thousands of feet above us and spilled its fresh white substance over the vari-colored rocks.[32]

Camp Three was set up even higher at an elevation of 2,476 feet in the upper Gregory Valley. From there, they were able to see the "Mystery Lakes" down a side valley between the Jaette and Gregory Glaciers. After several

Suess Land, Greenland. Photograph taken by Louise in the late 1930s.

weeks filled with long days and back-breaking work, the scientific team later reconvened on the *Veslekari*.

At the end of August, the weather shifted and the warm sunshine they had enjoyed for weeks was replaced by dense fog. Mother Nature was telling them it was time to depart this wondrous land. Taking a last long look at Franz Josef Fjord, they weighed anchor and began the journey back. The *Veslekari* was sailing slowly through the fjord when suddenly, without warning, she was grounded. They waited for high tide to come and go, hoping that this might shift the ship. Instead, the ship settled in even more, although they were relieved to see she remained upright. At this late stage in the season, all other ships had left East Greenland, so *Veslekari* was completely on her own in a desolate region of the world. Desperate measures were called for. Captain Olsen ordered the immediate removal of thirty tons of seawater ballast, two motor boats, one rowboat, three and one-half tons of fuel oil, and seventeen barrels of petrol. No change. Then fifteen tons of coals were thrown overboard. Overall, fifty-four and one-half tons were removed from *Veslekari* with no change in their situation. Captain Olsen's solution to the problem was typically innovative, as Louise related:

> About 720 feet away there happened to be an iceberg, some 20 feet long, 10 feet wide and 6 feet high. Around this, a cable was put and connected with the ship's winch. The motor dory shoved the berg as the winch pulled on the cable and the iceberg was grounded in a desired position aft of us. Fortunately for us, the next tide was the spring tide and at high water on September 4, with the engines full speed astern and the winch pulling on the cable connected with the iceberg, the ship was floated undamaged. Here was a case when an iceberg was a friend! We anchored and took onboard our petrol barrels and boats. Luckily we had ample coal left for the homeward journey. By 12:30 p.m., the ship was cleared and we left for Muskox Fiord.[33]

Travelling back through the fjords, snow had started falling and they knew they needed to be on their way. Louise remarked: "Nature was closing

Louise in parka. Photograph likely taken in the late 1930s. Unknown location.

her doors on us. We had arrived in early July when the last winter's ice was still blocking the entrance to the fiords and on shore spring flowers were in full bloom. Extending from summit to sea level, as far as one could see, Greenland was white."[34]

All scientists were eager for home, but Louise wanted to conduct more fieldwork. Bretz commented with derision: "Wish we could leave her with a can of beans in her beloved Greenland for the winter and beat it."[35]

Despite her failure to capture the respect of her scientific team, Louise ensured that the objectives of the expedition were met and all team members returned home safely. The list of scientific accomplishments was a long one. Most significantly, the physiographic studies yielded critical data documenting ongoing glacial recession. This would be a continuing professional interest of Louise's. With prescience, she stated:

> With the peak of glaciation throughout the world definitely on the wane, probably there is nowhere that one can see this ice recession in more varied and striking evidences in Greenland, and in locations accessible for observations. We included studies of this phenomenon as one of the principal objectives of our 1933, 1937, and 1938 expeditions.[36]

The team's use of photogrammetrical equipment highlighted its efficacy in exploratory surveys in inaccessible places, and would be adopted by other scientists. The surveyors' data and Louise's photographs would be used to create a series of useful maps published by the American Geographical Society. The recordings from the echo-sounder provided valuable information about the ocean depths. In addition, the specific adaptations that Louise had ordered prior to the expedition resulted in the development of the Hughes "*Veslekari* Model" — considered by many to be the first deep-water recording echo-sounder. The tidal gauge records sent to the U.S. Coast and Geodetic Survey were deemed to be of "special interest" by the government. Over thirty-one varieties of botanical specimens were collected in Jan Mayen and eighty varieties in East Greenland. The list of scientific accomplishments went on and on.

Traversing broken polar ice and stormy seas, *Veslekari* sailed home and docked at Ålesund on September 16. The expedition had taken eighty days. The scientific team disembarked and the crew began the laborious and unenviable task of unloading the cargo and equipment. Team members chatted about the prospect of seeing loved ones again. Certainly, the scientists were pleased to part company with Louise. By the end of the journey, some of the scientists were privately discussing an unfounded rumour that there was insanity in Louise's family with Bretz speculating that she was mentally unbalanced. They had all had enough of women in charge. Bretz confided in his journal that he, Miller, and Wood swore a solemn vow never again to travel to the Arctic with a woman. Over the coming weeks, expedition members went their separate ways and resumed their old lives.

As leader, Louise was not finished with the work of the expedition. She had no idea what was waiting for her when she resumed this work months later. Academic reputations would be challenged, egos would be bruised, and legal suits threatened as Louise attempted to bring this expedition, and the scientific results of their work, to a satisfactory conclusion.

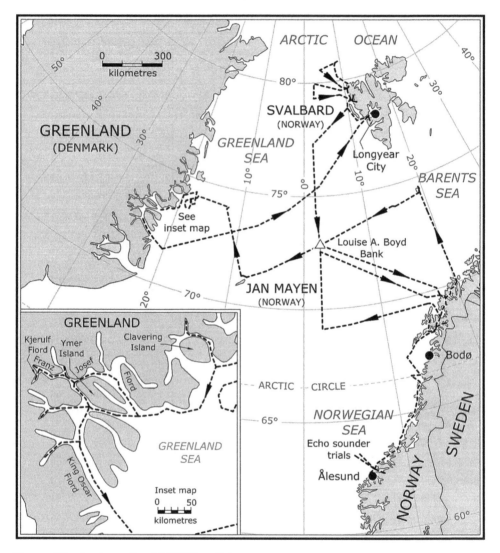

Route of Louise Arner Boyd 1937 Expedition.

CHAPTER SEVEN

AN OBSESSIVE PURSUIT

What is the strange attraction of these polar regions … so strong
and enduring that once having left … one's only idea is to go back?
— JEAN-BAPTISTE CHARCOT

Upon returning to Maple Lawn, Louise immediately began making new plans. Hardly were her travelling trunks unpacked and her maps, books, and scientific equipment safely stored away when she was off again. She wrote to a colleague: "I quite feel as though I were attached to the tail of a comet, when judging the speed with which this world seems to be taking me from almost one end of it to another!"[1] As she journeyed through Europe during the winter of 1933, Louise's diaries document the places she was visiting, the unique customs of local people, the ever-changing landscape. While somewhat lacking in introspection, her writing reflects an observant woman intensely curious about the world around her. Travelling by bus, horse and sleigh, and even reindeer, this trip exposed her to a different side of the northern Scandinavia she loved:

Tried skiing today. Hard work — not successful! Wish I were younger and good at it. It must be great sport. Superb day! Off about 3:30 p.m. with the reindeer and pulka. Went about 13 kilometres in moonlight. Such sparkling, glistening snow. Through shadows of trees cast by the moon on the snow! Through the forests — too beautiful![2]

When she arrived back in the United States in the spring of 1934, Louise's reputation as a bonafide polar explorer had preceded her. She had published another article, "Further Explorations in East Greenland, 1933," in *The Geographical Review*, and had been invited to participate in the Fourteenth International Geographical Congress in Warsaw, Poland. By now, Louise was skilled at getting what she wanted. She contacted relevant scientific organizations to obtain official letters of recommendation, since formal affiliation would open doors for her at the Warsaw Congress. Her persistence paid off. She arrived in Poland with credentials in hand as a delegate for three prestigious organizations — the Society of Woman Geographers, the California Academy of Sciences, and the National Research Council.

The letter from the Society of Woman Geographers emphasized Louise's accomplishments, stating that her attainments eminently qualified her to represent the Society. But Louise's interest in Poland extended beyond the Congress. She stated: "My objective, in addition to attendance at the Congress, was to make a photographic record of the rural life of the country, as revealed in representative portraits of peasant types and in representative views illustrating methods of farming and other land uses, native industries, transportation, architecture and market scenes. This was somewhat of a departure for me after long devotion to photography in the Arctic.... It seemed to me that the opportunity offered of doing photographic work in Poland was one that should not be missed."[3]

It isn't known if she had visited Poland before or if she simply took advantage of the opportunity to travel in a country that was largely ignored by the West. Certainly, she had the funds to go wherever she wanted. Poland was the only country she studied and worked in outside of the circumpolar north.

Louise had been warned that private cars were scarce in Poland so she imported her reliable Packard from California. She also brought over chauffeur Percy Cameron, who had worked for the Boyd family for over twenty years. Louise entered Poland at the southwest corner of the country at Cieszyn. For the next eleven days, she travelled throughout the industrial region of Polish Silesia, visited the sacred shrine at Czestochowa, and explored Polish Pomerania and East Prussia before returning to Warsaw in time for the Congress.

Since 1922, the International Geographical Union had promoted the study of geographical problems and coordinated geographical research requiring international co-operation. Louise was one of six hundred participating delegates and members representing thirty-six countries. She was one of only a handful of women who had been invited to present. Her paper, entitled "Report on Two Expeditions to the Franz Josef and King Oscar Fjord Region of East Greenland (1931 and 1933)," was given as a special lecture. Following the conclusion of the Congress, Louise continued her motor trip throughout the country.

International Geographical Congress building in Warsaw, Poland, with Louise's Packard parked in front in late August 1934.

Initially, she travelled to northeastern Poland with other Congress participants and their Polish hosts, Professors Limanowski and Rewienska of the University of Wilno. She then drove throughout the southern and eastern regions of Poland, where she explored the landscape and visited the Prypec marshes. This land and its people captured her imagination, inspiring another scholarly article in *The Geographical Review* and another American Geographical Society book, *Polish Countrysides*, both published in 1936.

While in Europe, Louise was thrilled to represent the United States once again at the Fourth International Photogrammetry Congress in Paris, where her expedition maps, prepared with new photogrammetric techniques, were displayed. Following these official functions, she returned to the United States and plunged into fulfilling obligations relating to the 1933 Expedition. Work on another book based on her 1931 and 1933 expeditions was ongoing and required many visits to the AGS office to consult with staff. *The Fiord Region of East Greenland* was published by the American Geographical Society in January 1935 and received widespread attention. Louise was confident enough in its significance to send the book out personally to polar organizations, scientists, and explorers, including Ejnar Mikkelsen, James Wordie, Harriet Chalmers Adams, and Vilhjalmur Stefansson. The British Admiralty "expressed their admiration for Miss Boyd's work" and founder of the French photogrammetry industry Georges Poivilliers wrote: "I don't know which I admire most, your scientific faith or the courage you needed to undertake such expeditions ... I carefully keep your book and maps as a precious souvenir of a great explorer of artic [sic] regions."[4]

Louise also sent a copy to French explorer Jean-Baptiste Charcot, whom she had likely first met in 1928 when Charcot and his ship the *Pourquoi Pas?* assumed an active role in the Amundsen rescue mission. He heartily congratulated her for the "really splendid scientific work it contains. I never saw anything better," and signed himself, "Believe me dear Miss Boyd yours gratefully and very respectfully, Charcot."[5] Louise's letter to him is easy and comradely — discussing ice conditions that *Veslekari* had encountered in 1933 and joking about other explorers. Clearly, there was mutual respect between the two. Louise was shocked when she received the news of Charcot's tragic death when the *Pourquoi Pas?* foundered on rocks in September 1936. She kept a copy of Charcot's obituary in her files for the rest of her life. It was a sobering reminder of the toll exacted on daring polar explorers.

Mait Miller, back at his job with the American Geographical Society, wrote her in 1936: "Your book has received more reviews and press notices than almost any other book published by the Society."[6] Louise's introduction to *The Fiord Region of East Greenland* graciously acknowledged the contributions of the team: "For the effective work done in the field by the members of the scientific staff of the expedition — Messrs. Bretz, Miller, Wood, Odell, and Drew, and Mrs. Odell — and for the contributions contained in this volume no words can adequately express my appreciation, nor can the whole-hearted devotion of Captain Olsen and the *Veslekari's* crew be too highly praised."[7] This statement masked the ongoing antagonism between Louise and Noel Odell following the conclusion of the expedition. It highlights Louise's maturity as an expedition leader and her recognition that each team member contributed to the overall success of the mission.

Written accounts portray Noel Odell as calm, genial, and easy-going, but Louise clearly drove him to distraction. Caught up in their conflict, Dr. Bowman reported that Odell "has gone quite wild and sassy."[8]

Odell wrote to Bretz:

> It is no good his [Louise's lawyer] trying to impress me with all that Louise has done with her money for members of the Expedition when one's work in the field was definitely restricted in scope by her incompetence and selfishness, and into the bargain one's wife, a not inexperienced traveler, returned with a nervous breakdown.... Nor is it much good your reminding me that Louise is a woman and that women's decisions are largely emotional reactions! Surely if a woman assumes man's responsibilities and wishes to acquire the credit of leadership, she has definitely got to display more faculties than emotional reaction and garrulity?[9]

Odell's disagreement with Louise extended beyond the tension between her and his wife, Mona, and Louise's stubborn refusal to allow him to conduct as much mountaineering as he wanted to during the expedition. From her earliest voyages, Louise demanded absolute control over the taking and use of photographs. In signing the required contract, all expedition members agreed to this. Additionally, the scientists agreed to obtain Louise's permission prior to publishing any article about the expedition results. Despite his earlier agreement to these terms, Odell decided to play by his own rules. He published a series of scholarly papers based on his 1933 Greenland fieldwork without her approval. Even more egregiously, he failed to mention that his data was collected during the Louise A. Boyd Expedition. He also did not submit an expedition report in a timely manner, so that the new American Geographical Society book was published without his contribution. The messy argument took three years to resolve and enmeshed the AGS, the Scott Polar Research Institute, and Louise's lawyer. At the end of it, Odell referred to Louise as "Mrs. Satan" in his correspondence. While only partial documentation of this conflict exists, it seems likely that both parties were at fault, for different reasons.

Both Odell and Louise sought Harlen Bretz as an ally, and he convincingly played the role of confidant to Louise. Her letters to him in 1933 and for many years thereafter refer to her fond visits with his family and mention thoughtful gifts between her and Bretz's wife. Bretz's hypocritical attitude toward her continued unabated. While he maintained a public façade of goodwill toward Louise, in private it was a different matter. Two years after the expedition, he invited Louise to speak to his students at the University of Chicago and wrote to Odell about it. In preparing his students for Louise's lecture, Bretz undermined her authority as a polar explorer as he had two years earlier to junior team members on *Veslekari*:

> I do not recall telling you of the Queen's [his private nickname for Louise] lecture here last spring. I had talked about her so much that she drew a capacity crowd at the open meeting of our graduate students' geological fraternity. She fulfilled every expectation I had awakened. She wore a diamond dog-collar, sundry finger diamonds and two

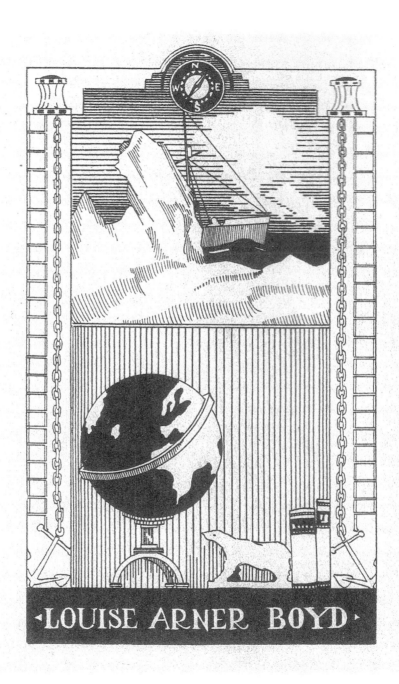

One of Louise's bookplates.

huge orchids (plus the conventional elements of dress). Plenty of the boys asked me if I bought her the orchids! She <u>read</u> her lecture, so its English was not too awful. But she <u>said</u> "exposition" consistently throughout. But before and after — especially after — we had the favorite Boydian stimulants. I had warned everybody not to slip — never to address her or to refer to her in her presence as "The Queen." Oh well, it's all over now and we have learned something more about the infinite possibilities for variety in human personalities.[10]

Despite being hard at work on her upcoming *Polish Countrysides* book and guest lectures at Stanford University, the Century Club, the American Geographical Society, the Society of Woman Geographers, and the San Rafael Improvement Club, Louise's thoughts had already returned to the Arctic. As early as January 1936, she had queried Captain Olsen to see if he would be available that summer. At the same time, she sent a telegram soliciting advice from Adolf Hoel:

> Louise Boyd considering charter of *Veslekari* this sum-
> mer for photographic study of glaciers and soundings
> along coast and fjords, Spitzbergen, Northeastland, King
> Carlsland and Jan Mayen. Stop. She does not wish to
> interfere with your use of vessel or work done by you for
> Norwegian government and uncertain how far you have
> covered subject. She feels this work related to her East
> Greenland and Jan Mayen studies and would appreciate
> your views and suggestions.[11]

Since no expedition in 1936 transpired, it is likely that either Hoel or Olsen advised against it. Louise was not deterred and moved forward with detailed plans for 1937. This came as a surprise to Harlen Bretz, since he and Mait Miller doubted the seriousness of Louise's intentions. After the 1933 Expedition, Bretz had commented: "Miller thinks there'll never be another; that further explorations by the Queen will be cruises without recalcitrant scientists and their funny notions onboard."[12] But Louise proved them wrong. Her letters to Bretz demonstrate a more advanced understanding of the scientific requirements for an expedition, as well as an awareness of the personal dynamics involved. She explicitly wanted to avoid hiring another scientist who was more committed to his own agenda than to the work of the expedition as a unit:

> In going over the plans for next year and the year afterward, don't you think that the best person to do the geological work would be one who would go on the expedition in connection with the physiographer — in other words, an Assistant Physiographer? Those of us at the A.G.S. and myself feel this would concentrate the work and avoid the unfortunate conditions (we hope there will never be a second repeat on them) as we had with O'Dell. He never tied in the geological work or cooperated with the physiographic work.[13]

By November 1936, Captain Olsen's services and the *Veslekari* were secured. Louise was delighted to learn that several men who had previously worked as her crew had signed up again. This group included Olsen's two sons and chief engineer Peder Strand, who wrote to Louise: "I have been at sea about thirty years but the trips with you to East Greenland was the most splendid trips I ever have had. It was a pleasure to work in your service."[14]

Olsen also hired Louise's good friend Captain Peder Eliassen as first mate. Louise had kept in contact with many of the Norwegian crew and could not think more highly of them:

> Greater loyalty and greater efforts than theirs on our behalf could not have been possible. Their long hours of work, their tenacity in getting the ship through difficult ice conditions, their interest in making it possible for us to reach our objectives, often under the most trying circumstances, deserve the highest admiration and respect.[15]

Back in the United States, the search for the first member of the scientific team was under way. Bretz wrote to Louise:

> I talked with Prof. Richard F. Flint of Yale University … and found him receptive to the idea of going with you. He is my first choice as a physiographer for you. He has an established and growing reputation, is between 30 and 35 years old, vigorous, an excellent field man, and a good scout to work with. His father before his death was a faculty member here; his mother is Professor of English now in our University. I feel sure you will like him.[16]

Employing a successful strategy she had used in 1933, once Flint had agreed to join the expedition as geologist and glaciologist, Louise used his name and reputation to attract others. Flint's twenty-six-year-old graduate student Lincoln Washburn would act as his assistant. "Link" Washburn had competed in the 1936 Olympics as part of the U.S. skiing team and participated in a National Geographic expedition to Mount McKinley. Link's wife, Tahoe Washburn, later wrote: "In January, 1937, his professor, R.F. Flint asked him to be his field assistant on explorer Louise Boyd's expedition to the magnificent fjord region of North Eastern Greenland during the following summer. I was devastated not to be with him."[17] But Louise had learned her lesson. From 1937 onwards, there would be no friends *or* wives tagging along for the ride.

Botanists from Yale University suggested the name of another potential team member — thirty-four-year-old plant ecologist Henry J. Oosting from the Department of Botany at Duke University. Although he was highly recommended, he had no northern experience and his correspondence with Louise prior to the trip highlighted his trepidation about travelling abroad. His feelings are reflected in the title he chose for his expedition diary, "To Greenland in 105 Days or Why Did I Ever Leave Home?" Louise's generous offer to share her cameras and technical equipment with him, to send him her extensive library on Greenland botany, and to write introductory letters to noted botanists Johannes Lid of the Norwegian Botanical Association and Dr. Anderson of the Herbarium in Finland did much to assuage his concerns. To round out the scientific crew, twenty-six-year-old James M. Leroy from Elizabeth City, North Carolina, accepted the position of hydrographer, thirty-one-year-old New Yorker Fred W. Buhler was hired as surveyor, and Norwegian Sverre Remoy signed on as radio operator.

Finally, the Louise A. Boyd 1937 Expedition plans were revealed publicly. While some reporters discussed the scientific objectives of the expedition, others still focused on Louise's charismatic personality and the seemingly startling fact that she was a woman. The *New York Times* referred to her as "the only woman polar explorer … whose Arctic explorations in the last ten years have rivaled those conducted by men."[18] According to the *Montreal Gazette*: "Women do about everything that men try to do these days. Even such things as Arctic exploration are no longer sacred monopolies of the so-called stronger sex. Miss Louise Boyd, the only woman polar explorer has just sailed to do a bit of Arctic exploration."[19] By now, Louise's expeditions were also announced in polar publications, including the *Polar Record* — the official journal of the Scott Polar Research Institute, affiliated with Cambridge University:

> Miss Louise A. Boyd, of San Francisco, proposes to lead an expedition to East Greenland and the waters between Greenland and Spitsbergen during the summer of 1937. It will be remembered that her last expedition in 1933 carried out much useful work in the fjord region of East Greenland. The work of the expedition will be along two different lines: (1) oceanographical work (and also magnetic work if arrangements can be made for including this); and (2) geomorphological and ecological studies of glacial marginal features in the fjord region of East Greenland.[20]

More important than the media coverage were the letters of congratulation she received from her peers, including Sir James Wordie of the Scott Polar Research Institute and Adolf Hoel. Hoel wrote that her plans were of "great scientific interest and practical importance."

Louise planned two ambitious expeditions to take place in 1937 and 1938. She had decided that a multi-year scientific program, conducting fieldwork in overlapping sites over the course of several seasons, would yield more productive results. One of the main goals of the 1937 Expedition would be the continuing investigation of glacial recession. This would be conducted by Flint and Oosting, who would study major plant communities associated with recessional features. Hydrographer Leroy would supervise the echo-sounding program, tidal gauge recordings, and magnetic observations. Buhler would undertake plane-table mapping, supplemented by Louise's detailed photographs. A further goal in 1937 was to travel as far north as possible given whatever ice and weather conditions the *Veslekari* would encounter. Louise commented:

> It was planned, if weather and ice conditions permitted, that the work of these two seasons would be carried on progressively northward from the King Oscar–Franz Josef Fiord area. On the other hand, it was felt that the latter area had by no means been exhausted, and our plans were suffi-ciently flexible — as plans for a summer expedition to East Greenland must always be because of the uncertainty of ice conditions — to permit our return there, assured of finding no lack of worth-while work to do, in case it proved impos-sible to spend the whole of either season farther north.[21]

In early 1937, Louise, Leroy, and Buhler left Ålesund on the *Veslekari*, sailing northward along the coast to meet with the rest of the scientific team — Flint, Washburn, and Oosting — in Tromsø. By the time *Veslekari* was ready to leave, Oosting was already regretting his decision to participate. He said ruefully:

> After various and sundry goodbyes not unmixed with regret — a sober supper — and then quickly down to the depot — I get started on the big adventure. Frankly I'm not particularly anxious to go now that the time has come — adventure of any sort has never been my line — and the thought of the rolling sea gives me no great cheer. But — we're off![22]

At 5:15 p.m. on June 30, *Veslekari* sailed out of Tromsø harbour. Grateful for the calm seas, the scientists were entranced by the magnificent fjords and the antics of puffins wheeling and circling overhead. As midnight approached, the wind quickened the waves and *Veslekari* continued on its northward course. Almost immediately, they encountered a violent storm, which proved daunting for the new scientific team. Strong waves swept over the decks. Louise described the harrowing scene:

> Heavy seas sweeping over our decks put so much water on them that the iron door of the galley had to be closed to keep the water from splashing on the stove and scalding the cook. Hip rubber boots were an absolute necessity, not only on deck but even in our mess room, where, despite the closing of the iron door, the sea surged in around our legs, often knee-deep. Such days as these were too rough for the sounder to work and the ship had to be navigated at from half to slow speed much of the time. In spite of the bad weather, however, we ran Old Glory up to the masthead on the Fourth of July.[23]

Oosting was rattled, and confided to his journal, "I am undoubtedly the world's worst sailor — if it can be avoided I shall never go off on a trek like this again."[24]

The storm lasted more than four days, and *Veslekari* rode through it on a course toward Jan Mayen. As the seas calmed, the ship was enveloped by banks of low-lying fog. They had arrived at Jan Mayen at last.

Overcome by seasickness, several of the scientists spent their time onboard lying flat on their backs on their bunks, reading and writing letters. As usual, Louise was a competent sailor with little tolerance for expedition members who were feeling under the weather. She was anxious to begin fieldwork. Although Captain Olsen deemed the seas too rough to land, Louise suggested taking the motor boat for a scout around. While the boat was out the weather cleared, and the boat was able to land. Oosting related:

Back comes the captain and says he is to go in for them at 6:00. Feeling rotten anyhow it made me feel no better and the only thing left was to pack for the afternoon. Upon their return, B [Miss Boyd] had collected a mess of plants for me. Perhaps I showed too little enthusiasm — at least she chose to twist one of my remarks and left me no end of embarrassment trying to explain myself. Well I pressed the plants — no data of any kind to go with them.... It happens that the relief boat is in now. I hope to send Cornie [Oosting's wife Cornelia] a letter on it tomorrow. I still say "Nuts to expeditions!"[25]

As the favourable weather continued, the decision was made to remain in the area for several days. The anchor was dropped in Jameson Bay and the expedition participants organized themselves according to their respective tasks. After a full day of fieldwork, the unpredictable weather conditions on Jan Mayen changed and Captain Olsen suggested shifting their position. Oosting remarked:

The sea began kicking up around 5:00 p.m. and when we came in at 6:00 we had a wild ride although not dangerous for the motor dories are very seaworthy and these boys can handle them. The *Veslekari* was rolling as usual — she would go up and down with the speed of an express train — whoosh! All the time the boys were trying to get the tackle hooked so the winches could go — big danger of catching the rear tackle and not the front because then the dory would simply dive under water and fill up.[26]

By then, the scientists were keen to reach Greenland — the ultimate destination for the expedition. After a day of calm sailing, the temperature began dropping precipitously. Then, *Veslekari* encountered the dreaded pack ice. The scientists were initially enthralled by the sight. Oosting stated: "We are at half speed and turn back and forth a good deal since they try to avoid larger pieces. Now and then there is a gentle bump as *Veslekari* nudges the floes aside. A little while back we hit one with a resounding thump! The men say that's nothing — wait till we head due W. into the real ice and begin bucking the floes."[27] *Veslekari* skirted the ice for hours, which turned into days. Although Captain Olsen and Louise knew what to expect, it caused consternation amongst the scientific team as they saw their agendas being diminished by the unrelenting weather conditions. Louise reported:

> In one 30-hour period we drifted 15 miles southwestward. The speed of the ship likewise varied. Rarely could we make more than half speed; often we made less, and there were days when we spent a good part of the time anchored to large ice fields. The captain and crew were tireless in their efforts. While in difficult ice Captain Olsen or Captain Eliassen, the mate, were always in the crows-nest. Frequent use was made of ice anchors imbedded in the heavy ice to give the engines additional pulling and pushing power. Narrow, seemingly impossibly small lanes were in this way pushed open into leads through which the ship could move. Great care had to be taken at all times lest the ship be beset or shut off from the first available opening. There was no sparing of the ship's hull as she continually bumped and pushed the ice.[28]

Captain Olsen and Louise knew well that all plans were at Mother Nature's mercy. Travel by ship to this region was already narrowly restricted to a few precious summer months, but those wishing to enter the Greenland Sea often encountered impenetrable ice. On this 1937 expedition, it took fourteen days for Captain Olsen and his valiant crew to break through.

Finally, in late July, *Veslekari* forced her way in. With *Veslekari* off Clavering Island, Flint, Washburn, Oosting, and Buhler went ashore to obtain data and collect specimens while Louise and Leroy travelled a short distance in *Veslekari* to the head of the Tyroler Fjord. The whole scientific team later moved to Louise's position for a short sojourn. Working from the ship, the team conducted fieldwork each day, often from great distances away. It was tough, dirty, often back-breaking work. Oosting related a typical day in the field:

> What a day! Started at 7:00 a.m. returned 7:30 p.m. … Up down and vice versa. Sand, water, moraine, rock and more rock plus a glacier. Been on a glacier for first time — not a very tough one to cross but it's a walloping big one and it was quite an experience. Crevices, streams and up and down everywhere. A great lateral moraine to cross on each side. After the big glacier another valley of outwash from three glaciers higher up — braided streams all through it and I don't really know how many times I had my shoes off to wring out my sox.[29]

The scientists welcomed their first real opportunity to conduct in-depth fieldwork. Lack of exercise, rich food and drink, and close quarters with strangers were taking their toll on all onboard. As had occurred during the 1933 expedition, several of the scientists held "bull

Louise coming onboard after fieldwork during the late 1930s. Unknown location.

sessions," during which they confided their feelings about Louise. Like Harlen Bretz before him, Oosting was not accustomed to taking orders from a woman:

> B. and her train of packers went off across the glacier first thing and have not reappeared. Fortunately she and Fred [Buhler] get along very nicely. Perhaps because of his innate politeness, perhaps obsequiousness, he never seems to cross her. Since he is the one who must work most with her in the field it is very fortunate. Our meal time periods sometimes get rather tiresome. Consequently, when like last night and, we hope, tonight, she stays out till after seven we have a pleasant break with routine eating without La femme atmosphere.[30]

On their last day in the area, the exhausted team trudged back to *Veslekari*, and learned that the *Polarbjørn* had run aground. Unable to pull his ship free, *Polarbjørn*'s captain was urgently requesting *Veslekari*'s aid. *Veslekari* responded immediately, hauling up its anchor and sailing at full speed. Oosting described the scene:

> We reached the *Polarbjørn* about 3:30 a.m. and found her perched at a crazy angle on a mud bank — the tide was still fairly low so she looked especially bad. People sleeping on board must, on one side, have had their beds on the wall, on the other side, they couldn't have slept without hammocks. They had already unloaded about 50 tons of cargo and equipment. There were long lines of fuel oil barrels tied together floating at anchor some distance off and all of their half-dozen boats were floating about just loaded to the gunwales with everything they could conveniently take off.[31]

Eight hours later, with the use of double cables and the manpower of the crews of both ships, *Veslekari* succeeded in pulling *Polarbjørn* free.

Louise, Captain Olsen, and the crew received the grateful thanks of all onboard *Polarbjørn*. Once the rescue mission had been concluded, *Veslekari* steamed out of Young Sound and resumed its original course. After a short visit to the men at the station at Sandodden, *Veslekari* started off only to encounter heavy fog and poor ice conditions. Captain Olsen concluded it was unlikely the ship would be able to travel any farther north. The decision was made to try to reach Franz Josef Fjord. This was familiar territory for Louise. She remarked:

> It was with renewed pleasure that I looked forward to seeing once more the 120-odd miles of this fiord's winding waterways. This was my third visit, but repeated visits increase rather than diminish the thrill that one experiences at the grandeur of this fiord, the magnificence of its towering walls and snow-covered mountain borders with summits rising to from 7,000 to 11,000 feet. The brilliant colouring of the walls, whether seen in dull light or full sun, has a beauty and vividness quite beyond imagination.[32]

After several stops, *Veslekari* anchored in a safe location near the entrance to Kjerulf Fjord. Louise knew the fjord as a "veritable graveyard of icebergs," and the sight was daunting for the scientists who had never experienced this before. Oosting stated wondrously:

> The bergs are almost all large — some unbelievably immense — 150 feet high and all shapes imaginable. Until this afternoon I wondered why *Veslekari* couldn't go in between them but — when we were far in there — we began to hear them crack — like a great cannon — a piece would slide off the side of one about the size of a small house and slide into the water — then the parent behemoth being unbalanced gradually turns half over and usually part way back. Can't believe it till seen for they are so big. Remoy told us last night about one tipping under a

ship and the ship capsizing — perfectly possible for *Vesklekari* is only a toy.[33]

This region would provide the site of a four-day camp for the scientific team, with the exception of Leroy, who travelled farther on to extend the sounding program. A camp was set up on the north side of the Agassiz Valley and provided one of the few opportunities on the expedition to conduct fieldwork. However, some of the scientists were becoming peevish over the limited progress they were making on their respective projects. Though the ship's passage had been stymied by poor weather and heavy pack ice, Oosting blamed Boyd for the limitations to his work. He commented: "I try my level best never to contradict her — even when I know she is wrong; try and remember that every arctic nut is cracked; sit back and chuckle over her childish simple-mindedness."[34] However, his criticism was not just directed toward Boyd, but also toward what he perceived as the scientific bias of the expedition:

One of Louise's cameras (left) and altimeter (right).

For an ecologist to hope to do anything within a Boyd expedition is practically hopeless. First, because of the fixed notions about places to visit and lack of comprehension of what it's all about. Second, because the geologists get first consideration — which is as it should be on the trip. I realize I'm only an accessory and shouldn't get much consideration with the set up but can't help but wish it were otherwise."[35]

On the last day of fieldwork, the weather shifted. A few days were spent exploring the outer reaches of the fjord with a few forays for Flint and Washburn to conduct geological work. As *Veslekari* sailed into King Oscar Fjord, they encountered pack ice once again. Proceeding slowly, *Veslekari* dropped anchor in a bay on Lyell Land at the end of Narwhal Sound. All aboard knew that their time was limited. Flint and Washburn worked feverishly for several days studying glaciers; Buhler was busy mapping, Leroy was carrying out a sounding survey of the fjord floor, and Louise was taking photographs.

They remained working at this site until late August. Finally, Captain Olsen became increasingly alarmed by the drifting pack ice appearing in the fjord. Afraid that winter was making an early appearance, he ordered the team back to the ship. By 6:30 that night they were under way. Sailing through Narwhal Sound they entered the north end of King Oscar Fjord, and then continued to Antarctic Sound. A quick stop was made at the Ella Island wireless station, and then, yielding to entreaties by the scientific team, *Veslekari* anchored so one day of fieldwork could be conducted on Ymer Island. As the scientists scrambled to complete their work, Louise spent a last long day exploring the island, which she had visited several times before. This was to be the last trip ashore for the expedition. Several scientists were disgruntled, since their work had to be curtailed.

As the ship set off once more, the size of ice floes and drifting ice they encountered increased. *Veslekari* was able to travel only three miles in ten hours, and then could move no farther. Louise described the scene:

As far as Captain Olsen could see from the crows-nest, north to Hold-With-Hope and south as far as Traill Island, heavy polar ice fields and floes blocked the coast. The men at the Myggbukta wireless station, who went up on high ground to make a survey of conditions for us, reported by radio that they could see no open water anywhere. Heavy polar ice had come south and, moving in to the coast, had closed it to navigation for miles. The ship was moved whenever there was the slightest opening, but all such moves were in vain, and finally at 10:00 p.m., our worst fear was realized. The ship was "pinched" and tipped several degrees on her side.[36]

Drastic measures were required. By attaching two kilograms of dynamite to a pole, placing it in an opening in the ice under the ship and then detonating it, the crew was able to free the ship. But *Veslekari* was able to make only minimal progress before being trapped in the ice again.

Tensions began to rise on the ship, particularly amongst the less-experienced scientists. Captain Olsen was faced with a dilemma. There was no way to return to Franz Josef Land, since the way they had come was now completely blocked. Although it would take them a hundred miles out of their way, the captain determined that the best route was to reach Sofia Sound, sail into King Oscar Fjord, and from there to the sea. On August 26, *Veslekari* traversed Sofia Sound with little difficulty, but found King Oscar Fjord significantly blocked by ice. Louise remarked:

> Ours had come to be a struggle against time. Not only was there a possibility that the ice might close in so tightly that we should be unable to get out that season, but there was also the even greater danger that the ship might be beset in the heavy ice and crushed. All hands, including the special assistants, were pressed into service and willingly and cheerfully manned the ice anchors, leaping from floe to floe with the heavy equipment and hammering into the ice the anchors by which the ship got leverage for pulling and

shoving. Many of the floes were as high as the *Veslekari*'s bow, 15 feet above the sea.[37]

The crew worked around the clock and no one onboard *Veslekari* slept much during that tense period. Over several days, *Veslekari* advanced painfully slowly by following marginal leads. As the weather improved, the vessel finally emerged from King Oscar Fjord. By being flexible, imaginative, and determined, Captain Olsen was able to sail *Veslekari* out of the treacherous ice fields of Greenland and head toward Spitsbergen. Louise was thankful for the expertise of her captain and crew and commented:

> Though the ice conditions which we had experienced were unusual for that time of year, they do exist in some years. All expeditions going into these waters should be aware of the possibility and prepared to meet it. There is a chance, although a rare one, of disaster befalling a ship, for the records show that the ice fields of the Greenland coast have taken their toll. There is also the possibility of having to winter in the ice. We got out, although there were certainly long hours when it was doubtful if we should; but others at Clavering Island that summer did not get out, and no ship was able to get through to them until the following mid-summer. That we got through was due to the great skill of Captain Olsen and his assistant Captain Eliassen; to the tireless hours that our engineer, Peter Strand, and his assistant put in the engine room and fire hole; to the work of the crew and finally to the *Veslekari*'s sturdy construction. Both our captains counted it their "most difficult ice job" and our gratitude to them and to the crew is deep.[38]

As *Veslekari* approached Spitsbergen, the weather continued to worsen. Arriving at Longyear City in early September, Louise and the crew bade farewell to three of the scientists — Flint, Washburn, and Oosting — who left the ship at that point. Despite the weather and lateness of the season,

The elegant Louise Arner Boyd.

Louise was determined to continue the echo-sounding program with Leroy and Buhler and see how far north they could go. Leaving Advent Bay, they reached the edge of the pack ice only three days later. For a few more days, *Veslekari* kept to the edge of the ice, studying ice conditions and obtaining soundings whenever possible. Finally, when no further data could be gathered, *Veslekari* turned south once more and conducted soundings until arriving at Tromsø and then Ålesund in late September. Leroy and Buhler departed the ship and left Louise to take charge of storing the equipment and supplies that would be used the following year.

The polar ice conditions that summer prevented the 1937 Louise A. Boyd Expedition and all other expeditions from carrying out their full programs of work. Louise was thankful that she had already secured the *Veslekari* and made tentative plans for the following summer. However, despite the challenging conditions, the scientific contributions of this expedition were remarkable. The documentation of the general morphology of the fjord region of East Greenland focused on the origin and history of fjords and glaciated valleys. This geological work was augmented by an examination of major plant communities associated with these landforms as well as the collection of botanical specimens. Detailed surveys using the plane table and photography were made of the Tyroler Valley, Narwhal Glacier, and glacier fill remnants in Agassiz Valley. Extensive hydrographic surveys were developed of the Greenland Sea along the East Greenland coast and around Jan Mayen. Furthermore, a previously unknown underwater bank measuring seven nautical miles long and one nautical mile wide was discovered halfway between Jan Mayen and Bjørnøya using the new "*Veslekari* Model" echo-sounder. This new feature would later be officially named the Louise A. Boyd Bank. Louise was delighted with what she had accomplished with her team, but there was still more to do the next year.

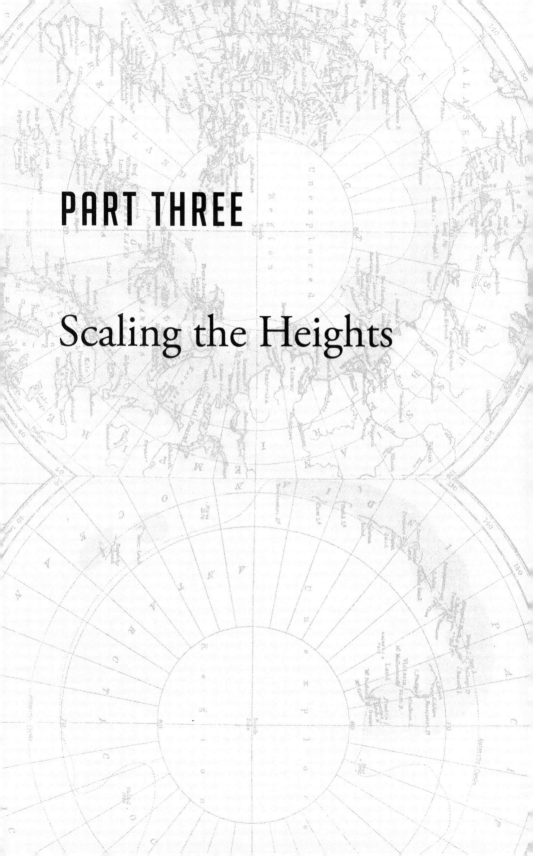

PART THREE

Scaling the Heights

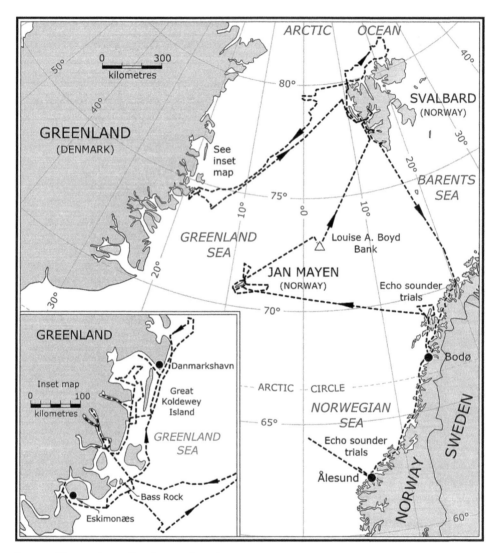

Route of Louise Arner Boyd 1938 Expedition.

CHAPTER EIGHT

CONTRIBUTING TO SCIENCE

I never see what has been done; I only see what remains to be done.
— MARIE CURIE

W hen an exhausted but elated Louise returned home to California, newspaper headlines announcing her accomplishments blazed: "A Woman Makes Her Mark in a Man's Domain."[1] Journalists clamoured to interview this elegant, self-assured woman whose life was committed to polar exploration but who still managed to fit in a hectic social life and philanthropic activities. She confided to Pulitzer Prize–winning *New York Times* reporter Russell Owen:

> I haven't wanted to talk about myself for I didn't know when I set out that I could do the job ... I had to learn first whether I was suited for leadership, particularly with a group of men, and see whether I could contribute anything of value. I think I have produced something worthwhile, of which I can be proud and as for the men, most of them go along with me each voyage. We get along fine.[2]

Louise posing for sculptor Cathe Wallendahl. Photograph likely taken in the late 1930s. Unknown location.

Louise maintained a full-time staff at Maple Lawn, and her personal secretary provided assistance with her voluminous correspondence. Her secretary also helped with the frequent requests for Louise to give lectures. Louise was the principal speaker at the annual dinner for the Society of Woman Geographers in 1938, where she mingled with other polar "celebrities," including Marie Peary Stafford and Captain Robert "Bob" Bartlett of the *Effie M. Morrissey*. She regaled the faculty and students of the Princeton Engineering and Geological Association with rollicking tales about "dining in a 135-foot Norwegian fishing boat where meals have to be taken in hip-boots in a galley flooded with two feet of water"[3] and "the expedition's narrow escape from the North when the ship was nearly crushed during a blizzard during rapidly freezing ice." In turn, Association members hailed her as "the greatest woman Arctic explorer of her time."

She was gratified by reviews of her latest book, *Polish Countrysides*. As with her earlier American Geographical Society volume, *The Fiord Region of East Greenland*, Louise had footed the bill for its publication. Although AGS staff member John Wright expressed privately that he felt it was "from a scientific point of view, one of the weakest of the A.G.S. publications,"[4] *Polish Countrysides* was well reviewed in scholarly journals. K.C. Edwards stated: "In producing such a full pictorial record ... Miss Boyd is not only to be congratulated upon the work of her camera, but must be warmly thanked for compiling a permanent record of so many of the distinctive features of a country where changes are taking place rapidly from day to day."[5] W. Elmer Ekblaw remarked: "Every photograph reveals superior craftsmanship, and a keen discernment of geographic values," and "this book is a tribute to Miss Boyd's skill as a photographer and to her geographic sense."[6]

Louise took time out for an American cross-country road trip, with her chauffeur, Percy Cameron, at the wheel. Upon her return, she was delighted by a *Washington Post* article entitled "American Women Explorers Carry Torch of Science All Over World." Louise was one of eight daring American women profiled. Author Viyella Wilson wrote glowingly:

> When the story of women's achievements in the twentieth century is written, the record of American women in the field of exploration will form a most important chapter....

> Miss Boyd claims San Francisco as her home but she is at home in many corners of the world as an explorer and hunter and has been in Washington many times as a member of the Society of Woman Geographers. Not only does Miss Boyd rank high in the field of women explorers but she has distinguished herself as a writer of scientific subjects related to her explorations.[7]

When her plans for the 1938 Expedition were under way, Louise stayed in contact with several members of the 1937 team. As before, she insisted on exclusive rights to all discoveries and complete control over the dissemination and publication of expedition data, including photographs. This included giving presentations about the expedition. As had Noel Odell several years previously, Duke University Professor Henry Oosting decided to try his luck — but he contacted Louise using diplomacy and tact.

> Since returning I have had several invitations to speak to different groups about our trip. Since I am not interested in that sort of thing in general, I have been able to escape conveniently by saying our contracts do not permit public presentation of the work until publication. However, I have an invitation to speak to the Duke Chapter of the Society of Sigma XI and I can scarcely evade it. Sigma XI is a national honorary scientific organization and an invitation to be on one of their programs is to me something of an honor because the speakers are usually older men.... It is customary to give reviews of research in progress to these organizations and most frequently such reports precede publication so that I do not believe there is anything irregular in my request. I would appreciate having Miss Boyd's reactions at her earliest convenience.[8]

Louise did not respond until a month later and her telegram was sharp and to the point:

218

Cable from Miss Boyd Quote No objections if guarantees to confine lecture to limitations of botanical work but will not grant request to do so on expedition as whole Stop Photographs not yet ready cannot be released until my return Unquote Would it be possible to send us resume of report before lecture is given.[9]

Louise knew that lecturing on and publishing recent fieldwork results were critical to academics. For professors such as Henry Oosting, it was "publish or perish," and the quicker he was able to get the expedition fieldwork results into print or give a lecture to a distinguished gathering, the sooner he was on the fast track to a tenured full-time position at a prestigious university. In limiting Oosting's freedom to present on a topic of his own choice, forbidding him from using original photographs, and requesting editorial rights prior to the lecture, Louise exercised a degree of control over his professional work unheard of for most scientists. It is unclear exactly why this was of such significance to her, but it remained a consistent practice throughout and following all of her expeditions. Highly territorial, she jealously guarded expedition data in a way that was intolerable to scholars such as Oosting and Odell before him. But, as Oosting recognized, all team members had already agreed to these terms when they signed their expedition contracts.

During the planning stages, Louise was a meticulous organizer. The extant correspondence between Louise and her network of advisors underscores her formidable ability to manage all technical and scientific aspects of the expedition. In an April 1938 letter to Elling Aarseth, *Veslekari's* owner, she demonstrated a keen grasp of topics as varied as the storage requirements of cameras and survey instruments, the appropriate footwear for ice climbing, the workings of the Marconi wireless, and the exact dimensions of the perfect darkroom. She compiled an exhaustive list of thirty-five questions, one of which read:

In 1933, on the forward deck, starboard side, there was an excellent cabin in which we kept our survey instruments, phototheodolites, cameras, film, etc. This cabin would be excellent to use on the coming two expeditions, providing that bunk space elsewhere can be given for two men.... The small dark room, next to Miss Boyd's cabin will remain as it is, for a developing room. Can't the ice and break box be put near our galley? Can't the entire space, as well as the large developing room, be put into one cabin, for camp supplies? It would be possible for me to give up the 1933 cabin used for cameras and tide gauges and have it made available for two bunks for porters, providing there will be space near the crew's galley or elsewhere on the decks for these instruments. How about on the starboard deck aft, in opposite position to the former developing room? I am enclosing a rough draft, explaining the 1933 layout, and a separate one, asking questions on it.[10]

There was no detail that escaped her attention and no evidence that anything was ever forgotten on an expedition. Although it rendered her an outstanding organizer, her perfectionist nature was likely challenging for others.

As in past years, Louise received queries from interesting characters wishing to join her in exploring the remote circumpolar north. This group included Richard Browning Catto from San Mateo, California, who applied as expedition photographer, although he admitted he was "a person of limited training" who possessed only a "somewhat adventurous nature"; Wayne Belles from Ann Arbor, Michigan, who applied for the position of radio operator and eagerly asserted that his code speed was increasing under continuous practice; as well as more promising candidates such as Lillemor Grimsgaard of Oslo, who had served as cook on the *Isbjorn* during a 1932 hunting expedition, and Swedish Professor Major H.N. Pallin, who wished to pursue studies into glaciological phenomena focusing on polygonal markings based on his earlier work in Northwest Greenland. All were summarily rejected. There is no evidence that Louise ever took any of these unsolicited queries very seriously as she relied almost exclusively on her own extensive network, previous crew members, or recommendations by the American Geographical Society.

Her ambitious plans were to return to Norway in early May and sail on the *Veslekari* from Ålesund on June 1. Captain Olsen had agreed to sail with *Veslekari* once again with Peder Eliassen as first mate and Olsen's son Jonas as second mate. Louise wanted to spend all of July conducting hydrographical work in north and northwest Spitsbergen, going as far north as *Veslekari* was able, based on the ice and weather conditions. Then the team would spend August in East Greenland, primarily along the coast north of Clavering Island.

The next step was the careful selection of the scientific team. Jim Leroy and Fred Buhler had proven to be satisfactory team members in 1937, and both of them were rehired. Fred Buhler knew of a young Norwegian-born American geologist named Finn Eyolf Bronner who was just starting his career at Rutgers University. Leroy, Buhler, and Bronner would be firm friends and stayed in contact after the expedition was over. Although Bronner was to become one of Louise's staunchest supporters, his early relationship with her got off to a rocky start. Once hired, an eager Bronner immediately met with other geologists who had worked in Greenland including Richard Foster Flint and Charles Schuchert from Yale. Much to Louise's dismay, he began to barrage her with requests for equipment and books that he would need for the expedition. Misinterpreting his initiative, Louise worried that Bronner was pursuing his own agenda and that he would not be a good team player. Clearly, she was particularly sensitive after her conflict with Odell. Bronner's letters to Louise are contrite. He apologized for any misunderstanding and confirmed his commitment to the objectives of the expedition. Matters continued to escalate, though, and his participation was in jeopardy. To his alarm, in late April, Bronner received a letter from Louise's lawyer, William F. Humphrey. Bronner sent his answer by special delivery:

> I have every intention of fulfilling my contract with Miss Boyd, in spirit as well as in letter. I have never thought otherwise. However, no geologist would consider going into the field — especially unknown territory — without formulating several plans of investigation, any or all of which may prove feasible of execution. A trained geologist would be of little constructive value to Miss Boyd until he

had acquainted himself with problems of special and general application, which I have been at some pains to do.… I am certain that no one has a fuller understanding of it than Miss Boyd herself. I hope that Miss Boyd is permanently reassured of my sincerity in this matter, and that further clarification will be unnecessary.[11]

This letter sufficiently assuaged Louise's concerns and nothing more came of the matter.

Twenty-five-year-old radio expert Anthony Hilferty from New York was hired to be in charge of the radio equipment. Although still a young man, he had been in the U.S. Navy for the last four years and had been discharged only in January. He was ready for a new challenge. Louise herself bore a heavier burden than usual as she assumed the roles of expedition leader, photographer, and botanist.

The team gathered in Ålesund in late May. As usual, the loading of supplies and equipment on *Veslekari* was hectic and noisy. Shortly before departure, geologist Finn Bronner wrote to his parents:

> *Veslekari* is a good and practiced boat. She rolls like a bathtub. Fred Buhler and I share a cabin astern, right above the propeller. Our enormous room is seven ft long, five ft wide and barely six ft high. We each have a cupboard in the room between the berth wall and the side of the ship itself, which is a meter thick! We have both electrical and kerosene lamps, an extremely small washing place, a small drop-leaf table, a mirror and various shelves and hooks. When I lie on my back, there is hardly four inches from the tip of my nose to the bottom of Fred's cot.… See you in October! A thousand kisses and hugs from your son, Eyolf the Greenland traveler.[12]

Veslekari sailed from Ålesund on June 1, 1938, a year to the day since she had sailed in 1937. However, it proved a false start as the echo-sounding equipment failed and the ship was forced to return to harbour. Setting off again on June 8 toward Jan Mayen, they arrived there a week later — about three weeks earlier than in previous years. Louise and the scientific team were happy to have reached their destination so quickly. Bronner referred to Jan Mayen as "the world's stormiest, most Godforsaken and most beautiful island." After dropping anchor at Jameson Bay, Louise and the scientific team brought mail and newspapers to the grateful men at the wireless station.

A full fieldwork program was planned for Jan Mayen. This included intensive hydrographical studies with close observations of tides and currents made with the echo-sounder and magnetic observations. Much of the largely uncharted area off the southwest end of Jan Mayen was characterized by hazardous hidden reefs and rocks, so the team's contributions in this area would be beneficial to mariners. The next day, soundings continued as *Veslekari* sailed to Walrus Bay on the eastern side of the island, where Buhler and Leroy set up a tidal gauge off Brielle Tower. While this was under way, Louise went ashore with two assistants. She remarked:

> This was really wild country. We crossed much water-soaked ground, tramping over thick moss under which were hidden rocks which caused frequent turning of ankles. The island is famous for its blue foxes and not only did we see their footprints everywhere on the moss and in the snowbanks but our only paths were fox trails. Their predilection for birds and birds' eggs was indicated by the way in which these trails followed the bird cliffs for miles. It was a raw, cold day. The fog became very thick and it was so cold that the moisture froze on the twill of my hiking breeches. Mr. Bronner and one of the crew were also out on this high ground and appeared like moving silhouettes when we met them in the fog.[13]

Although Leroy and Buhler were familiar with Louise and knew how she worked, this was the first time that Bronner had seen her in action.

Described by a journalist as still looking like a girl, "wide-eyed, free-striding, quick-smiling and straight as a spear," there was no question that she impressed him.[14] Bronner related:

> Louise A. Boyd was, by far, the most energetic person on the expedition. She was operating in high gear all of the time she was awake.... During shore excursions, Miss Boyd could outwalk and outlast all of her porters and aides. She knew exactly where she wanted to go to do her work, and seldom let herself be deflected from her goal. Her work ethic was one of total dedication to her work: I have rarely encountered anyone with such singlemindedness.[15]

Louise's vigour and commitment to accomplishing her goals were admirable. They are even more so when one remembers she turned fifty that year.

A sudden squall with gusty winds and blowing snow took everyone by surprise. Plans to leave Walrus Bay and sail to another location were abandoned until the storm blew over. According to Louise: "A storm from the

Louise and crew onboard *Veslekari* in the late 1930s.

northeast was rolling such heavy seas even into this small bay that we were obliged to move farther in and put out both anchors."[16]

The next day the storm continued with no signs of abating. All day, the *Veslekari* rode a hard gale at anchor and there was no possibility of moving. Finally, the weather improved enough so that *Veslekari* was able to sail to the other side of the island. Shortly after the landing party was put ashore, the wind began whipping up again. Louise reported that: "it was already blowing so hard that even with the help of the men, I had difficulty in keeping my footing, and sharp, wind-blown pebbles stung our faces."[17] The heavy winds deposited a coat of silt over the whole ship. When the storm passed, they set a northerly course for the newly anointed Louise A. Boyd Bank, which Louise and the *Veslekari* team had discovered the previous year. Repeated soundings there revealed additional scientific details. Over the new few days, they stayed close to Spitsbergen, loading up on fuel, fresh water, and cleaning the boilers at King's Bay.

They made a short stop at Amsterdamøya and then sailed southwest toward Greenland. Although at times the fog was thick and the pack ice challenging, *Veslekari* reached Greenland in only four days. This was an astonishing feat compared to the fourteen days it had taken in 1937. When they landed on the east face of Bass Rock, the team encountered melting ice and surface water that they had to wade through knee-deep to get to shore.

On shore, they encountered two octagonal wooden cabins built in 1901 by members of the American Baldwin-Ziegler Expedition during their quest for the North Pole. While searching for ethnographer Ludvig Mylius-Erichsen and his colleague Hoeg-Hagen, Danish explorers Ejnar Mikkelsen and Iver P. Iversen from the *Alabama* Expedition had been forced to overwinter there in 1909–10. They were rescued only in 1912, in the direst of circumstances. Louise was delighted to find some pemmican left there, which she considered to be still edible after thirty-seven years.

When they departed, *Veslekari* headed to the southwest end of Clavering Island and the Danish wireless station at Eskimonæs — at the time the northernmost wireless station on the east coast of Greenland. Louise and her team visited with the men there for a day and then sailed toward the Norwegian hunting station at Revet in Payer Land. This was a visit that Louise and everyone on *Veslekari* was looking forward to, as it was the home

Louise handling a camera at Eskimonæs, Greenland, in the late 1930s.

of Gerhard Antonssen, who had a reputation for being the most skilled trapper on East Greenland.

Known as the "King of Revet," Antonssen had heard about the *Veslekari's* upcoming visit. More particularly, he had heard there was a woman onboard and wanted to look his best. Bronner reported that in his eagerness to look presentable, Antonssen had hastily hacked off a year's growth of beard with his hunting knife. Unbeknownst to Louise, he raised *Veslekari's* crew on the radio and asked to be brought onboard unobtrusively so he could be given a haircut. Bronner relates the startling sight of the burly trapper hauling himself over the side of *Veslekari* with his furrowed face covered with hundreds of bleeding nicks. A chair, sheet, and scissors were provided and porter Samson Vestnes volunteered for the daunting task. According to Bronner: "When all this secret grooming was finished, someone notified Miss Boyd that she had a visitor and the two met on deck with obvious delight."[18] Antonssen invited Louise to visit his cabin and they spent several happy hours together as she cast a knowing and experienced eye over his many furs. The next year, Antonssen's already colourful reputation flourished. Bronner related the tale:

> Antonssen had a very long trapline and several small huts strategically placed so that he always was within reach of a safe haven to spend the night…. Antonssen had reached this hut with his dogteam in a raging blizzard and extremely low temperatures, but he found the door heavily glazed. Battling gale force winds and stinging snow, he drew his big sheath knife and drove it into the door, but the blade glanced off the glaze and the force of the blow swung the knife directly into Antonssen's left eye. One can hardly imagine a more frightening situation, but Antonssen knew that his one hope of survival lay in reaching the meteorological station at Eskimonæs. He also knew that he could trust his dogs' instinct to remember the way from many previous trips from Revet so he bundled himself into the sled and pointed the team toward Clavering Island. He was right and the team brought him safely to the station. The personnel there radioed Norway and were put in two-way

communication with a surgeon who guided them step by step in emergency treatment. The following summer, Antonssen returned to Norway for proper medical treatment and to discover what it was like to be a folk hero.[19]

Hoping for an early start, *Veslekari* was just about to set sail when she received a distress call from the *Polarbjørn*, which had arrived a short time earlier and was anchored not far from them. Their radio had failed and no one onboard could repair it. *Veslekari's* radio expert, Anthony Hilferty, was dispatched to help them. After eight hours, the repairs were made and finally their ship was able to sail. Louise's goal then was to continue to find the farthest north possible. Passing Shannon Island, Great Koldewey Island, and Germania Land, *Veslekari* encountered more ice and snow but was able to proceed. They sailed along the coast of Ile de France until the ship was stopped by impenetrable polar ice just south of Cape Montpensier at 77°50' North, where Louise and the team disembarked. According to the *Polar Record*, this was the "second farthest north landing ever made from a ship on this coast. *Veslekari* was the only ship to go that far north in 1938."[20] Louise described the scene:

> At 9:00 a.m., a short distance south of Cape Montpensier, we anchored to a field of polar ice which was grounded and frozen to the shore. The ice was as high as the bow of our ship, 15 feet above the water, and its many hummocks were higher still. We used a ladder to get from the ship to the ice and then went over its rough surface to the land.[21]

This was a major accomplishment for Louise and the *Veslekari*. During each expedition, she diligently tracked how far north *Veslekari* travelled compared to other polar vessels, thus demonstrating one subtle way she measured her accomplishments against those of other explorers of her time.

Captain Olsen remained ever-vigilant about getting caught in the ice, so the *Veslekari* stayed only a few hours. Louise remained hopeful that another path northward would be found, but it was not to be. She stated sadly, "All

The *Veslekari* during the late 1930s. Unknown location.

that we could do this far north had been accomplished. I had spent profitable hours ashore with my cameras at our one stop and had continued my photography from the deck of the ship both going and returning, in order to get as full a record as possible of this seldom-visited coast."[22]

Sailing past Cape Bismarck, *Veslekari* anchored off Danmarkshavn, which had previously been frozen in. According to Louise, this was one of the best harbours to winter a ship at that northerly location since it was protected by a long peninsula. It was early August. An extended fieldwork period was planned, including tidal gauge soundings, collecting botanical specimens, and filming. As had occurred so many times before, Louise and her companions encountered traces of other explorers who had come before them. After disembarking, the team found the deteriorating remains of the station used by the ill-fated 1906 *Danmark* Expedition. Louise, Bronner, and the other members of the shore party wandered through the scattered debris — all that was left of the men who had been there before them. Luckily, the weather was in their favour and the team was able to stay and work there for nine days. Louise remained dedicated to her photographic work and strived to obtain the best results possible. She stated:

> No matter how long my days had been, constantly photographing from the shore or from the ship: no matter how fatigued I was at the time one usually calls bed time, I never terminated my day's work until I had thoroughly cleaned all used photographic equipment and packed all exposed film. My hours often were not those of round the clock, but it was a case of boots on till boots off that constituted my day, and hours that often took me well into those of the following morning.[23]

Once fieldwork had been completed, *Veslekari* travelled to Hvalrosodden and explored the Marke Fjord where extensive soundings were taken by Leroy. Returning to Hvalrosodden, they continued sailing to the north end of Great Koldewey Island where *Veslekari* anchored in Dagmar Harbour. After taking the motor dory to shore, Louise and the scientists had a difficult time climbing the precipitous rocky slopes. Reconnaisance of this part of the island revealed a small lake unrecorded on the maps. Just after returning to *Veslekari*, Louise was surprised by the arrival of two other polar vessels in that remote region. One visitor was the *En Avant*, led by American-born explorer Willie Knutsen and his benefactor, Count Gaston Micard, whom Louise had encountered on the *Quest* in Greenland during the 1933 Expedition. Earlier that year, Knutsen had written to Louise suggesting that he and Micard should join forces with her on an upcoming expedition. Knutsen was primarily interested in the "redoubtable Miss Louise Boyd" assuming half the expenses of such a voyage, but it was clear he did not expect her to be a silent partner. In suggesting a French-American-Norwegian Expedition, he had outlined an ambitious plan of sailing to Danmarkshavn and then flying to Independence Fjord. There, a weather station would be established in preparation for later sledge journeys into Peary Land. Louise did not agree to this plan, nor did she agree to Micard's earlier request that she transport his expedition to Greenland. She had written a curt "Impossible" as a directive to her assistant, but there were no hard feelings. In fact, Louise and Willie

Finn Bronner onboard *Veslekari* during the summer of 1938.

would be friends for over thirty years. Knutsen later recalled his memorable 1938 encounter with Louise:

> When we drew within shouting distance she suggested — rather, commanded — we all meet on shore for a shin-dig. She shouted that she would supply "the goddamn booze!" There we were on shore, three crews of toughened sailors and arctic expedition men and it was she who was barking orders that we all assemble for a historic photo. It was difficult to ignore her. We assembled. Then the party began. When she spoke — occasionally taking a swig from a bottle of brandy she carried around with her under her arm — I was reminded of a brothel owner in a Hollywood western. This in no way detracted from her professionalism, nor from the years of important research she did in the Arctic; quite the contrary. She was a great scientist and a wonderful person.[24]

Louise and crew onshore during the summer of 1938. Unknown location.

Surprisingly, in the same location, Louise met another eminent polar explorer. This was Count Eigil Knuth, a Danish archaeologist who had worked with Helge Larsen excavating Eskimo ruins on the 1935 Courtauld Expedition to East Greenland and who had crossed the Greenlandic inland ice with French explorer Paul-Emil Victor.

Knuth shared his itinerary with Louise. He planned to determine the northernmost limit of southern Eskimo culture; conduct a botanical, geological, and meteorological investigation of Northeast Greenland, and study muskoxen. As usual, the meeting of the three ships provided ample opportunities for Louise to learn more about current weather and ice conditions as well as hear the personal stories and experiences of those she met.

After the socializing had concluded and the *Veslekari* scientists, ever-anxious to expand their fieldwork program, could stand it no more, *Veslekari* lifted anchor and sailed down the east coast of Great Koldewey Island to Traek Pass.

Anchoring off the entrance to Traek Pass, Louise and the scientific team and several porters went ashore. As always, Louise was filled with enthusiasm. She related:

> With two of my special assistants I climbed to the summit of Mt. Petersberg, the highest ground on the south side of the lake. It was a steep climb, and loose stones made footing difficult. Also, it was so warm that for the first time that summer I removed my sweater shirt and continued the climb wearing my wind jacket as a blouse. The climb was, however, very much worthwhile.[25]

From the summit, it was apparent that the waters in the region all around were ice-free, so after they returned to the ship, *Veslekari* proceeded to Bessel Fjord opposite the southern tip of Great Koldewey Island. The head of the fjord widened into a bay and the crew anchored there. Members of the scientific team went ashore and Louise was delighted, since Bessel Fjord was often impassable due to the ice.

Louise, Washburn, and Bronner were struck by the glacial changes evident there. She remarked with authority: "There were a number of glaciers on the north wall, the majority of which had cut deep ravines. All were in a state of recession, with large lateral moraines showing their former extent."[26] Muskoxen grazed throughout the area and Louise took advantage of the opportunity to gather the discarded wool. She was keen to promote the economic opportunities this wool offered, but neither the Danish nor Norwegians seemed interested. She extolled its virtues:

> On one of my early expeditions to East Greenland, I gath-
> ered enough of this wool to have two mufflers handwo-
> ven by members of the Norwegian Home Industries in
> Åalesund. On subsequent expeditions I have made a point
> of gathering the wool whenever I found it. The natural
> color is beige, shading in places into light brown. It is warm
> and soft except that where not all of the coarse hairs were
> removed before weaving it is somewhat scratchy. I found
> no evidence that the Danish or Norwegian hunters or other
> visitors to Greenland gathered this wool; even when I told
> the hunters of its merits.[27]

Louise's interest in the potential value of this wool showed foresight. It would be another twenty years before the qiviut industry, based on the processed underwool from muskoxen, became a thriving economic enter-prise in the North.

Because of time constraints, *Veslekari* left the area and travelled farther north in Dove Bay, where the men wanted to conduct some research. They anchored off the Orientering Islands, where Bronner wanted to get to work. Louise also conducted a thorough photographic survey of these small islands and was later able to create a small-scale topographic map from her photo-graphs. From there, *Veslekari* sailed and anchored in several more fjords, the team conducting as much fieldwork as possible in the time remaining.

The grandeur of the landscape around them never ceased to fill Louise with wonder:

Glaciers of all kinds and descriptions covered the walls of this fiord, completely dominating the scene. Some were hanging glaciers with avalanche ice below them; others had descended only a short distance; while some had receded up the walls into narrow channels, leaving only relatively large lateral moraines to show their former extent. We entered the fiord in the face of a strong wind which swirled snow off the highland icecap and whipped the water into whitecaps.[28]

By early September, the ice and weather conditions were shifting and it was time to return home. *Veslekari* set sail, arriving at Ålesund harbour on the evening of September 12. The 1938 Louise A. Boyd Expedition was at an end.

As Louise had planned, the scientific data gathered by the team augmented the 1937 Expedition results through providing more extensive and detailed hydrographic, tidal, and geological observations. Improvements to the scientific equipment and the manner in which this equipment was used had helped to garner more accurate results. One of the highlights of this expedition was reaching the farthest north at Ile de France. Not only was this an achievement in and of itself, but it yielded other results, including the northernmost botanical collection made on the east coast of Greenland.

Louise's accomplishments on this journey won her even more praise. The September 9, 1938, edition of the *New York Times* heralded "Boyd Expedition Sets Arctic Mark." John Wright of the American Geographical Society wrote:

> In penetrating to Lat. 77 degrees 50 minutes N. Long 17 degrees 10 minutes W., off the icebound coast of East Greenland, Miss Boyd came to within about thirty miles of the northernmost latitude (78 degrees 16 minutes N., 16 degrees 21 minutes W.) reached in this area by the Duc d'Orleans in the *Belgica* in 1905. The Ile de France on

which she landed, lies some fifty-five miles due north of the point off Germania Land where Captain Bob Bartlett turned back in the *Morrissey* in 1930. Thus Miss Boyd may claim the credit of having gone farther north in a ship along the East Greenland shore than any other American and of having attained what is probably the second highest latitude ever reached by a vessel in these waters.[29]

Louise, Finn Bronner (right, middle), and other crew onboard *Veslekari* during the summer of 1938.

Louise spent time in New York City exchanging polar tales with her friend and colleague Vilhjalmur Stefansson before returning to California. Louise was pleased by her profile in the *San Francisco Call-Bulletin* in which Edwin C. Hill wrote: "This writer, buttonholing explorers inward or outward bound, has found that showmanship is apt to be an important detail of the undertaking, with its build-up for books and lectures. We can be indulgent as to this, as most of them are up to something worthwhile, but it is interesting to note that it is the one woman among them who brings back the cold, unadorned, factual account which science esteems."[30]

Louise had already received many honours from foreign governments, but her diverse contributions to science and her relentless exploration of Greenland, Svalbard, and Jan Mayen remained unrecognized by her own country. Months after returning home, Louise received the momentous news that she had been awarded the illustrious Cullum Geographical Medal from the American Geographical Society. First awarded in 1896, the Cullum Medal was presented to "those who distinguish themselves by geographical discoveries, or in the advancement of geographical science." Other Cullum Medal winners included Robert Peary, Fridtjof Nansen, Ernest Shackleton, Robert Falcon Scott, and Jean-Baptiste Charcot. In its long history, the Cullum Geographical Medal has still been awarded to only three women — Ellen Churchill Semple in 1932, Louise Arner Boyd in 1938, and Rachel Carson in 1967. Louise's humble acceptance speech given on December 20, 1938, at a meeting of the American Geographical Society, captures her joy in receiving the award, her passion for the North, and her love for the work she did:

> It gives me the greatest pleasure to accept the Cullum Geographical Medal, the award of which I deem a greater honor than I ever expected. If I have made Arctic exploration my life work, it is because it has been for me the most fascinating field of endeavor I could have entered. I hope that my modest efforts, which have been sincerely devoted to scientific ends, have been of some use to those who are interested in that part of the world. And I also want to say that in my various expeditions to the north it

Louise receiving the Cullum Medal on December 20, 1938.

Louise's Cullum Medal from the American Geographical Society.

would have been impossible for me to have done the work without the loyal and cooperative staff of men who have been with me. Their help, both during the expedition and when we returned, in correlating data, have done everything to make the results of the trips worthwhile.... It is very difficult for anyone who has been on an Arctic trip to evaluate their work. I will make no attempt to do so. But I must say that the charm of the Arctic, its infinite diversity, its aloofness from the rest of the world, made it a field which gives its own reward. Only those who have been in the Greenland Fjords, who have seen the magnificent sunsets over the ice, who have drifted for days in the misty fields of pack looking always for a lead toward the shore, who have been buffeted by storms and made lame by continuous movement, can appreciate the spell which always draws us back there.[31]

While in New York, Louise was asked to sign the prized Fliers and Explorers Globe at the American Geographical Society. This globe had been signed by the major explorers and aviators of the twentieth century and commemorated their routes and accomplishments. She was delighted to accept this invitation.

The year 1938 ended on a personal high for Louise and marked a turning point in her career and in the public acceptance of her as a polar explorer. As 1939 dawned, the newly minted Cullum Medal winner started making plans for the publication of her next American Geographical Society book, based on the 1937 and 1938 expeditions. The scientists were busily analyzing their data, working up their results and preparing their own contributions for the book. Team members stayed in close contact. Finn Bronner had married Wibecke, his Norwegian sweetheart who had waited anxiously for his return, and he was keen to open up his New York home to his friends. Bronner wrote to Louise, using his affectionate title for her:

> Dear Chief.... Jim [Leroy] and Jack [unknown] came down
> to see us about two weeks ago but Fred [Buhler] had a

previous engagement and Tony [Hilferty] was probably prevented from coming by a very heavy snowstorm that tied up traffic over the whole East. Lincoln Washburn and Tahoe came to the G.S.A. [Geological Society of America] meeting and we had lunch together one day. Wibecke agrees with me that they are a charming couple. Lincoln worked on Victoria Island last summer, so you see, the Arctic draws him back too. For that matter, I feel an ever stronger desire to return — there is a strange and powerful urge to see more ice, more dwarf birch reddening with frost, more precipitous granite walls.[32]

Louise wrote excitedly to her good friend Adolf Hoel in Oslo informing him that she had been asked by the American Geographical Society to exhibit at the International Congress of Polar Exploration, to be held in Bergen, Norway, in two years' time. An article in the April 1939 issue of *The Geographical Review* entitled *Recent Exploration in the Polar Regions* related the accomplishments of Lincoln Ellsworth's 1938–39 fourth Antarctic expedition, the British Graham Land Expedition in 1937, and other Soviet, Polish, British, Scandinavian, and American expeditions. Louise was thrilled to see the "Louise A. Boyd Arctic expeditions of 1937 and 1938" included in the illustrious list.

She was also celebrated by her own community and state, which recognized her work as an explorer and a notable civic-minded individual. Her impressive philanthropic resume at that time included significant work conducted for the American Red Cross, the San Rafael Improvement Club, the Marin Music Chest Chorus, the San Francisco Garden Club, the San Francisco Opera Association, the San Francisco Symphony Orchestra, the San Francisco Community Chest, and the Woman's Athletic Club.

At a lively ceremony at the Marin Golf and Country Club, the mayor proclaimed Louise an honorary citizen of her hometown of San Rafael. Dr. Lynn White said of her: "She might have stayed home, enjoyed the comforts of her fine home, enjoyed the company of her friends, but she could not. There was no choice left to her … Miss Boyd has the disposition which makes idleness impossible, she must always be doing."[33]

Not to be outdone, the mayor of San Francisco hosted a reception in her honour. A local newspaper commented that she was "no sportswoman seeking thrills in the white wilderness, no dilettante fleeing from social boredom, no amateur trail breaker gathering material for a travel book or a lecture tour. Louise Boyd is a seasoned, poised explorer, far more capable

Louise signing the Fliers and Explorers Globe at the American Geographical Society office in 1938.

and courageous than many a man."[34] Other awards were bestowed upon her later that year, including honorary Doctor of Laws degrees from Mills College and the University of California–Berkeley.

Apart from being lauded on the public stage, Louise's growing stature also reflected well on the small Norwegian communities of Ålesund, Tromsø, and Vartdal, and on the men who sailed with her. Her glory was their glory, too, and she could not have succeeded without them. In *The Fiord Region of East Greenland*, she stated: "Able seamen — men with sterling characters — none are finer than the sons of Norway. I have sailed the northern waters and the Arctic Seas with them now many times, and they have won my highest respect and admiration."[35]

Media attention was at its peak, attracting prospective expedition members, none of whom were suited to the task at hand. These individuals included Everett R. Peters, who proudly stated he had a "supply of high grade dented can goods on hand including Red Salmon and fruits that I am willing to share for the Cause of Exploration you are conducting."[36] Applicant Richard B. Beam from Helena, Montana, had been "trying to discover an expedition leaving for the northland which would want a landscape artist along. I am anxious to paint up in that country, especially in Alaska, and am not afraid of hard work and thus earn a birth [*sic*]. Being thirty years old and in perfect health I ought to be able to hold up my end of the stick even though I have spent too many years in college to be exactly muscle bound."[37]

Joseph Eden wrote:

> I presume with your standing as a explorer you could get the government or the Museum of Natural History to finance you with funds and planes to find and explore new land for the United States. I would be willing to go with you any time; I'm a dependable and game fellow. I know that if you and I would get together we would make fame and fortune. I'm a single man age 30 and a native of Michigan. I came to Florida about a week ago to visit my brother here. I expect to go back to Michigan soon. I prefer the cold north to these tropics.[38]

It was during this time that Louise entered into negotiations with New York–based publisher Ives Washburn Inc. to write her autobiography, tentatively titled *A Woman in the Arctic*. For some unknown reason the project never came to fruition. Following a presentation to the San Rafael Chamber of Commerce, she was asked about her future plans. Louise replied somewhat disingenuously: "It is too soon after the last expedition really to know. The best part of half a year or more will be required to work up and sift the results of the last two expeditions, and until this work is done, nothing further can be contemplated, but this much at least I can tell you — I hope Fate will enable me to continue my work in the polar regions, and that 1940 or 1941 will see me again in Arctic waters."[39]

A letter written from Louise to Captain Johan Olsen around this time reveals her clear intention to launch another expedition to Greenland in 1940. She said feelingly:

> One thing I can say very frankly, and that is, whatever ship
> I have, I hope you will be my skipper and that Mr. Eliassen,
> Johan, Jonas, Sam and Rudi will again sail with me. In fact,
> I unhesitatingly say that I consider *Veslekari* has sailed with
> me with a prize crew of officers and men and I am devoted
> to them individually and collectively.[40]

In fact, Louise would never sail on the *Veslekari* or work with Captain Olsen and his Norwegian crew ever again.

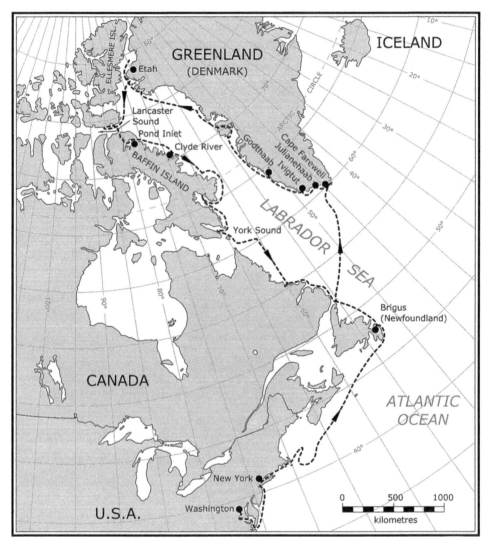

Route of Louise Arner Boyd 1941 Expedition.

CHAPTER NINE

HONOUR AND GLORY

And come WWII,
her pictures strategic to the effort. Obsession,
this once and at last, turned asset.
— ELIZABETH BRADFIELD[1]

When Louise returned to the United States, it was to an uncertain and much-changed world. Throughout the past year, she had been oblivious to the political tumult around her as she concentrated on expedition plans. Now it was impossible to ignore. Hitler had occupied Austria and his aggressive posturing toward other European nations had escalated despite the Munich Agreement. The Spanish Civil War had torn apart the fabric of that nation and hostilities between China and Japan were ongoing. On September 1, 1939, German forces invaded Poland and the Second World War began. But for Louise, world events seemed to hardly impact her plans for her next expedition. By chance, she had met Dr. J.H. Dellinger, Chief of the Radio Section of the National Bureau of Standards in the Department of Commerce, while both were returning from Europe on an ocean liner. Louise had been impressed by his energy and enthusiasm for her work.

Dellinger stated:

> [T]he proposal very rapidly developed that she would take
> an expedition up along West Greenland for the Bureau. I
> had explained to her that one of our greatest troubles was
> trying to do something about the auroral zone, because we
> hadn't been able to get any data from there, radio condi-
> tions there were very special and radio transmission across
> there was difficult and of unique commercial and military
> importance. She said, "I'll go up there and get you some
> data: you detail some of your men to go with me. I will hire
> a ship and a crew and take them up for as long as you like."[2]

By late 1940, the United States had recognized the strategic geopolitical
nature of Greenland after the German invasion of Denmark that April. By
1941, the U.S. assumed full responsibility for Greenland's defence. Suddenly,
previously little-known Greenland assumed pivotal importance on the world
stage. The significance of Louise's scientific contributions became apparent to the American government. Realizing that her vast knowledge about
Greenland could be of assistance to enemy forces, officials in Washington
advised Louise to stop lecturing about her expeditions. Louise cancelled presentations to the American Society of Photogrammetry and the University of
California. Her upcoming AGS publication on her 1937 and 1938 expeditions, entitled *The Coast of Northeast Greenland*, was put on hold indefinitely.
Rear Admiral Edward "Iceberg" Smith related:

> The motives which withheld from publication the material
> of Miss Boyd's 1937 and 1938 expeditions naturally sug-
> gested its value to our own country. Information regard-
> ing Northeast Greenland prior to our entering the war
> was extremely scanty, and in preparing for a mission there
> during the summer of 1940, I was advised to consult Miss
> Boyd. The opportunity quite happily arose while the old
> cutter *Northland* was being hurriedly recommissioned at
> Oakland, California, prior to proceeding via the east coast

of the United States to Greenland. Miss Boyd and her staff were exceedingly cooperative and helpful in supplying me with voluminous photographs, identifying splendid panoramic views of important headlands, and in identifying topographic features. This information was of great assistance in the navigation of those little-known, ice-infested waters. Even this isolated corner of the globe was not free of World War II activities.[3]

After conferring with Dellinger, Louise agreed to conduct her next expedition to Greenland on behalf of the National Bureau of Standards. A government source stated that: "Miss Boyd is a wealthy California woman who is one of the best-informed people in the United States on the polar regions. She is completely trustworthy and the State Department has every confidence in her."[4] Working for the United States government for the first time, Louise prepared to undertake a dangerous voyage into an active wartime region.

Discovering that Captain Johan Olsen and the *Veslekari* were unavailable for hire would have been a hard blow. Louise also learned that technical equipment and supplies she had stored two years previously in Ålesund, Norway, in anticipation of her next voyage, had been commandeered by agents sympathetic to the Nazi invaders. But there was little she could do about it. For her most ambitious undertaking yet, Louise would have wanted to work with the ship that she loved and a captain and crew that she trusted. But it was not to be. By November 1940, Louise had contacted Captain Bob Bartlett to ask if he and his ship, the *Effie M. Morrissey*, were available for a 1941 voyage. She wrote:

> Possibly it surprised you, but we Arctic people are apt to head north at any time — are we not? The idea of my taking out another Arctic expedition, and this time going to northwest Greenland near the axis magnetic pole in Smith Sound and near the dip magnetic pole in the Gulf of Boothia taking ionosphere equipment and one or two staff members of the Bureau of Standards had been planned

Cigarette card showing young Captain Bob Bartlett, likely during the 1920s.

as far back as 1938 for the coming year, 1941, by myself and the Bureau of Standards. The Bureau of Standards is very anxious that I carry out my plans because they and members of the Government consider that additional radio information, which can best be had at the above mentioned geographical points, is of more value than ever in connection with national defence and they want me to go ahead with my plans if I can possibly do so.[5]

Captain Robert Abram Bartlett (1875–46), known as "Captain Bob," was a gruff, straight-talking ice-master from Newfoundland who descended from a distinguished line of whaling and sealing captains:

He had survived several shipwrecks and, thanks to his skill and perseverance, prevented a number of others, and he saved the lives of many shipmates. An eccentric who played Chopin gramophone records as his ship was about to sink below the arctic ice, a man frequently inconsistent in accounts of his own voyages, a man blessed with incredible good luck when at sea, a known drinker who professed to be a teetotaler, Bartlett was, nevertheless, an exceptional leader of men.[6]

Bartlett was brash and outspoken and had strong feelings about the qualities of a true explorer:

For the post of leader, endurance and courage are especially important. If the man in charge breaks down under the strain of cold or hunger or hardship, his whole crew will break with him. He must be the one who goes on and on, without giving a sign of flinching. The indomitable courage of the leader has saved many an expedition that seemed doomed. Does all this sound as if Arctic exploration is too tough an assignment to yield real fun? It may, but there are still in this world many men with the sturdy qualities of mind, body, and heart that will find great satisfaction in going through these battles with nature and attaining the goal.[7]

Bartlett was a staunch man's man. He and Louise had known each other since at least 1932 and their early correspondence was cordial. In a 1940 note, she confided: "I know you and I as good friends now will get along grand and come back at the end of the journey with the warmest of friendship which I think only the Arctic can give one."[8]

Writing from his usual New York base in the Murray Hill Hotel, Bartlett replied, "I really think before doing or making any commitments that you should come to New York and see the *Morrissey*; we could do a better job by thrashing things out together."[9]

She agreed. "I like your attitude and quite see your point." After Louise hired Bartlett as skipper, Dellinger from the National Bureau of Standards had reservations due to Bartlett's reputation for profanity even amongst seafaring men. Dellinger related that Louise was unconcerned. Later in the trip, she declared: "I don't think there remains any cuss words for me to learn — think the full vocabulary has been recited on this trip!"[10]

The 1941 Louise A. Boyd Expedition operated under the auspices of the National Bureau of Standards (NBS) with co-operation from the United States Coast Guard and the Carnegie Institution. According to a government report:

> The principal purpose of the expedition was to secure data on radio transmission in the Arctic regions. There is urgent need of such data because evidence has accumulated that conditions there differ radically from those elsewhere and exact knowledge would yield the means of increasing the efficiency of radio communication across the Arctic regions, particularly to Europe and the Orient.[11]

The NBS chose two of their best men for the job: twenty-six-year-old Archer S. Taylor and twenty-nine-year-old Frederick R. Gracely. Taylor was a physicist who had worked in radio at the Signal Corps Aircraft Radio

Captain Bob Bartlett onboard the *Effie M. Morrissey*. Photograph likely taken during the early 1940s. Unknown location.

Laboratory. His job was to make continuous soundings of the ionosphere as determined by radio measurements and auroral manifestations. Frederick Gracely had degrees in physics and electrical engineering and would be primarily responsible for making magnetic observations. Both men would measure the intensities of ultraviolet light and cosmic rays.

In letters sent to the United States Selective Service Board, NBS Chief Lyman Briggs stated that Gracely and Taylor represented the Bureau on a voyage to the Arctic regions from May 20 to October 31, 1941. However, while Gracely's letter stated that he would be doing work important to national defence, no such phrase appeared in Taylor's letter. Unbeknownst to all onboard, Archer Taylor was a Quaker who refused to conduct work that would aid in the war effort. This was a matter that had been discussed between Briggs, Dellinger, and Taylor, but likely was not shared even with Louise. As Taylor related in his journal, it was virtually impossible to escape talk about war and this likely contributed to his discomfort onboard.

A twenty-one-year-old Coast Guardsman named Tom Carroll held the position of radio operator while twenty-three-year-old Dr. John A. Schilling was hired as ship's physician and assistant to the other scientists. Missouri-born Schilling had just graduated from Harvard Medical School a few months earlier. This was the first time Louise had sailed with a doctor, but he was present at Bartlett's insistence. According to Schilling, "The captain has a great faith in a doctor and would not take a trip without one, as he said he owed it to his crew, having been in early years on ships himself with no doctor." As captain, Robert Bartlett hired his usual dedicated crew of family and friends from his small and close-knit hometown of Brigus, Newfoundland.

> Few skippers have ever been more considerate of their crews than Bob Bartlett. There was no military smartness about the ship, but morale was high and the competence of the crew and their readiness for any task proved that he had the kind of discipline that makes men happy and at the same time eager and efficient.[12]

The crew included his younger brother, fifty-four-year-old William Bartlett, as first mate; forty-seven-year-old Leonard Gushue as First Engineer; and Leonard's son, twenty-six-year-old Bart Gushue, as Second Engineer. The captain's young nephew, fifteen-year-old Sam Bartlett, was a deckhand, while thirty-six-year-old Tommy Pritchard acted as steward and his father, fifty-six-year-old Bill "Billy" Pritchard, was cook. As a young boy, Billy Pritchard had worked as cabin boy for Robert E. Peary on the *Roosevelt* during Peary's 1908–09 bid to reach the North Pole. On that same expedition, Robert A. Bartlett had been captain and Leonard Gushue's father, Thomas, had been Bartlett's first mate. The *Morrissey*'s crew also included Jim Dooling, Charles Batten, Reg Wilcox, and George Bartlett. Dr. Schilling was impressed by these men, and wrote:

> The crew are amazing men of the old sailing type. Quite a rare crew because of it. Jim Dooley [Dooling] is 70 years old and still climbs the mast and does a real day's work, quiet but a long ways from being through. George is 65 and works and looks like a young man. A life of hardship with continual activity don't lessen a long life; they tend to make one.[13]

These men had sailed with Bartlett on his previous expeditions, and, like Captain Olsen's crew in Norway, were dependent on sealing, whaling, and fishing during other seasons. They descended from a long line of hardy Newfoundland families who lived and worked by the sea. While Captain Olsen from Ålesund and Captain Bob from Brigus are dominant figures in maritime history, the men (and very occasionally women) who formed their crews served with honour, even though their contributions have not been formally recognized.

During late spring, Bartlett was busy readying the *Morrissey* for her next voyage. Louise was named as a consulting expert to the National Bureau of Standards and spent much of her time in Washington and New York meeting with government officials in the two months before setting sail. She was diligent about concealing the true nature of the expedition. Information about it was released to the public only in April, mere weeks before their departure date. No mention was made of where the expedition was going or for how long:

> Miss Louise A. Boyd will conduct an expedition into Arctic waters this summer for the purpose of carrying on radio and geomagnetic investigations sponsored by the National Bureau of Standards. The expedition will be in the schooner *Effie M. Morrissey* under the captaincy of Captain Bob Bartlett. Miss Boyd and Captain Bartlett are both Arctic explorers of long experience.[14]

Following this announcement, Captain Bartlett received an official government letter advising of the risk of undertaking an expedition to Greenland at such a time:

> The Navy Department considers that the backers of the expedition should realize that under existing circumstances there may conceivably be some jeopardy in

Captain Bob Bartlett at the Peary Monument during the summer of 1932.

connection with their operations and that any attendant risks are taken entirely upon their own responsibility. Also, conditions may make it impossible for the Navy Department to render assistance in the event of unforeseen contingency. Subject to the foregoing remarks, the Navy Department has no objection to the proposed expedition provided it is undertaken with the following conditions, which should be agreed to in writing by the master of the ship and by the sponsors:

a) She will not proceed east of longitude 43 degrees W.
b) She will not transmit any meteorological information.
c) She will keep the Navy Department informed of her position when practicable.[15]

It was a solemn reminder that this would be no ordinary expedition, and it is evident that Louise was aware of the particular threats that might await. But, to the world at large, this was just another Arctic expedition and only a select group of people knew its true purpose. Shortly before leaving, Louise received a warm handwritten note from Vilhjalmur Stefansson expressing his best wishes for a successful expedition: "May the shores and seas of Greenland yield to you this summer even more of their secrets than in past years. A pleasant voyage and a safe return. Greetings to Captain Bob and to all your company."[16]

On June 11, the *Effie M. Morrissey*, with Louise, the scientific team, and the crew onboard, cast off from the Coast Guard dock in Washington.

It was the first time that Louise had sailed on the *Morrissey*, a ship dear to Captain Bob Bartlett's heart. Years earlier, Bartlett quoted Robert Peary: "Of all the special tools that a polar explorer requires for the successful prosecution of his work, his ship stands first and preeminent. This is the tool which is to place him and his party and supplies within striking distance of his goal, the tool without which he can accomplish nothing."[17] The *Morrissey* was Bartlett's special tool and his best girl all in one. He would later say that "she was the greatest bloody bargain of my life." Built as a sailing schooner during the winter of 1893–94, she measured 152 feet long with a hull length of 112 feet and a breadth of 24 feet, 5 inches. In 1913, she was purchased by Harold Bartlett of Brigus, who sold *Morrissey* to his brother Bob in 1925. She had bravely sailed with Captain Bob Bartlett and his Brigus crew on more than thirty Arctic voyages.

Travelling down the Potomac River and Chesapeake Bay and then north along the eastern seaboard, the *Morrissey* passed many freighters and destroyers before docking on the East River in New York to pick up additional supplies. By the time *Morrissey* lifted anchor, Dr. John Schilling had already formed early views of his shipmates:

> It will be most interesting to watch the personal developments this summer; what with a crazy woman, two scientists with slightly inverted personalities, and a nervous radio operator. The crew, although uneducated, are all fine men. They are hardworking and don't complain; rough yet kind; clean living and — to date — not very profane.

A model of the *Effie M. Morrissey.*

Most of them do not drink. Of course they reflect their captain for whom they have been working for years. Many of the men's fathers and grandfathers have worked for past generations of Bartletts.[18]

As was customary with Captain Bartlett on all his Arctic voyages, another stop was made at his home port in Brigus, Newfoundland. Clearing customs there proved a grim reminder of the dramatic international events:

> The town is very bustling due to war activity and building the U.S. bases.… The harbor was full of freighters, tankers and warships. One with a tremendous hole in its side due to a torpedo. There is much war talk and I finally realized that here is a country really at war. The people are 100 per cent behind Churchill.[19]

As they left Brigus, bad weather was on the horizon. The *Morrissey* headed toward the North Atlantic, encountering crashing waves that swamped the lower decks. After a few tense days at sea, radio operator Tom Carroll received a partial radio message for the two scientists, Archer Taylor and Fred Gracely, that stated tersely: "Your salaries will be withheld unless you …" The two scientists had to wait uncomfortably for almost two weeks before Carroll was able to receive the last part of the transmission, which demanded they sign an affidavit swearing that they did not advocate the violent overthrow of the United States government. It was a ludicrous request: there was no way to sign and deliver an affidavit at sea. A document attesting to their good faith and intentions was duly prepared and signed by Louise and Captain Bartlett, who acted as witnesses. It was later transmitted by radio operator Tom Carroll to Washington in Morse code. The incident kept the *Morrissey* crew laughing at Washington bureaucracy for days.

During the first weeks of the expedition, it became apparent that the budding friendship between Bartlett and Louise was becoming strained. And where Captain Bob led, his crew was sure to follow. Bartlett had rarely sailed with women on the *Morrissey*, and the maritime tradition that it was unlucky to have a woman onboard ship was alive and well as far as he was concerned.

Marie Peary Stafford had sailed with Captain Bob in the summer of 1932 on a voyage to erect a monument to her late father, explorer Robert Peary. Despite the fact that Bartlett had sailed with and deeply respected her father, Bartlett and Stafford did not develop a collegial relationship. Louise wrote:

> The one and only woman that ever went on the *Morrissey* is Mary [*sic*] Peary Stafford, who did not get on with either Captain Bartlett or anyone else on the ship. There was mutual scrapping and dislike, so I have to live down her reputation and make a good one for myself.[20]

Only time would tell if the strained relations would improve. This was the sixth expedition that Louise had organized, financed, and led. She was fifty-four, the author of several books, and had many awards and honours to her name. As an experienced explorer and leader, Louise had

Louise onboard the *Effie M. Morrissey* with scientists (left to right) Frederick Gracely, Archer Taylor, and Tom Carroll during the summer of 1941.

no qualms now about directing men onboard or imposing her will. She worked effectively with scientists Gracely and Taylor, but young, intemperate Dr. Schilling was a different matter. Less than half her age and fresh out of school, Schilling was unwilling to accord Louise the respect she was due. In his diary, he confided:

> Had my first run-in with Miss B. today. She informed me I was to do recording work for these scientists. My answer was in the affirmative only to the extent that they got so far behind they couldn't do it themselves. It's funny; if the captain asked me to do it I would never have hesitated and done it whole-heartedly. His secret of leadership is the respect he commands of his men and there isn't a one of the crew that wouldn't jump overboard if the captain told him to, whereas, with Miss B., I don't give a damn about her or her whole scientific project which is so insincere on her part, her motivation being purely selfish and self-promoting. Well, it takes all kinds of people to make a world, and I suppose the Miss Boyds with all their money, scattered brains and loose tongues have their place. It's humorous how she always starts in by saying she is the leader and that the captain is her hireling. Well, that's mighty wrong; perhaps she will learn something from him before the trip is over.[21]

By refusing to assist Taylor, Gracely, and Carroll with their work on an as-needs basis, Schilling disregarded the terms of the contract he had signed with Louise. As documented in his expedition diary, he was patronizing toward her and refers to other mature, single women as "pitiful and frustrated." Ignoring her impressive accomplishments, he stated about Louise: "She has missed everything that has been worthwhile. I think this has been true of a great many things in her life, notably a husband."[22]

Schilling's attitude made life onboard uncomfortable. Archer Taylor commented in his logbook: "Miss Boyd accuses Dr. J [of] having a swelled head. And sometimes I think she is right. In any case, she has handled this very well, though it is hard for me to have to work with the doctor now under the circumstances."[23]

Louise was responsible for providing leadership to the men in her charge as well as ensuring that the scientific agenda was followed. For the first time in her working life, the captain and crew did not support her. Schilling's expedition journal is rife with negative comments made by Captain Bartlett and the crew about Louise. He also suggested that the crew was not committed to the scientific program of the expedition. Archer Taylor's log corroborates this. He stated: "They had trouble getting the mainsail up without getting caught in the antenna. Personally I think the trouble is with the people giving the orders rather than with the antenna installation itself. They are a stubborn and determined bunch and I think they are not keen about trying to make the antenna work."[24] Later, Taylor suspected that the collection of aurora borealis data might have been compromised since there was no watch specifically designated for this. Rather, the scientists relied on the regular crew carrying out the watch to report any sightings. Taylor commented: "It is a clear night. Maybe there will be an aurora. I think that if it were my responsibility I would stand personally on clear nights and not depend on the ship's watch to tell me about it."[25] Later he commented acerbically: "I guess there was no aurora at all though it was a clear night."

As the *Effie M. Morrissey* approached Greenland, Schilling and the other scientists were awestruck by the stark beauty of the landscape.

> When I looked out at 4 am., there was one of the most wonderful sights I've ever seen. To the north lay the rugged, tremendous peaks of Cape Farewell, rising out of the ocean. Large, precipitous crags rising out of the mountains as skyscrapers that are dwarfed to nothingness by comparison. They were snow-covered and layers of clouds scudded past them. I thought of Shangri-la in *Lost Horizons* and certainly this appeared like the last outpost of the world.[26]

Only a few hours later, the previously calm weather took a sudden turn for the worse. The skies darkened, rain that began as a light drizzle began to pelt, and the wind changed into a full gale. Captain Bartlett decided to take *Morrissey* close in to shore to shelter from the storm, and to drop anchor. With the wind howling down the narrow pass separating two mountains, the *Morrissey* tugged fiercely this way and that, eventually hauling the one-thousand-pound anchor from the depths of the ocean. As the ship was being pulled precipitously, Bartlett gave orders for the motor to be started. The foresail was reefed, hoisted, and promptly blew away. But Captain Bartlett was in his element. His face blackened with grease, he bellowed so loudly he could even be heard above the gale. While the crew worked together in unison, Louise and the scientists hung on for dear life — exhilarated and terrified in equal measure. When the dramatic squall passed, everyone was exhausted. Louise gave orders for the ship to harbour at Cape Farewell, the southernmost tip of Greenland. A few days were spent there on fieldwork while the crew conducted repairs.

After *Morrissey* was ship-shape once more, she sailed to a few nearby communities before dropping anchor at Julianehaab. It was a hive of activity, with several ships moored there. Soon after *Morrissey's* arrival, they were hailed by Commander Donald Macmillan of the Arctic vessel *Bowdoin*. Macmillan was an experienced explorer who had been a "tenderfoot" member of the Peary Expedition in 1908–09 with Captain Bartlett. Louise, the

The *Effie M. Morrissey* in Greenland. Unknown date.

crew, and the scientists were invited aboard *Bowdoin*, where they enjoyed Macmillan's hospitality as well as the chance to explore the smaller, but, in Taylor's estimation, newer and better-equipped vessel.

The U.S. Coast Guard ship *Comanche* was also moored nearby. Both the *Comanche* and the *Bowdoin* had been assigned to the Greenland Patrol that defended Greenland and supported the U.S. Army in setting up air bases there to assist the Allied efforts. Commanded by Edward "Iceberg" Smith, the *Comanche* patrolled that region along with the USS *Bear* and *Northland*. As usual, Louise was caught up in history. The Greenland Patrol played a critical role during Second World War military activities in the North Atlantic region. Years later, Louise received a letter from retired captain Frank Meals, who commanded the *Comanche* later in the war. In November 1962, he thanked her "for the great assistance you unknowingly gave to me and others of the United States Naval Forces operating in Greenland during World War II":

> As you know, Greenland had long been a Danish "closed" colony and charts of the colony were not made available to other countries. The best our Government could do was to supply the ships with reprints of old charts based on early British and French explorations; these charts were incomplete and inaccurate, but they were the only charts available. Fortunately, for us all we were able to obtain a copy of your book *The Fiord Region of Northeast Greenland*, which proved to be of the utmost value to us in our work. I do not know the circumstances in which your book was made available to United States vessels operating in Northeast Greenland during the war years, nor if you have had from official sources acknowledgement of and thanks for the service it rendered. But I would like you to know, and belated although it be, extend to you my personal thanks for the aid it gave me, as commanding officer of a vessel of the Northeast Greenland Patrol in those hazardous war days. Not only did your book provide us with knowledge of the region, which tended to safeguard our navigation of these

largely unsurveyed waters, but it awakened in me, at least, an appreciation of and a love for the beautiful fiord region which I will retain to the end of my days. For this, I thank you, and wish for you every happiness in the years ahead.[27]

Louise responded:

I am deeply grateful for your letter and appreciate your taking the trouble to tell me personally how much good the work I, and my fine associates, did for you and your men, in the use of my book *The Fiord Region of Northeast Greenland*. I had the pleasure of knowing Commander E.H. "Iceberg" Smith, and in fact, gave him a lot of photographs and other data before his ship left San Francisco on its way to the Atlantic and East Greenland. He had me come on the Coast Guard boat and go over several details with him. Regarding Northeast Greenland, I am glad that some of our work was successful; because I did say repeatedly that I thought the Germans would use submarines and airplanes and would land near northeast Greenland. The information in my book also had a great deal to do with locating one of their submarine stations near Koldewey Island, Northeast Greenland.

I will be perfectly frank and say that I have not had much official acknowledgement nor thanks for the services I have rendered … but then I did not do it for thanks but because I felt that my knowledge should be put to the very best use in the defense of our country and of our allies. I served with the War Department for nearly three years.…

I am going to keep your letter with my records because I value it. I will be pleased to hear from you.[28]

The *Morrissey* stayed in Julianehaab for several days, enabling Louise to spend time meeting government representatives. It was during this visit that she met Army Air Corps Colonel Benjamin Giles, and offered him hospitality onboard *Morrissey*. In a later letter, Giles acknowledged the significance of Louise's contributions to the war effort as a result of her 1941 Expedition:

> I was very glad indeed to receive the photographic negatives of KIPISAKO air field and position of the main base, both as to longitude and latitude and magnetic declination. Both the pictures and the exact position of the air base serve a very useful purpose, and on behalf of the War Department, I wish to personally thank you for your splendid spirit of cooperation in obtaining these data.[29]

A few days later, *Morrissey* sailed to a nearby fjord where Gracely and Taylor continued collecting data. Then, it was on to Ivigtut — the world's only source for cryolite, used in the production of aluminum. As such, the protection of Ivigtut had immense significance during the war. The Coast Guard vessel *Modoc* was anchored there and assisted *Morrissey*'s radio operator Tom Carroll in sending reports back to Washington. *Modoc* was one of four Tampa-class 240-foot cutters responsible for keeping the convoy routes open around Greenland.

The next community to be visited was Godthaab, where a new consulate was being built. Several days were spent there with Louise visiting the American consul to Greenland, government representative James K. Penfield. As they sailed through dangerous waters, it was only through contact with other military vessels and government officials that Louise kept herself apprised of the war's progress. A letter forwarded by a Maple Lawn staff member indicates how worried her friends were:

> Poor Mrs. Rutherford has been like a chicken on a hot stove about your being up there in the Arctic — not to mention a few others — of course they all have an idea you are very close to Iceland and the East Coast of Greenland (never having been given the slightest bit of information they have just assumed I guess that you are in that vicinity). Of course Iceland to us (according to the papers) is a very

dangerous spot right now what with German submarines etc. not to mention the sinking of some of our ships and really you can't blame them for worrying especially when they do not know your itinerary.[30]

After leaving Godthaab, *Morrissey* crossed the Arctic Circle and visited several more local communities. After encountering icebergs of all sizes, *Morrissey* met pack ice in Melville Bay. From afar, all onboard could see the Peary Memorial cairn that had been erected on the promontory at Cape York by Marie Peary Stafford as a memorial to her late father, Robert Peary. Stafford had travelled on the *Morrissey* to the site in 1938 to erect the cairn with Bartlett as captain. After a short visit to the village of Thule, *Morrissey* steamed into Inglefield Gulf toward Northumberland Island, where the ship anchored off Etah.

By this stage in the expedition, the tension on the ship between the crew and the scientific team was palpable. A clear division existed between Captain Bartlett, and Louise and the scientists she employed. Schilling was a notable exception, and he made his allegiance clear:

> I quite often smile inwardly when I think of the odd personalities gathered on this trip. An old wealthy eccentric sexless spinster, a hard old bachelor sea captain, one scientist that is hopeless as a man, a mildly neurotic nervous radio operator, and a delicate, sensitive, though pleasant and hard working 2nd scientist. No doubt they have me in some such odd category in their own minds, too, so I guess it all evens out in the end, and after all if it weren't for the diversity of characters this would be a pretty drab society.[31]

Schilling may have felt humbled by the knowledge that existing documents by other expedition members do not record such scathing comments about him. Archer Taylor was quite discreet in comparison. Schilling's criticism was particularly directed toward Louise and Frederick Gracely. Condemning Gracely's weight, listless behaviour, and diet, he also mocked the scientist's intellectual abilities. In doing so, he displayed his inexperience, as Gracely had three advanced degrees and later worked for both the Central Intelligence Agency and the Mercury Project at NASA. Taylor records that the onboard strain came to a head when Louise attempted to assert her rights as expedition leader and informed Captain Bartlett that the scientific team was not supposed to perform shipboard labour. While this was likely an attempt to establish clear lines of responsibility, it backfired and succeeded only in creating further unpleasantness:

> Bobby [Louise's private nickname for Bartlett] has a bad disposition not at all nice…. I had it right out with him yesterday when he said no one but L.A.B. and himself could go to the aft part of the ship — that that was his Holy Domain! I told him a charterer had the entire ship not part of it and that meant the staff and the wireless man, and with that he went off the handle completely…. Today he said he intended to make the Staff [the scientific team] work on the ship and I said no not one bit, they have a more than full program to carry out. Will see they do not either![32]

Louise's constant comparisons to her previous ship *Veslekari* caused further tension as Bartlett and his crew were understandably biased in their opinions that the *Effie M. Morrissey* — the ship that had served them faithfully for so many years — was the superior vessel. In their diaries, both Schilling and Taylor record frequent attempts of their onboard colleagues to avoid encountering specific individuals. Schilling reported:

> I had to laugh, literally openly, at the captain this evening, though felt embarrassed for doing so, even though I couldn't help it. I looked up and saw him sneaking down the port rail behind the dory and duck into the aft hatch, just to avoid Miss B. who was sitting with her back to that quarter. The comedy was too great for me to constrain my features, to think of an old sea captain,

fearless of the Arctic, yet avoiding a bothersome talkative old maid who was trying unintelligently to make her mark in the world was too much.[33]

Etah, a renowned destination in the lore of many Arctic expeditions, is the most northerly harbour in West Greenland. When the *Morrissey* team visited Etah, it appeared most unlovely, presenting a vast landscape of discarded beer cans, batteries, and other waste from a previous expedition. Taylor and Schilling were unimpressed. The team spent four days on Etah. Several side trips were made, including to Littleton Island, where American explorer Elisha Kent Kane had cached a small boat and provisions in 1853. Finding her way blocked by ice, the *Morrissey* had to wind through the massive bergs before finally heading into Lancaster Sound:

> We were entering the Lancaster Sound, so famous in the Search for the Northwest Passage. What mixed feelings of awe, wonder, fear, admiration, adventure, those old explorers some 200 years ago must have had. Many never returned and all suffered hardships.[34]

Captain Bartlett was surprised to find so much snow and ice in the area at that time of year. On their way toward Beechey Island, the ship was stopped short by a solid barrier of ice.

> The ice was the heaviest sort of pack ice about 10–15 feet thick and the pans were about 20 yards on a side, so their weight alone is tremendous and the push of a whole pack almost amounts to an irresistible force. We proceeded westward as far as we could to see if there was any open water beyond or a safe opening. There was none and we turned the vessel east again, and I might add I was not sorry either.[35]

Given Bartlett's decision that the ice was inpenetrable, *Morrissey* was forced to abandon plans to visit Beechey Island and headed back toward Dundas Harbour. Louise was disappointed and made her feelings clear to the captain. Taylor confided in his journal: "Personally, I was satisfied to accept the Captain's judgement, although I recognized that it might have been affected by the negative attitude he had apparently developed toward Miss Boyd."[36]

The *Morrissey* remained in the area for three days with all onboard hoping that the ice conditions and the foggy, overcast weather would shift. Time was spent gathering data and visiting a Royal Canadian Mounted Police station. Schilling and Taylor remained unaware of the significance of the data that was being gathered. Schilling commented: "The scientific magnetic measurements may be of some importance, but Gracely is so stupid about everything else and so slovenly in his way of life that I cannot get much enthusiasm over the project that was really manufactured to give a little prestige, purpose and publicity to the trip, though of course enthusiastically welcomed by the N.B.S."[37]

The expedition diaries of both Taylor and Schilling remain oblivious of the true significance and purpose of the expedition. It is almost certain that Louise successfully concealed the fact that the expedition was directly assisting the American war effort.

In late August, the ship sailed and anchored at Pond Inlet on the north coast of Baffin Island in Canada. A few days were spent there and data was gathered about a large active sunspot that was passing across the face of the sun. This resulted in the complete blackout of all radio communication for two weeks, and a spectacular display of the aurora borealis. Several other stops were made, including at Clyde River and Pangnirtung. Miss Boyd made good use of this time to visit with the RCMP and the local clergy who ran both the hospital and a ladies mission society.

Taylor and Schilling agreed in their respective journals that Louise overstayed her welcome there. Shortly after they finally left, the ship's gyro compass — a critical piece of equipment — failed. Despite his lack of experience, Taylor fixed the compass and found his credibility onboard much improved. *Morrissey* then entered Frobisher Bay and anchored at York Sound. This was a particularly important site for Louise, as she had agreed to photograph and gather data there. The United States government was considering building in the vicinity and her information and photographs would be critical. Louise, Gracely, and Taylor went ashore to take photographs and obtain magnetic measurements.

Once they left York Sound, a summer storm descended suddenly. With a strong northwesterly wind blowing, it began to snow and visibility was reduced. The captain's gruff voice pierced the fog, "Hard to port: Hard to port" as the *Morrissey* narrowly missed hitting the cliffs of the Button Islands off Cape Chidley. The storm lasted twenty-four long hours. Taylor commented:

> It was rough. No one could sleep. It was hard even to eat.... You straddled the bench with one foot braced against the bulkhead. Ironically, soup was the only thing that could be cooked. A large kettle, maybe 15 inches deep, was lashed to the top of the coal stove with soup only 6–8 inches deep so it could slop around without going over the top. Soup bowls were only partly filled. The strategy was to hold the bowl in your hand while you tried to transfer some of it to your mouth. Then you would set the bowl down, just before the ship's roll reached its zenith; butter a ship's biscuit and quickly retrieve the soup bowl before the ship begins to roll again. It sounds fun, but it got old very fast.[38]

When it seemed the storm had left them — the skies cleared and the sun broke through — wet clothing was hung out to dry and repairs to the scientific equipment and the hull got under way. But just hours later the storm returned, and even more ferociously than before. The *Morrissey* was in sight of land, but the storm was too great to move closer in and find shelter. This was the most desperate situation they had encountered yet. Usually a seasoned sailor, but lacking confidence in *Morrissey*'s captain and crew, even Louise was tense. In her panic, she asked Archer Taylor to get the radio operator to send an SOS message that the ship was about to sink. The U.S. Coast Guard radio operator Tom Carroll knew that such a message could be sent only by the Captain. Although there was a lot of shouting and dashing about by the crew, Taylor and Carroll correctly surmised that the ship's demise was not imminent. Carroll wisely held off on sending the SOS message.

Finally the storm subsided and *Morrissey* limped into the nearest harbour at Hopedale, Labrador. Later, much recovered from the ordeal, Louise exchanged social visits with the Moravian minister and his wife.

Sailing southward along the Labrador coast, the *Morrissey* made brief stops at the communities of Turnavik and Battle Harbour, where Gracely and Taylor made magnetic observations and collected aurora borealis data. Leaving Battle Harbour and entering the Strait of Belle Isle, they counted over fifty vessels in the area. Later they learned that a German submarine had been sighted close to Conception Bay. On October 10, the *Morrissey* reached Brigus Harbour in Newfoundland.

The rest of those onboard visited with Bartlett's mother and sisters while Louise travelled to the American naval base at Argentia, where Roosevelt and Churchill had held meetings a few months previously.

Memorial to Captain Bob Bartlett in Brigus, Newfoundland. Photograph taken in 2015.

This was followed by another unpleasant incident on the ship that caused tempers to flare once again:

> Since she [Louise] did not go to St. John's, she asked Gracely to obtain for her a substantial quantity of fresh fruits and vegetables — fresh foods we had not experienced for several months. This resulted in a painfully unpleasant scene when Billy not only served them to us at dinner in the saloon but to the forecastle crew as well. Miss Boyd made it quite clear that she had not meant to provide the fresh foods to the working crew but only as a special treat for the Captain, his aide, the NBS scientists, the doctor and the radio operator. It was a thoughtlessly élitist gesture that could only aggravate the tensions that had been developing onboard for some time.[39]

It is hard to see this as anything other than an "élitist gesture." However, Louise was known as a generous woman who rewarded loyalty and good service. While sailing on the *Veslekari*, the Norwegian captain and crew received bonuses and she kept in contact with many of them for years. Louise also provided references for previous crews and expedition participants and hosted them at her Maple Lawn home in California. It is possible that, at that stage in the journey, she was aware of the derogatory things that the Captain and his crew said about her. Taylor confided to his journal that he overheard many comments about Louise that were disrespectful and indecent. Perhaps the withholding of fresh produce would have been one way of expressing her displeasure with the crew.

The *Morrissey* continued sailing in a southerly direction past Cape Race and Cape Cod. Steaming through Long Island Sound, they went ashore in New York before arriving at the United States Coast Guard pier in Washington on November 3, 1941. The headlines spoke glowingly of their return: "San Rafael Explorer Returns" and "Gains Data on Radio on Arctic Expedition — Boyd Group Is Praised for Work for Bureau of Standards." But one *New York Times* headline, "Bartlett's Craft Back But Captain Bob Is Nowhere to Be Found after Ship Gets In" referred not to the expedition but likely to Bartlett's feelings about it. It seems that soon after the *Morrissey* docked, Captain Bob Bartlett could not get away fast enough.

But Louise had had a fine time. She wrote to a friend: "We are all in grand health — have just adored every day we have been out and it has been a most fascinating and instructive summer! Really I am just thrilled with all I have seen and done.... The *Morrissey* is a fine sea boat; rides huge seas like a gull does."[40] As always, she was gracious in acknowledging the contributions of all expedition members. Louise ignored the conflict that had arisen between herself and Captain Bob, as well as the tension with Dr. Schilling. She later stated resolutely: "Fate was more than kind to me in the

The *Effie M. Morrissey* docked with Captain Bartlett onboard. Photograph likely taken in the early 1940s.

splendid staffs of scientists whose results prove their outstanding abilities and qualifications. The same high caliber, I am proud to say, existed with my skippers and crew. To all of them I give the greatest credit."[41]

Following the return to Washington, she and the scientific team were busy tabulating valuable data and conveying it to government authorities. The scientific contributions were lauded by many government departments, including the head of the Department of Terrestrial Magnetism at the Carnegie Institution, who told Louise that her data had solved many of the transmission problems his department had grappled with. Chief of the Radio Section Dellinger's faith in Louise had not been misplaced. He commented that the data gathered within the auroral zone "constituted the missing link in NBS's [National Bureau of Standards] emerging radio weather forecasting service."[42]

Louise was relieved that the objectives of the expedition had been met and that her work had not been cut short due to wartime hostilities. As always, luck had been on her side. All agreed that the timing of the expedition had been fortuitous. Louise wrote: "I am sure you all feel as I do, that it was a kind fate that allowed us to go north last year, as with the present war bursting on us so suddenly, I personally think the data we obtained is more valuable than ever."[43]

Only a few weeks later, on December 7, 1941, the Japanese attacked Pearl Harbor and the United States officially entered the war. Louise had left the Arctic region just in the nick of time.

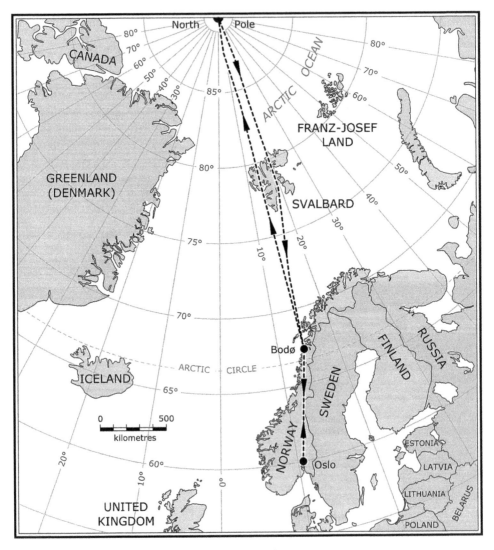

Route of Louise Arner Boyd's 1955 North Pole Flight.

CHAPTER TEN

THE NORTH POLE AND BEYOND

Just like jumping blindfolded into the universe.
— ROALD AMUNDSEN

There was not a moment to lose. As soon as Louise arrived back in the United States, she settled into an executive apartment at the Broadmoor, home to a select cross-section of Washington bigwigs. Her position as an expert consultant for the National Bureau of Standards and the War Department was officially confirmed. As with all government employees, her background and personal history were heavily scrutinized. Louise's personnel file reported that she was "a member of a well-known and well-regarded pioneer family and she is one of the most prominent residents of San Rafael. There is no alien influence. All associations and affiliations are favorable and she is known in the best of social circles."[1] As a patriotic American whose ancestors had fought in the American Revolution and the Civil War, Louise was thrilled to assume an active role in the war effort. She wrote to Secretary of State Cordell Hull: "I consider it an honor and privilege to have served our Government last year as leader of the Louise A. Boyd Arctic Expedition, and shall continue to serve at all times to the best of my ability in any capacity in which I am requested."[2] Cordell Hull would become known as the longest-serving Secretary of State; he held the position from 1933 to 1944. He would later be awarded the Nobel Peace Prize in 1945 for spearheading the establishment of the United Nations.

Documentation indicates that Louise worked for several branches of military intelligence during the war. Her assistance was solicited by high-ranking officials from different departments, including the office of the Coordinator of Information (later known as the Office of Special Services, or OSS), the Corps of Engineers, and the Troops Division. Like her parents before her, Louise took her responsibilities seriously. She wrote to her friend Stefansson:

> While I am still attached to the National Bureau of Standards, my work really has been transferred to the War Department where I am signed up for the duration as Expert Consultant, Office of the Chief of Staff. I am returning to Washington the middle of August. In other words, I am home on a very short furlough. Because I expect to leave here for Washington on August 11, I will appreciate hearing from you as soon as possible. Next time you come to Washington, I hope I will surely see you. I have a temporary apartment at the Broadmoor, 3601 Connecticut Avenue, so be sure to let me know when you come. And plan to have dinner with me, or a Sunday lunch, as my working hours are 8:15 A.M. to 5:00 P.M., like the rest of them in the War Department.[3]

Louise was initially paid $10 (USD) per day, although this was later increased to $25. One of her first assignments was writing a study on the feasibility of York Sound on Baffin Island as a military landing field. Using data she had collected as well as detailed photographs, Louise completed the classified report and submitted it to Hull. Louise also put at the government's disposal her file of several thousand photographs of Greenland, Jan Mayen, and the surrounding region; extensive scientific data in hydrography, geology, glaciology, botany, ecology, radio, and magnetic transmission; and her large library of maps and Arctic publications. In Washington, Louise annotated photographs selected by military intelligence and assisted in data analysis and the preparation of intelligence reports. Former expedition participant Finn Bronner, then a major in the Topographic Detachment, stated of her work: "Even though her photography collection was amazing in its very scope, its intelligence value was greatly enhanced by Miss Boyd's profound familiarity with the areas she had visited and by her incredibly copious notes. Her contribution permitted a detailed study of hundreds of miles of coast line and enabled the Aeronautical Chart Service and the Army Map Service to revise charts and maps and to locate additional features not available from other sources."[4]

Louise worked for military intelligence throughout 1942 to 1944. Colonel Hamilton Maguire, Chief of the Central European Branch of the Military Intelligence Branch, commended her: "Your research work here as Expert Consultant has also included conferences which were helpful to the Navy and the Air, as well as the Army. Your industry, accuracy and long background of scientific exploration enables you to make a major contribution."[5] Lieutenant-Colonel S.P. Poole of the Geographic Section of the Military Intelligence Service referred to her as the most competent American authority in her field.

On October 3, 1944, Louise was notified that the services of expert consultants such as her were no longer required. In thanking her, Poole stated: "I can't begin to tell you how much we really have appreciated your fine and patriotic devotion to duty while in this office. Several of the officers have commented on it — many of them outside our Section entirely."[6] Louise accepted this decision gracefully and indicated her willingness to again serve her country in the future.

During this same period, Louise's attention was often diverted from important war work. The long-simmering tensions between Louise and Captain Bartlett that had developed onboard the *Morrissey* continued long after the ship had docked. Voluminous correspondence exists between Louise, Bartlett, National Bureau of Standards Director Lyman J. Briggs, and Louise's lawyer, F. Sanford Smith. Amongst other matters, Bartlett claimed he had not been reimbursed for additional expenses, while Louise shot back that he had not handed over the expedition logbook and maps as stipulated in his contract. Over time, this correspondence became increasingly acrimonious, with Louise tartly declaring: "I have lost all respect for

R.A.B. ... He'll never over my dead body get that money I call his 'bonus' for good behavior — not a cent of it!"[7]

The matter took more than six months to resolve and the goodwill between them was never restored. There is no record that the paths of Louise and Bartlett ever crossed again. On April 28, 1946, Captain Robert A. Bartlett died at the age of 70.

Adjusting to life after the completion of her 1941 expedition and her stimulating wartime service must have been challenging for an active woman such as Louise. There was no expedition on the horizon to plan, though she continued to express her desire to return north.

Her expert knowledge of Greenland and her assistance to the Allied effort was acknowledged by Denmark shortly after the conclusion of the war. In March 1946, she received the King Christian X Liberty Medal, which was "conferred upon persons of foreign nationality, who during the years of occupation have made special contribution towards Denmark's cause by making known the Danish people's national position ... or by putting their working power at the disposal of the Danish Legations and Consulates; and upon such who have proved to be especially deserving, when the hour of the liberation came, by their efforts on Denmark's behalf."[8]

Since the Amundsen rescue mission in 1928, Louise had received awards and honours from Denmark, Norway, France, and Italy. She had represented her country honourably in leading six Arctic expeditions and had provided assistance to her fellow explorers and scientists in the field, often under dangerous circumstances. She had served her country well, but, by the late 1940s, Louise had received no formal recognition from her own government.

After the war, she resumed work on her manuscript about her 1937 and 1938 voyages to Greenland. *The Coast of Northeast Greenland with Hydrographical Studies in the Greenland Sea* was published by the American Geographical Society in 1948 to glowing reviews. The long, mutually beneficial relationship between Louise and the American Geographical Society continued, although privately some grumbling about her was expressed. In an in-house memo, John Wright wrote:

AGS is under no obligation to L.A.B. We have benefitted through her by being able to publish two books and distribute them to Fellows but this has been done at cost in editorial time that fully balances our indebtedness. More largely through the sponsorship of the AGS, L.A.B. has gained her present reputation and recognition. It is not unjust to say that she is interested in the AGS only in so far as it will further her personal interests and ambitions. Experience has shown that she has many admirable and even lovable qualities but that she is also extraordinarily self-centred and rather dictatorial.[9]

Despite these feelings on the part of some AGS staff members, on the surface, the relationship between the AGS and Louise remained amicable.

Louise Arner Boyd receiving award from the Department of the Army. Photograph taken in New York in 1949.

Good news was on the horizon. In the spring of 1949, Louise received a Certificate of Appreciation from the Department of the Army recognizing her "outstanding patriotic service to the Department of the Army as a contributor of geographic knowledge and as a consultant during the critical months immediately before and after the start of World War II."[10] Upon presenting the certificate to her, Major General Roscoe Woodruff acknowledged that Louise's actions had benefitted the cause of victory. The Army was the only branch of the government to formally acknowledge this, even though her work had been an asset to diverse government departments at all levels.

As usual, Louise kept herself busy. A journalist described a typical day: "She dictated letters and notes all morning, received her certificate in the afternoon, attended a dinner of the board of directors of the American

Louise and her dog on Maple Lawn's Magnolia Terrace. Photograph likely taken in the 1960s.

Polar Society and gave an illustrated address at the Polar Society's fourteenth annual meeting at the American Museum of Natural History. She is also preparing to sail for Portugal next week where she will address the International Geographical Congress in Lisbon."[11]

Over the coming years, Louise's time was consumed with speaking engagements and writing assignments. She also returned with vigour to her longtime philanthropic endeavours, which included working tirelessly as president of the Marin Music Chest Organization, leading the membership drive for Guide Dogs for the Blind, serving as a director of the San Francisco Symphony Orchestra, a park commissioner of San Rafael, and a trustee of Mills College. She stated, "Though I'm a geographer and an explorer, I've never neglected my civic duties."[12] She was a member of myriad other organizations, including the American Society of the Legion of Honor, the M.H. de Young Museum Society, and the Children's Hospital. She was also still president of the Boyd Investment Company. However, her work with scientific organizations remained a priority. In 1949, she was elected an honorary member of the California Academy of Sciences, which recognized her many years as a trustee. In 1951, she published an article on her Arctic expeditions in *Photogrammetric Engineering* as well as one in *The Geographical Review* about her 1934 travels throughout Poland. Around this time, Louise learned about a project that Vilhjalmur Stefansson was spearheading — a twenty-volume scholarly work about the Arctic and Subarctic regions called the *Encyclopedia Arctica*. The biographies of only three women — Lady Jane Franklin, Josephine Diebitsch Peary, and Louise Arner Boyd — were featured:

> Miss Boyd's contributions to knowledge of the Arctic, in addition to the great collection of her own photographs which she has accumulated, and her venturesome use and experimentation with ultramodern equipment and techniques, including adaptation and personal use of the camera for mapping purposes, are the published reports on geological, glaciological, physiological, ecological, and hydrographical investigations and the topographical

and hydrographical surveys carried out by the competent experts whom she selected for her field staffs and for whom she furnished the best of modern equipment.[13]

It was a fitting tribute to Louise and all she had accomplished.

In 1952, Louise travelled throughout Germany and Austria, and completed extensive renovations at her San Rafael home. These renovations included the installation of an outdoor swimming pool and sauna so she could better entertain her guests, as well as a grand banquet-sized dining room and a huge living room/office. In her newly renovated quarters, she surrounded herself with oversized wall maps of her expeditions, signed photographs of explorers and prominent world figures she had worked closely with, and artifacts from her travels abroad. One visitor commented: "Miss Boyd's outfit tonight is a far cry from that of the Arctic explorer as she gracefully accompanies us into her huge library where all kinds of tropical and subtropical flowers in gorgeous containers temper the gust from the numerous Arctic souvenirs. For the house is rich in these souvenirs — there are maps of '*Veslekari*'s' ice-filled and dangerous hunting grounds, objects made of walrus tusks, polished medals, diplomas, and other distinctions which she has won for her outstanding research in Arctic science."[14] And always, there were portraits of her beloved parents and brothers.

Louise's hospitality was legendary and she regularly opened her home to her friends for parties. A close friend commented: "She is never too busy to welcome old friends or to take an active part in Marin county affairs. She nearly always has house guests and with her charm and warm personality, she attracts anyone who meets her."[15]

No matter how engaged she was with social and philanthropic activities, Louise's sharp mind was always focused on the North. In early 1952, she learned that the Boyd Bank — the underwater feature between Jan Mayen and Bjørnøya she had discovered during her 1937 Expedition — had been renamed the Veslekari Seamount by the U.S. Board of Geographic Names. Louise was furious and wrote to the American Geographical Society: "I am most disappointed that as an American citizen I am left out entirely in favor of a foreign ship. The ship had nothing to do with it but was in my service and that of my staff."[16] Due to her tenacity, and after six months of negotiating, the board reversed its decision and this feature is still known today as the Boyd Seamount.

In a 1954 profile entitled "Arctic Call Is Strong," Louise mused to a reporter about how "the march of events since World War II has made the independent Arctic explorer a vanishing species."[17] She was now sixty-seven years of age and knew that her own exploring days were behind her. And yet, she still had one more expedition in mind. Throughout 1954, she corresponded with Norwegian Polar Institute Director and good friend Harald Sverdrup. Like many of her high-profile friends, Sverdrup had an illustrious past. Described as "honest, unassuming and pious," Harald Sverdrup was an accomplished oceanographer and meteorologist who developed the first accurate theory of ocean circulation, known as the "Sverdrup balance." He had also participated in many Arctic voyages, including Roald Amundsen's 1918–25 expedition on the *Maud* through the Northeast Passage. Louise corresponded with Sverdrup about her recent appointment as Chairman of the Committee on Geographical Explorations for the American Society of Photogrammetry. At the end of that year, she wrote to him with momentous news.

In a letter boldly marked "TOP SECRET," Louise confided to Sverdrup a long-held dream to fly to the North Pole. This dream to reach the Pole was remarkable, given that she did not care for flying. Unlike her previous trips, where she hired the ship and the staff and developed an appropriate scientific agenda, this plan put her entirely at the mercy of others. There is documentary evidence that Louise lobbied her network of friends and supporters for three years to bring this dream to fruition. She wrote to American Geographical Society president and fellow explorer Richard U. Light:

> Incidentally, I do know the new Secretary of Air, Harold Talbot's sister Mrs. Church very intimately although I have not seen her for a number of years. As he has just stepped into office, am sure he has too much to do in getting

started and organized for me to try to put an iron in the fire with my wishes. However, if worse comes to worse, I will see what I can do along those lines.[18]

She spoke to Walter Wood and Lincoln Washburn — two previous expedition members with whom she kept in touch and whose opinions she valued. They enthusiastically endorsed her ambitious plan. Louise also secured the support of renowned pilots Bernt Balchen and Finn Lambrechts. Lambrechts was one of the two Norwegian aviators who had been on the *Hobby* with Louise during the 1928 Amundsen rescue mission. Now a lieutenant-general in the Royal Norwegian Air Force, Lambrechts had remained in contact with Louise. Once he knew her plans, he introduced her to Thor Solberg of the Solberg Aviation Company. Both men agreed to fly Louise to the North Pole. She referred to this new adventure as "The Louise A. Boyd North Pole Flight" and it is evident that she intended to make this her eighth expedition. She told Sverdrup: "I plan to take no so-called laymen — women or men — but will take a couple of scientists along. For your information, I will pay no salaries nor assume any responsibility for accidents, loss of life, etc. Realizing you are the world's greatest authority on Polar Ice besides heading your splendid Polar Institute there in Norway, is there some one or even two people you would like to send along?"[19]

While she had been in contact with Charles Hitchcock, the new director of the American Geographical Society, there is no indication that he considered it to be a true scientific undertaking. Louise also wrote to Calvin J. Heusser in the Department of Exploration and Field Research at the American Geographical Society regarding a pollen and spore collecting study. Her National Bureau of Standards contact (and now friend) J.H. Dellinger put her in touch with physicist Dr. Serge A. Korff at New York University about the possibility of collecting cosmic ray measurements. With the assistance of her finely honed network of prestigious colleagues and friends and with an admirable ability to go straight to the top, she approached only those scientists who were at the pinnacle of their careers or who demonstrated outstanding potential. But for various reasons none of these scientific plans worked out, and even Louise's invitation to Harald Sverdrup himself to accompany her was courteously declined.

Louise would be one of the first women to fly to the Pole and the first person to fly there on a non-military and non-commercial flight. As with her expeditions by sea, this long flight was not without its inherent risks. But, most significantly, this was the culmination of her personal dream to finally reach the goal of so many polar explorers — the fabled North Pole.

Louise worked hard organizing the event. She wrote to her friends, Cathe and Nino Mowinckel: "Frankly it was a big undertaking. But as with my other expeditions that were all with ships, I went thoroughly into every detail long before I even signed up for the flight."[20] She also displayed the same secretiveness regarding what information she shared with people and when it was divulged. She believed in the significance of what she was about to do and carefully composed the message that would be sent out to the world. When the time was right, she made sure that all the world knew about this North Pole flight.

Accompanied by her maid, Miss Boyd flew from New York to Oslo in June 1955. As always, she stayed at the stately Grand Hotel, which had hosted the Nobel Peace Prize winner every year since its inception.

Louise planning her North Pole flight in early 1955.

A dinner was given at the Grand in her honour by the American ambassador to Norway and his wife, and the noteworthy guest list included officials from both Norway and the United States: Admiral Jacobsen, Commander-in-Chief of the Royal Norwegian Navy; Major General Sanders and Colonel Sam Westbrook from the United States Air Force; Lloyd Larson, U.S. Chief of Mission to Norway; and Mr. Nielsen from the Norwegian Ministry of Defence. On June 17, U.S. Ambassador Corrin Strong and Rear Admiral John Carson from the American Embassy bade farewell to Louise at the Oslo airfield and watched as she boarded the DC-4 with ten people onboard. Accompanying her were Lieutenant Colonels Finn Lambrechts and Steffan Olsen.

The weather in Oslo and Bodø was poor that day, with rain pouring down. All onboard feared the worst. As Louise knew well, Arctic weather was unpredictable at best and it was more than possible that the lack of visibility would jeopardize the success of this journey. But the skies cleared and the plane took off from Oslo around 7:35 p.m., and arrived in Bodø for refuelling. Setting off once more, Louise was in the co-pilot's seat taking photographs. As they approached the Pole, the clouds vanished and the DC-4 emerged into perfect sunshine. Louise was elated as the plane crossed the North Pole. As she gazed down, a cheer went up onboard and a glass of champagne appeared in front of her to mark the occasion. Years later, she recalled the experience:

> North, north, north, we flew. Soon we left all land behind us. From the cabin window I saw great stretches of ocean flecked with patches of white floating ice. Now the ice became denser, its jagged edges surrounding open pools of seas. And as I saw the ocean change to massive fields of solid white, my heart leaped up. I knew we were approaching my goal. Then, in a moment of happiness which I shall never forget, our instruments told me we were there. For directly below us, 9,000 feet down, lay the North Pole! No cloud in the brilliant blue sky hid our view of this glorious field of shining ice.... In a moment of silence and reverent awe the crew and I gave thanks for this priceless

sight. We crossed the Pole, then circled it, flying "around the world" in a matter of minutes. Then we departed. My Arctic dream had come true.[21]

From takeoff at Bodø to the North Pole and back to Oslo took a total of 16 hours of continual flying. Upon hearing the news, the wife of her lawyer, F. Sanford Smith, exclaimed:

> The excitement in our house was terrific and when the news did come through by radio that you had actually crossed the Pole, Sanford and I were so thrilled, we danced for joy! Wish you could have seen us we were jumping up and down hugging each other, just as though we had lost our senses — We are certainly proud of you, Louise, in fact we think you are wonderful! No other woman can claim the distinction of having flown over the Pole and

Louise returning from her 1955 North Pole flight.

you are indeed a great geographer and have certainly made a name for yourself.[22]

It was the fulfillment of a lifetime's dream. She confided to friends: "For me, even with 7 expeditions to my credit to the Arctic, this was a big undertaking — it far exceeded my greatest expectations! And I expected a lot!"[23]

After arriving back in Oslo, Louise set to work informing the world of her accomplishment. She issued a press release to the major U.S. newspapers and sent off a flurry of telegrams to the Norwegian Polar Institute, the Society of Woman Geographers, and the American Embassy, as well as to her friends. Her secretary responded: "Hallelujah! Was that ever a happy moment when your voice came over the phone this afternoon! Ah ... and a relief too, for while we had the feeling of every assurance you were going to make it — still, there were anxious moments and we can now relax. We are all mighty proud of you and thrilled to the very marrow."[24]

The letters that poured in attested to her popularity and the loyalty of those who knew and loved her. She received warm congratulatory notes from Maple Lawn staff members, high-ranking officials from the American Embassy and U.S. Army, and close friends from around the world. Likely the most touching were the roses sent by former Norwegian crew member Captain Astrup Holm and a letter from Samson Vestnes, who acted as porter on her 1931 and 1933 expeditions on the *Veslekari*. She also received a telegram from Captain Herr, commander of the French polar ship the *Strasbourg* and coordinator of the 1928 Amundsen rescue attempt. It was several decades later, but this distinguished French naval officer and Louise's former *Hobby* crew members still regarded her with great respect:

It is with great emotion that Mrs Herr and I have read about your latest polar expedition in the *Figaro*. We did not read anything about your return and we wish to know if that trip ended well. We looked at the photographs from your research in 1928 and a flow of memories, situations and details came back to us. We thought about you and your friends and we have once again felt great admiration and praises for the courage and perseverance you have shown, as always.[25]

Now approaching her seventies, Louise's Arctic expeditions were behind her.

Following her momentous 1955 North Pole flight, Miss Boyd returned to her philanthropic causes in San Rafael, and to her work with geographic and scientific organizations. She had been involved with the American Polar Society for many years. Unlike the Explorers Club, which did not admit women until later in its history, the American Polar Society had always welcomed female members. Louise sat on the Board of Governors and was active in the western branch in California. In the summer of 1959, she was elected an Honorary Member, joining such luminaries as Lincoln Ellsworth, Richard Byrd, and Vilhjalmur Stefansson. To this day, she is still the only female Honorary Member in the APS. In nominating her, Treasurer William Briesemeister wrote that she was without a doubt one of the foremost explorers.

The twice-yearly Polar Society meetings were often held at Maple Lawn, where Louise's skills as a hostess were on full display. The agenda of the October 24, 1959, meeting at Maple Lawn offered members a late afternoon swim followed by cocktails and a delightful picnic supper in the luxuriant gardens. This was followed by the scientific program, during which members discussed APS member Peter Gluckman's plan to fly a single-engine airplane around the world through the polar regions. The group, including Louise, engaged in an animated discussion about weather conditions at both poles. Tragically, at the next meeting in May, it was announced that Gluckman was presumed lost at sea after he attempted to fly from Tokyo to the United States non-stop. He was never heard from again.

Louise was honoured when the western section of the American Polar Society changed its name to the Louise A. Boyd branch. And another surprise was on the way. On February 8, 1960, the *New York Times* announced "First Woman Elected to Top Geographic Post." Although Louise received no further recognition from the United States government, she was honoured by the American Geographical Society as they elected her to their council:

She is Mrs. [*sic*] Louise A. Boyd who has been named to the chief policy-making body of the American Geographical Society, the first woman to be so honored in the more than a century the society has existed.

It was a belated recognition for contributions to the knowledge of the world for which Mrs. Boyd is responsible, especially those parts of the world which have for so long been great mysteries, the polar regions.

Mrs. Boyd has led eight expeditions to the Arctic, the first in 1924. She was the first [woman] to fly over the North Pole, in 1955. She has been cited by the American Polar Society for having contributed more to the knowledge of much of the Arctic than any other explorer.

Louise looking at a map depicting her expeditions. Photograph taken at Maple Lawn, San Rafael, California, in the late 1950s.

The American Geographical Society is to be congratulated on having seen fit to include Mrs. Boyd in their
policy making. They'll be getting superb advice.[26]

David Lowenthal, secretary to the AGS during the period of Louise's
tenure, reported that council members were primarily explorers not
geographers. He considered the AGS was somewhat progressive in
appointing women as staff, but admitted that their contributions were
not always welcome. According to Lowenthal, Louise was likely elected
because AGS officials believed she would leave money to the organization after her death. Many male councillors were surprised by her

Louise's desk at Maple Lawn. Photograph taken in the late 1960s by Ansel Adams.

dedication to her position, since she flew in from the west coast to the New York office for most meetings.

Her supporters, including former president of the American Geographical Society Dr. Richard Light, applauded this:

> I am delighted that this honor should come to you, who so richly deserved it. Please accept my warmest congratulations. To you, the succession of expeditions between 1926 and 1938 must seem like a blazing polar aurora, occupying a large segment of your life. I know that to me, participation in your 1938 expedition remains still as one of the brightest points in my career. I have often tried to understand what these expeditions meant to you, and invariably I come to the same answer: your boundless enthusiasm and intense dedication to the task of revealing the face of an unknown land.[27]

In 1961, Louise was named a Woman of Distinction by the Soroptimist International Federation of the Americas (SIA) and gave a presentation on whaling treaties at the American Polar Society. However, ill health began to curtail her activities. At age seventy-five, after living very comfortably at Maple Lawn, travelling the world in high style, and enjoying her life as a generous benefactor of geographic, educational, and cultural organizations, her finances were beginning to suffer. No records regarding the Boyd Investment Company, of which she was president, have survived. She had paid scrupulous attention to detail in planning her expeditions, but she was always lavish. She did not scrimp when buying the most modern equipment for her ships, and her expedition supplies were of the highest quality. Unlike other polar explorers such as Peary, Scott, and Byrd, Louise paid for all her expeditions and for the publication of her books.[28] She neither sought nor received commercial endorsements.

Despite having a long-standing financial advisor, drastic measures were needed. By the fall of 1962, Louise was forced to put her beloved Maple Lawn up for sale. Months later, a public announcement was made that the charitable organization the Elks Club had purchased the estate. Louise would be moving to her San Francisco apartment at 210 Post Street. The market value of the over ten-acre property at that time was $230,000 USD ($195,000 for the land and $35,000 for the buildings). One condition of the sale was that the exact selling price would not be disclosed, although Elks members related that the price had been more than reasonable. By that point, Louise's funds were running dangerously low. She wrote to the Elks, "In these circumstances, I have given careful consideration to the matter of selling and have decided to offer the property to you, exclusively, in view of the fact that my residence would be preserved and the grounds and facilities be maintained and used in substantially the same manner as heretofore."[29]

Thus began what must have been an agonizing period for Louise. Her great-grandfather had built Maple Lawn and all of her family memories centred on her life there. She was faced with losing her family home, but also with disposing of most of the furniture and mementoes that had been so precious to her. Due to her stature in the community, the reverence with which she and the Boyd family were held in California, and her reputation as an explorer, the sale of this San Rafael mansion was well publicized. As a result, she was contacted by many friends and acquaintances who knew how devastating this move would be for her.

Over the coming months, Louise began to dispose of her assets. The California Academy of Sciences, of which she had been a Fellow since 1939 and an Honorary Member since 1949, received more than fifty books, and the University of California received over a thousand. The Smithsonian Institute in Washington received a substantial number of early American history artifacts. Other books were donated to the University of Alaska Fairbanks, the Louise Arner Boyd Museum of Natural Science, and the Dominican University in California.

While sorting through her belongings and the precious antiques purchased by her ancestors, Louise continued to attend social functions. Once the sale of Maple Lawn was under way, she appeared reconciled to her upcoming move. Following an appreciation dinner given by the Elks, Louise wrote to Exalted Ruler Carl Clark:

To you and your associates go my heartfelt thanks and appreciate [*sic*] for the beautiful dinner you gave in my honor on March 27, 1963. I have had dinners, yes, but to me this was an outstanding event in my life, and at my time of life I feel that for what you did for me, I can never really express my great appreciation. On the lighter side, I have never had a better time! To you and your members may I say their friendship made me feel so at home. They brought out my laughter, my sense of humor and I never had a better time at a big dinner. I enjoyed every single minute of it!! … Some were afraid I might be an old dowager, without a sense of humor. I hope I discredited that feeling! I loved the "Hello, Louise" signs; I loved every bit of it and it made me extremely happy in my thoughts of giving up Maple Lawn!![30]

Louise and Elks at Maple Lawn, San Rafael, California, in 1962.

A few years later, Louise moved to another apartment, at 1055 California Street, considered "one of the most coveted addresses for a permanent home for the city dweller." The change of address did not seem to cramp her style. In a letter to her friend and American Polar Society colleague Marjorie Fountain, Miss Boyd wrote about a recent trip to the Sonar Laboratory of fellow APS member Dr. Tom Poulter. Louise was about to embark upon a three-day motor trip to the High Sierras and hinted that a trip to Alaska was on the horizon. Shortly after her return from the mountains, Louise made plans to go north again and flew to Alaska in August 1967. Her timing could not have been worse.

In Alaska, she was looking forward to reuniting with her old friend and 1931 expedition participant Dr. Walter Wood and his wife. At that time, Wood was president of both the Explorers Club and the American Geographical Society. Louise hoped to spend time at the Institute for Marine Sciences as well as the Arctic Research Laboratory at Point Barrow. But, shortly after she arrived, it became apparent that Fairbanks was on the brink of a national disaster. Overnight, the banks of the Chena River overflowed and began flooding the city. More than seven thousand residents were forced to flee their homes. Situated on high ground, the University of Alaska served as a flood evacuation centre for townsfolk for more than two weeks. Louise's planned itinerary was drastically curtailed as staff and students alike worked to provide shelter, food, and support to the beleaguered refugees who had fled their homes. Louise reported:

> Mud, mud, mud everywhere. People lined up in double rows as much as for two hours at the Commons which was where students were fed — on one day, 11,000 meals. These consisted of cold army K rations and coffee yes when electricity permitted use of stoves. Money or no money the University saw to it they were fed. Fresh water was flown in large planes to the airfield and from there in metal containers by helicopters to university grounds. Starving hungry dogs in great numbers were vicious and attacked people.[31]

Louise was a keen observer of everything that was going on. Upon leaving, she declared that "the spirit of Fairbanks, its courage and cheer, should forever be a motto on the official seal." Although she did not stay there long, Alaska had made an indelible impression upon her heart. Two years later, she was delighted when the University of Alaska awarded her an honorary doctor of science degree. In accepting the award, she said graciously, "I share this honor with the people I worked with. I used the word *we* not *I* in accepting it. We worked as a unit."[32] During this second visit, she also participated in a three-day symposium at the Naval Arctic Research Laboratory, which included the dedication of its new Point Barrow facility.

Louise's involvement in the world at large was diminishing along with her finances. By the fall of 1969, she had moved to another, less tony residence in San Francisco, at 2275 Broadway Ave. Soon it became apparent that her financial situation was dire. At that time, several of her San Francisco friends formed a group that assumed control of her affairs. Her longtime financial advisor Sanford Smith commented privately that Louise's wants and desires had exceeded her income for years. Several immediate measures were

One of Louise's last residences, at 2275 Broadway Avenue, San Francisco. Photograph taken in 2015.

put in place, including the termination of the employment of her chauffeur and the sale of her car. Her health continued to decline, necessitating an additional move to a convalescent care facility at 1359 Pine Street. This final move resulted in the disposal of most of her treasures at public auction in San Francisco in January of 1971. She wrote to a friend: "It breaks my heart to have to give up all the beautiful antiques I had, but I could do nothing else."[33] Her good friend Marjorie Fountain visited her regularly and handled her correspondence. She had kept in contact with photographer Ansel Adams, to whom she had sold many of her cameras and who had taken photographs of Maple Lawn several years earlier. He wrote to the American Geographical Society to see if they could do anything to assist her. AGS director Burton W. Adkinson responded:

> We are acutely aware of Miss Boyd's plight and wish the Society could be of some assistance. Members of the Society's Council have investigated her situation and feel that the Society is in no position to assist her. She receives a very small royalty from publications which the Society published on Greenland, but this does not relieve her financial condition. The Society, itself, is in severe financial straits, and, therefore, cannot aid in this manner.[34]

Relatives of Louise's last housekeeper, Pauline Franzini, recalled that Pauline maintained her relationship with Louise despite no longer being in her employ. In 1970–71, Louise began declining invitations to attend public events. But her mind appeared lively and inquisitive as always, as she evinced interest in receiving current publications from the Arctic Institute of North America, the French Embassy in New York, the Alumni Association of the University of Alaska, and the National Society of Colonial Dames. Louise's stature in society remained unaltered and she was elected an Honorary Board Member of the Strybing Arboretum Society in May 1971. In May 1972, she was elected to Honorary Membership in the Society of Woman Geographers. She wrote to her friend Virginia Pope, former fashion editor of the *New York Times*, "I have not had anything as delicious as the Portuguese plums that you sent me. They are perfectly marvellous. Someone was here and opened the carton for me, so that I do not know which store they came from, but they are the best I have ever tasted. I am getting on as well as can be expected after such a serious operation and having no home or apartment of my own."[35]

Louise Arner Boyd died on September 14, 1972, two days before her eighty-fifth birthday. News of her death circulated quickly amongst her many admirers. Finn Bronner, geologist on her 1938 Expedition, wrote: "So the Chief is dead. No matter how long one knows of an impending death, the event itself brings about a jarring of the soul. Bless her memory."[36]

Her memorial service took place at St. Paul's Episcopal Church in San Rafael with pallbearers from the Louise A. Boyd Science Museum, the California Academy of Sciences, and the City of San Rafael Police Department. Many letters of condolence were exchanged between her friends. Otis Taylor wrote to Marjorie Fountain: "I feel deeply Louise's death for it has been such a privilege and joy to have known her for her character and for all she has done to make her life count. I am glad she is now at rest after two long years of inactivity which I know must have at times been a great cross for her to bear but she never complained and always when I went to see her I came away feeling the inspiration of her strong and radiant personality."[37]

Louise's obituary appeared in all major U.S. newspapers, including the *New York Times*, the *Washington Post*, and the *San Francisco Chronicle*, as well as the *Fairbanks Daily Miner* and international papers such as Norway's *Bergen Arbeiderblad* (now *Bergensavisen*). It also appeared in major geographical and polar journals, including *The Geographical Review* and *The Polar Record*, in which polar writer and curator Alan Cooke wrote: "It would be difficult to overestimate the importance of her contribution, through participation and generous financial support, to knowledge of the Arctic regions. Probably no woman since Lady Jane Franklin had done so much in this cause."[38]

It is a testament to her abiding passion for the Arctic that she chose not to be buried next to her beloved parents and brothers in the Boyd family mausoleum in Mount Tamalpais Cemetery and Mortuary in San Rafael. Instead, she had asked her friend Walter Wood to ensure she was cremated and that her ashes would be scattered in the Arctic. According to correspondence exchanged between Louise's friends Peter McBean and Marjorie Fountain, Wood agreed to fly Miss Boyd's ashes to Point Barrow in Alaska in

May 1973. Finn Bronner wrote to Lincoln Washburn: "If the Chief's wish was to have her ashes scattered in the Arctic, it seems appropriate that some effort should be made to signal the event in a manner befitting her personal involvement in Arctic exploration. It seems to me that the United States government could be induced to honor her by diverting on the International Ice Patrol ships to the East Greenland fiord region to carry her ashes to one of her favorite places."[39] No formal record exists confirming that these instructions were carried out. The final resting place of this most remarkable and courageous woman remains unknown.

THE LEGACY OF LOUISE ARNER BOYD

> She must stand as one of the great persons of this century and we
> who have shared her life's adventures should hold ourselves to be
> highly privileged.
> — FINN EYOLF BRONNER[1]

More than forty years after her death, the name "Louise Arner Boyd" still stirs memories in some corners of San Rafael and San Francisco. The oldest and most culturally diverse city in Marin County, San Rafael is as prosperous and thriving as it was in Louise's time. Today, the streetscapes of San Rafael's vibrant and historic downtown core reflect the lives and generous philanthropic contributions of the illustrious Boyd family. Saint Paul's Episcopal Church, where Louise and her parents worshipped, is still a pillar of the community. Its beautiful memorial window, paying homage to her brothers Seth and Jack who died tragically young, still has the power to inspire regular churchgoers and visitors alike. The San Rafael Public Library, to which her parents, Louise Arner Boyd and John Franklin Boyd, were early subscribers, is a bustling hub of activity. The Boyd Gate House to the original Cook/Boyd estate housed the Marin

History Museum until recently. This museum, which contains one of the largest collections of artifacts belonging to Louise Arner Boyd, is currently closed. It is hoped that sufficient funding will be found to restart this museum and to conserve and revitalize the historic Gate House. Donated by Louise's parents in 1907 in memory of their dead sons and located next to the Gate House, Boyd Memorial Park continues to provide a soothing natural greenspace, children's recreational area, and haven for the neighbourhood. Most significantly, Maple Lawn, the magnificent home and sprawling estate that was Louise's birthplace, remains a dominant feature at Mission and C Streets in San Rafael.

Beloved by Louise, Maple Lawn has been owned by the San Rafael Elks #1108 since the early 1960s. Operating as the Elks' meeting place, clubhouse, and main office, Maple Lawn's grandeur has diminished over time and later renovations have blighted its splendour. Louise's award-winning camellias, lovingly nurtured in a cutting garden to the rear of the property, have been uprooted to make room for parking, the extensive, lavish grounds have been neglected, and many of the exotic trees Louise imported have been cut down or are diseased. Yet remnants of Louise's

Maple Lawn today. Photograph taken in 2014.

The Magnolia Terrace, Maple Lawn, designed by Louise and still in existence today. Photograph taken in 2015.

privileged life in Maple Lawn are everywhere for those who know where to look — the original sweeping staircase in the main hall; the treasured family portraits of Louise's great-grandparents hanging in the upstairs boardroom; the outdoor pool, sunny magnolia terrace, statuary, and sauna she installed in the 1950s to delight her guests; the abandoned servant quarters on the upper floor; the enormous safe in the basement; the panelled billiards room; and the imposing brass door knocker.

Longtime Elks believe that Louise never really left Maple Lawn. Several individuals who have stayed there late at night are startled by glimpses of the shadowy outline of a tall woman descending the once-majestic staircase.

Halfway across the world in small coastal towns in northern Norway, Louise Arner Boyd and her daring exploits are still remembered amongst its older citizenry. This is evident in fishing towns such as Tromsø, Ålesund, and Vartdal on the northwestern coast from which Louise embarked on her polar adventures. This region has strong ties to its proud maritime

The Louise Arner Boyd museum, in private hands in Vartdal, Norway.

history. Louise's unique status as a female polar explorer who earned the regard of notable Norwegian captains such as Johan Olsen, Paul Lillenes, Kristian Johannesen, Astrup Holm, and Peder Eliassen remains intact. Although their numbers are dwindling, there are still older Norwegians who recall the striking, confident American woman who handed out candies and ice cream to children at the dock prior to her departure on Arctic expeditions. The name "Louise Arner Boyd" is inextricably linked to the historic Norwegian polar vessels *Hobby* and *Veslekari*. These two ships, neither of which survive today, command great respect in northern Norway, where their position in Norwegian polar history is unrivalled. Indeed, many north Norwegians here evince a powerful attachment to *Hobby*, *Veslekari*, and other renowned polar vessels and all who sailed on them. Louise's history is, in part, the history of these two ships and the courageous Norwegians who sailed with her.

Sculpture of Louise Arner Boyd (and the subject herself) located in the Marin History Museum collection currently in Novato, California. A similar bust is held by the Universitetet i Bergen Bibliotek, Bergen, Norway.

Walking the streets of Ålesund does not immediately bring to mind the life and contributions of Louise Arner Boyd. She is not indelibly imprinted on this town as she is in her hometown of San Rafael. Overlooking the harbour, the Hotel Scandic, where Louise regularly stayed, is still one of the finest in town and is just a short walk from all the best restaurants. The pier from which the *Veslekari* departed is now used for cruise ships, which dwarf the town when in port. One local resident has worked for decades to keep Louise's memory alive. Educator and historian Brit Aanning Aarseth is married to the great-nephew of shipping magnate Elling Aarseth, who supplied ships to Louise during the 1930s. She developed a strong interest in Louise Arner Boyd and established a small museum in her memory in the village of Vartdal, where Elling Aarseth's shipyard was located. During a research trip following in Louise's footsteps, I was privileged to visit this privately run museum. The museum is housed in the original Aarseth shipping office, where the crew of the *Veslekari* received their hard-earned wages. Entering through the front door used by Louise herself, I walked past the peeling poster of Roald Amundsen that Louise gazed at whenever she visited the office and viewed treasures that pay homage to the adventurous American woman whose fate was bound to the North. Logbooks, *Veslekari*'s flag and buoy, and correspondence relating to the shipping company are all carefully preserved for perpetuity.

While bookshelves heave with biographies of her peers Roald Amundsen, Sir Hubert Wilkins, Vilhjalmur Stefansson, and Richard E. Byrd, no authoritative biography of Louise Arner Boyd has ever been published. There is no plaque or public statue in California, in Norway, or in Greenland recognizing the life and accomplishments of this extraordinary woman. Unusually, Belarus is the only country with plans to erect a public monument to Louise Arner Boyd. In 2015, the Pinsk District of Belarus's Brest Oblast initiated a tourism project commemorating Louise's 1934 road trip across what was then Poland. Certain areas of her trip now fall in Belarus and the Ukraine. The government project includes a monument and documentary about Louise and the creation of car and bicycle routes recreating Louise's journey.

A portrait of Louise. Unknown location and date.

And what is Louise Arner Boyd's lasting legacy? She was born into privileged high society in which rigid expectations of how a woman should live and behave existed. Her life was spent negotiating a tightrope — ensuring that she fulfilled her civic duties as a philanthropist and society doyenne, while at the same time pursuing her lifelong passion for the Arctic. She struggled to earn the respect and approbation of her peers and to overcome her own fears and shortcomings:

> The greatest handicap I have had in obtaining my present position is, first, my sex — being a woman. When I first went to the Arctic, people definitely seemed to feel, and openly told me so, the Arctic was a place only for men — that for me to go where I did was an eccentricity and hobby and not to be taken seriously. Secondly ... my not being a university woman and not having such a degree very definitely caused many people to look upon me as a person not having the proper education and training to make me worthy to be included in the rostrum of the scientific world. In many cases, it has happened that I have had far more actual experience and field work than those so-rated scientists whose knowledge was limited only to books and who did not have practical application of it.... I consider that hard work, determination to succeed and persistence have done more than anything else to bring me to the position I have achieved. A strong characteristic of mine is power of concentration and I also have the tendency to stick to things, and accomplish them. These traits eventually overcame my handicaps.[2]

Miss Boyd's voyages to Greenland were conducted during a transitional period in polar exploration between "the Golden Age," in which conquering the poles was accomplished by overland routes and by sea, and the modern technological era heralded by early polar flights by Amundsen, Ellsworth, and Byrd. Gillis wrote that Louise Arner Boyd "represented one of the last revivals of a Victorian phenomenon — the wealthy explorer who poured a personal fortune into expeditions aimed at advancing science and satisfying profound personal curiosity."[3] In rejecting a sedate and sheltered life as a wealthy wife and mother, she defied societal expectations. But she also challenged the ideal of a polar explorer as defined by manliness, stoicism, and heroism. Her seven daring expeditions to northern Norway and Greenland between 1926 and 1955 paved the way for later female polar explorers, including Americans Ann Bancroft and Helen Thayer, Norwegians Liv Arnesen and Cecilie Skog, and Englishwomen Ann Daniels, Caroline Hamilton, Felicity Aston, and Rosie Stancer. Meticulously planned by Louise, each hazardous voyage accomplished specific scientific objectives and was completed in a timely manner without loss of life. Her participation in the 1928 international mission to rescue Roald Amundsen, her geographic discoveries, and her military intelligence work for the American government during the Second World War won her awards and highlighted her commitment to representing her country honourably. Noted periglacial geologist and 1937 expedition member Dr. Lincoln Washburn stated:

> I grew to appreciate and respect Miss Boyd for her devotion to promoting scientific research. Much of her earlier career was devoted to fun trips with friends where scientific research was not part of the program as was the case subsequently. The participants of the 1933 expedition and their work became well known to me, and I have a high regard for their accomplishments. Without Miss Boyd's sponsorship and that of the American Geographical Society none of the 1933 research would have been undertaken and she deserves great credit for making it possible. I had not met her before the 1937 expedition but I grew to admire her for the vigor with which she promoted the work and did her share in walking over the countryside and contributing so much to the photographic record.... It is truly remarkable that a woman of Louise Boyd's background and times was able to organize and contribute to polar research under sometimes quite adverse environmental conditions.... The

many awards received by Miss Boyd from a number of governments clearly show the esteem in which her contributions to research were held.[4]

Louise's main contributions focus on her pioneering exploration of the coastal regions of Greenland. Significant results include her discovery of the area that became known as Louise Boyd Land (73°31'00" N, 28°00'00" W), and the topographical features Louise Gletscher (73°53.3'N, 27°43.0' W), Boyd Bastion (73°26.1' N, 28°34.9' W), and Boyd Seamount (72°41'00" N, 2°55'00" E), which still bear her name. Perhaps her most important contribution, and the one of which she herself was proudest, was her photography. She believed that her photographs of the coastlines and topographical features of Greenland were of significance, and her opinion was corroborated by the U.S. government during the Second World War. She would be delighted to know that contemporary scientists are using those of her Greenland photographs that have not been lost over time to learn more about the state of the environment today. Nobel Prize–winning American geographer Frederick Nelson commented: "Numbering in the thousands, Boyd's Arctic photographs have rich but untapped potential for documenting environmental change in a dynamic cryospheric environment."[5] Danish glaciologist Anders Anker Bjørk concurs, stating: "Louise Boyd's images ... offer a unique opportunity to track glacier change back in time, and this is of particular interest in modern times, as we are in urgent need of figuring out how large glacier changes have been in the past in order to better understand the changes that are happening right now."[6]

A collection of Louise's still photographs and films of North East Greenland and Poland is today housed in the National Archives in Washington, D.C., and in the American Geographical Society Library at the University of Wisconsin–Milwaukee. As noted throughout early volumes of the *Polar Record*, all her original negatives, films, logbooks, and diaries were donated to the American Geographical Society upon the completion of each expedition. Over time, most of the thousands of photographs and negatives she herself owned and loaned to the United States government, as well as original logbooks and diaries, have become unaccounted for. It is hoped that increased interest in Louise and her work will assist in uncovering these precious photographs and documents.

Through her expeditionary work, Louise generously and with intent provided unique opportunities to young, early-career scientists who made significant discoveries in their respective fields of study and who used the results of their fieldwork in Norway and Greenland to advance their careers. Richard Foster Flint, Lincoln Washburn, Noel Odell, J. Harlen Bretz, and Henry Oosting are all illustrious names in the scientific community. The research conducted during the Louise A. Boyd expeditions continues to be cited in academic journals in the fields of glaciology (Swithinbank, 1950; Wilson, 1953; Kinsman and Sheard, 1963; Lasca, 1966; Funder and Petersen, 1980; Anda, Orheim, et al., 1985; Hulbe, Wang, et al., 2010; Bjørk, Kjær, et al., 2012; Bjørk, Aagaard, et al., 2014), geology and geomorphology (Weidick, 1995; Bennicke, 1998; Higgins, Gilotti, et al., 2008), oceanography (Johnson and Eckhoff, 1966; Gulliksen, 1974) and botany/ecology (Lid, 1964; Bliss, Heal, et al., 1981; Barbour and Billings, 2000; Büntgen, Hellmann, et al., 2015).

Socialite. Philanthropist. Geographer. Photographer. Scientist. Explorer. During her lifetime, Louise Arner Boyd (1887–1972) was all of these. Ultimately, she should be remembered as an American original, an intrepid and adventurous woman who overcame the social constraints imposed on women of her class and her time and who defied what it meant to be a polar explorer. Spellbound by the North, Louise fearlessly pursued a relentless desire to penetrate deep into the circumpolar world and learn its secrets. Her seven expeditions and the scientific data that was generated as a result should ensure that the stature of Louise Arner Boyd is elevated to that of other outstanding explorers of the twentieth century.

Louise strolling at Drake's Bay in northern California. Unknown date.

Acknowledgements

Over the ten years it has taken this book to come to fruition, I have had the kind assistance of many individuals across the globe who have supported my quest. Two people were critical during the early stages of this project. Magnus Sefland of Gjøvik, Norway, spent many hours selflessly researching Miss Boyd's activities in northern Norway and provided me with details about those great Norwegian mariners whose heroic deeds on the sea went largely unnoticed. I would also like to thank educator, artist, actress, and producer Kate Campbell Stevenson of Maryland, U.S.A., who shares my commitment to telling the story of great women and who enthusiastically encouraged me from the very beginning. This story of Miss Boyd would not have been told without their interest, support, and encouragement.

The following people also went above and beyond in helping me understand Miss Boyd and her world. Their contributions, in the form of granting interviews, access to private family papers, or assistance to a keen researcher were greatly appreciated. Sincere thanks to Brit Aanning Aarseth and Aage Aarseth; Adolphus and Mrs. Andrews; Morton Beebe; Kjersti Bratseth; Janice Braun, Mills College; Eric Bronner; John Bronner; Carl Clark; the late Princess Genie di San Faustino; the late Marjorie Fountain; Jane Gilotti; Deborah Franzini; Gladys and Henry Franzini;

Daniel Hope, Bowdoin College Library; Laura Kissel, University Archives, Ohio State University; Will C. Knutsen; Bonnie Laforge, The Thacher School; Keith Martin, National Institute of Standards and Technology; Robert Menzies; the late Evelyn Stefansson Nef; Kay Noguchi, formerly of the San Rafael Public Library; Cynthia D. Redman; Iain Brownlie Roy; Don and Sharon Sanborn; Jolyon Schilling; Ana Stark, St. Paul's Episcopal Church, San Rafael; the late Archer S. Taylor; Sally Miller Wages and Dan Wages; Steve Woodhams and members of the Coleman family; Valerie Zamora.

I would also like to acknowledge with gratitude the contributions of the following individuals or organizations: Audrey Amidon, National Archives; Charlotte Clark Anderson; Ansel Adams Trust; Seth Adams, Save Mount Diablo; Caroline Atuk-Derrick, University of Alaska Fairbanks Library; Ann Kristin Balto, Norsk Polarinstitutt; Gina Bardi, San Francisco Maritime Heritage Museum; Lisa Benson, Norwegian Maritime Museum; Stephen R. Bown; Paul Brawley, formerly of the schooner *Ernestina*; Mary Brattesani; Yolanda Bustos and the staff of the California Academy of Sciences; California Historical Society; Nora Chidlow, U.S. Coast Guard Archives; Jane Clifton; Contra Costa County Historical Society; Richard Corville; Lisa DeCesare, Harvard Herbaria Botany Library; Andree Doiron for assistance with translation; Judith K. Farrar, Claire T. Carney University Library, University of Massachusetts Dartmouth; Margaret "Mugs" Freeman; Mark Gilbert, Scott Polar Research Institute; Terry Glenn; Fred Goldberg; Elena Govor; David Gracely; Anne Blix Gulstad, Norsk Luftfartsmuseum; Christopher Harney; Elisabeth Hartjens; Sarah Hartwell, Dartmouth College; Gerald Holdsworth, University of Calgary; Richard Hoye, Ojai Valley Museum; the late Augusta M. Hyde; Bob Jaeger; Loma Karklins, California Institute of Technology; Pamela Klein, San Rafael Public Library; Kjell-G. Kjær; Adam Kronegh, Danish State Archives; Beverly Lane, Museum of the San Ramon Valley; Peter Lewis, American Geographical Society; Library of Congress; Library and Archives Canada; Morton Lillenes; Marianne Lindvall for assistance with translation; Ingunn Løyning, Spitsbergen Airship Museum; the Marin History Museum; David Mackesey; Annie McDowell, formerly of the schooner *Ernestina*; Ken McGoogan; Memorial

University, Centre for Newfoundland Studies; Peter Schmidt Mikkelsen; David Miller, Smithsonian Institute; Marcie Miller; Eugene Morris, National Archives and Records Administration (College Park); Jocelyn Moss, Marin History Museum; Suzanne Nussey; Peter Odell; Knud Dankert Olsen; Lillian Percey; Susan M. Peschel, American Geographical Society Library, University of Wisconsin–Milwaukee; Michael Peterson, San Francisco Theological Seminary Library; Beryl Price; Provincial Archives, Newfoundland; Bert Riggs, Queen Elizabeth Library, Memorial University of Newfoundland; Jovanka Ristic, American Geographical Society Library, University of Wisconsin–Milwaukee Libraries; Amy Rule, formerly of The Centre for Creative Photography, University of Arizona; Becky Sedrel; Frode Skarstein; Tore Sorenson; Harold Gushue Sparkes; Statsarkivet i Tromsø; Laurie Thompson, Anne T. Kent California Room, Marin County Free Library; Torbjørn Trulssen, Polarmuseet i Tromsø; University of Calgary Press; University of California, Berkeley Library; University of Chicago Special Collections; Reina Williams, University of Chicago Library; the late Ivar Ytreland. I'd like to express my appreciation as well to to Elizabeth Bradfield and Persea Books for permission to quote from her fine collection *Approaching Ice: Poems*. Finally, thanks to the dedicated staff at Dundurn Press who did such a great job on this book.

For his expert mapmaking, computer skills, and technical support, but, more importantly, his patience, good humour, and willingness to share me with Miss Boyd for this past decade, I thank my partner in life, Duncan Payne. For their forbearance and courtesy in listening to Miss Boyd's story over and over again, I thank our children, Hannele Kafarowski-Payne and Eli Kafarowski-Payne. I extend my heartfelt thanks to all who helped me along this marvellous journey but whose names have not been recorded here.

Appendix

List of participants in Louise Arner Boyd Expeditions (1926–1941)[*]

NORWAY

Aarseth, Leif
Akselvold, Einar
Anstad, Ivar
Aune, Odd
Backman, Mr.
Bastøe, Jarl
Bjørge, Arthur
Bjørge, Olger
Bjørn, Hilda
Blindheim, Ivar
Botnen, F.

Cornelieusen, Karl
Eliassen, Peder
Ellingsen, Mr.
Frederiksen, Ingemand
Gambst, Alfred
Garshol, Ingard
Gjærde, Agnar
Gjærde, Knut
Hansen, Ingolf
Hoel, Holger
Holm, Astrup
Holm, Øvind

---

* The author apologizes for any names that have been inadvertently omitted or misspelled.

Bratseth, Erik

Høyberg, Sigvald

Ingebriktsen, Lars

Jensen, Arthur

Jensen, Ingvald

Jensen, Kirsten

Jensen, Leif

Johannesen, Captain Kristian

Johansen, Olaf

Jonsen, Mr.

Krogseth, Ragni

Lambrechts, Finn

Lillenes, Captain Paul

Lützow-Holm, Finn

Myhre, Svein

Olsen, Einar

Olsen, Captain Johan P.K.

Olsen, Johan E.

Olsen, Jonas

Olsen, Lars

Opsahl, Hans

Pederson, Pedar

Remoy, Sverre S.

Riiser-Larsen, Hjalmur

Röiset, Knut

Rövik, Olger

Rudi, Asbjørn

Rudi, Norman

Skjeldrup, Ingvald

Solbjørg, Oistein

Sørensen, Johan

Sørensen, Sverre

Stølen, Peder

Strand, Anders

Strand, K.

Strand, Peder

Synstenes, Torvald

Torgersen, Trygve

Ulveseter, Erling

Vestnes, Samson

Vik, Samson

Wiik, Ove

Wiik, Samson

Ystehede, Bjarne

NEWFOUNDLAND

Bartlett, George

Bartlett, Captain Robert "Bob"

Bartlett, Samuel

Bartlett, William

Batten, Charles

Dooling, Jim

Gushue, Bart

Gushue, Leonard

Pritchard, Bill

Wilcox, Reg

UNITED STATES

Bretz, J. Harlen

Bronner, Finn E.

Buhler, F.W.

Calhoun, John Harrison

Calhoun, Julia

Carroll, Tom

Stadsnes, Magnus
Coleman, Janet D.
Drew, William B.
Flint, Richard Foster
Gracely, Frederick R.
Hilferty, Anthony F.
Leroy, James M.
Menzies, Robert H.
Menzies, Winnifred
Miller, O. Maitland
Oosting, Henry J.
Roche, Rose
Schilling, John A.
Taylor, Archer S.
Washburn, A. Lincoln

Whitney, Harry C.
Wood, Walter A.

ENGLAND

de Gisbert, Francis J.
Odell, Gwladys "Mona"
Odell, Noel E.

SPAIN

Ribadavia, Count Ignacio
Ribadavia, Countess Blanca

SWEDEN

Anrick, Carl-Julius
Anrick, Calla

Notes

PROLOGUE

1. "No News About Amundsen," accessed August 21, 2012, www.hidden europe.co.uk/no-news-about-amundsen.

CHAPTER ONE: AN ADVENTURESS IS BORN

1. Arnold Blackmur, *Old Diablo: A Social History* (Redwood City: Ampex, 1981), 6. See also "Horses of California" by Joseph Cairn Simpson, *Sunset Magazine* 9 (1902), who extolled the virtues of the Oakwood Park Farm: "The best appointed of all the horse-breeding farms in California and so far as I have knowledge not a single establishment in the United States on which so much money has been expended for improvements — that is my judgement of Oakwood Farm," p. 29.
2. Judy and Rick Hornor, *The Golden Quest and Nevada's Silver Heritage* (Pilot Hill: Nineteenth Century Books, 2006), 69.
3. O.S. Fowler, *Phrenological Character Report of John Franklin Boyd* (Boston: O.S. Fowler, 1871), 1. It is likely that the personal details in this report were either accurate or consistent with John F. Boyd's self-assessment since the report was preserved by John Boyd himself and, upon his death, by Louise Arner Boyd.

4. "Yachts and Lots," unknown newspaper, n.d.

5. *Bodie Standard*, November 7, 1877.

6. "Boyd-Arner," *San Francisco Examiner*, April 29, 1883.

7. *Rochester Daily Union Advertiser*, June 30, 1876, 7. Theodocia Arner was the editor of *The Journal of the Home*, which was the monthly publication of the Rochester Association for the Relief of Homeless and Friendless Females. Advocating on behalf of the Home's clients, this journal was edited by Theodocia Arner until her departure to California in 1872.

8. *Hospital Review*, August 15, 1876, 3.

9. *Marin Journal*, unknown month and day, 1879.

10. *San Francisco Chronicle* (Sunday edition), n.d.

11. "Sad Accidental Death," *Marin Journal*, August 15, 1901, 6.

12. Letter from Mrs. Louise Arner Boyd to Sherman Thacher, February 9, 1902, The Thacher School Archives. Under Sherman Thacher's tutelage, the school program emphasized the link between a sound mind and a sound body. As quoted by Makepeace (p. 75), an 1891 advertisement for the school stated: "The aims of the place are in three directions: toward health and enjoyment, toward unselfish, manly character, and toward accurate, thorough, and self-reliant habits of thought and study; an object constantly in view is to help a boy towards the simplest way of living a happy, useful life — with other people."

13. Letter from Sherman Thacher to Mrs. Louise Arner Boyd, March 27, 1902, The Thacher School Archives. Mrs. Boyd is referring to Jack Franklin Boyd's 1902 application to The Thacher School. A reference letter sent by an unstated family friend to Sherman Thacher attested to Jack Boyd's upright and conscientious nature. Jack must have been an exceedingly truthful boy, since this is emphasized in the reference letter and application.

14. LeRoy McKim Makepeace, *Sherman Thacher and His School* (New Haven: Yale University Press, 1941), 113.

15. Letter from Mrs. Louise Arner Boyd to Sherman Thacher, May 9, 1902, The Thacher School Archives.

16. "Boyd Memorial Park Dedicated with Appropriate Ceremonies," *Daily Independent*, May 2, 1905. See also "John F. Boyd Gives Park to San Rafael," *San Francisco Chronicle*, December 7, 1904. The donation of

land was estimated at $25,000 USD. The only stipulation of the gift was that the Town Trustees employed a man to keep the Park in good condition. *Sherman Thacher and His School,* by Makepeace (p. 113), suggests that Mr. and Mrs. Boyd wanted to establish a memorial to Jack Boyd at The Thacher School but Sherman Thacher asserted that "our boys had too much already." It was Thacher's idea that a clubhouse in Jack's memory be presented to the Ojai community. As outlined in "Boyd Center Marks Centennial," the Jack Boyd Memorial Clubhouse served as a local hospital during the flu epidemic of 1918, a flood disaster centre in 1938 and a USO centre during the early years of the Second World War. In 1957, the clubhouse was moved to another location and is now part of the Ojai Parks and Recreation Department.

17. "The Ruins as Seen by Ed Soules," *Marin Journal,* April 24, 1906, 1. See also "Among the Homeless from San Francisco," *New York Times,* May 2, 1906. According to this article, at least a hundred San Francisco residents travelled back with the Boyds on the *Konprinz Wilhelm.* A day after arriving in San Francisco, these residents estimated their losses due to the disaster at $7,000,000 USD.

CHAPTER TWO: SHAPED BY ADVERSITY

1. "Sloop Gjøa Which Made NW Passage Here," *San Francisco Chronicle,* October 20, 1906, 9.

2. "Present Their Daughter to Marin County Society," *San Francisco Call,* August 19, 1906.

3. "Death Calls for Mrs. John F. Boyd," *Marin Journal,* October 2, 1919. According to one obituary of Mrs. Louise Arner Boyd, "… the mother never fully recovered from the shock of their [sons'] death." See also "Wife of Pioneer Broker Dies Here," *San Francisco Examiner,* October 5, 1919. According to Mrs. Louise Arner Boyd's San Francisco death certificate, the official cause of death was "encephalomalacia with contributing causes being myxedema and anemia secondary."

4. "Respected Citizen Called to Death," *Marin Journal,* May 6, 1920. See also "Aged Millionaire Near Death in Fall," *San Francisco Examiner,*

April 29, 1920. According to his San Francisco death certificate, the official cause of death was "diabetes with contributing factors being fracture of the left femur and bronchitis."

5. Untitled, undated document by Louise Arner Boyd, 1, Marin History Museum.

6. Ibid., 2.

7. Ibid., 3.

8. Clive Holland, *Farthest North: Endurance and Adventure in the Quest for the North Pole* (London: Robinson, 1999), 223.

9. Roald Amundsen, *My Life as an Explorer* (Cambridge: Cambridge University Press, 2014), 242.

10. "Presentation at Court," *San Francisco Newsletter*, July 4, 1925.

CHAPTER THREE: "DIANA OF THE ARCTIC"

1. Elizabeth Bradfield, *Approaching Ice: Poems* (New York: Persea Books, 2010), 73.

2. Robert Peary, quoted in Michael F. Robinson, *The Coldest Crucible: Arctic Exploration and American Culture* (Chicago: University of Chicago Press, 1966), 1.

3. Untitled, undated document by Louise Arner Boyd, 4, Marin History Museum.

4. Partial contract between Mr. Francis J. Gisbert and Louise Arner Boyd, Louise Arner Boyd Archive, San Rafael Public Library.

5. Ibid.

6. Letter from Frederick P. Hibbard to Louise Arner Boyd, September 28, 1926, Marin History Museum.

7. Count Ribadavia, *Chasses et Aventures dans les Regions Polaires* (Paris: Maisonneuve, 1927), 4.

8. Untitled, undated document by Louise Arner Boyd, RO-12, Marin History Museum.

9. Ibid., RO-13.

10. Ibid., RO-21.

11. Count Ribadavia, *Chasses et Aventures dans les Regions Polaires* (Paris: Maisonneuve, 1927), 33.

12. Untitled, undated document by Louise Arner Boyd, RO-18, Marin History Museum.

13. Louise Arner Boyd, "Sheets? No, Table Cloths!," n.d. Unpublished story, Marin History Museum.

14. Count Ribadavia, *Chasses et Aventures dans les Regions Polaires* (Paris: Maisonneuve, 1927), 29.

15. Louise Arner Boyd, "Naming the Polar Bear Cubs," n.d. Unpublished story, Marin History Museum.

16. Louise Arner Boyd, "Sticks of Candy? No, It's Dynamite," n.d. Unpublished story, Marin History Museum.

17. Julius Payer and Karl Weyprecht, *New Lands Within the Arctic Circle* (New York: D. Appleton, 1877), 175.

18. Janet Coleman, unpublished diary of 1926 trip, Coleman family papers.

19. Untitled, undated document by Louise Arner Boyd, RO-46, Marin History Museum.

20. Count Ribadavia, *Chasses et Aventures dans les Regions Polaires* (Paris: Maisonneuve, 1927), 50.

21. Letter from Mr. Francis J. de Gisbert to Louise Arner Boyd, May 19, 1927, Marin History Museum.

22. Janet Coleman, unpublished diary of 1926 trip, Coleman Family Papers.

23. Count Ribadavia, *Chasses et Aventures dans les Regions Polaires* (Paris: Maisonneuve, 1927), 62.

24. Ibid., 75.

25. "2 Bay Girls Safe After Polar Hunt," *Oakland Tribune,* September 25, 1926. At the time of her return, this "girl" was 39 years old. See also "American Girl Shot 11 Bears in Arctic," *New York Times*, September 26, 1926, and "American Girl Returns From Frozen North With Trophies," *Hamilton Journal* 40 (236), 1926.

CHAPTER FOUR: CHASING AMUNDSEN

1. Letter from Astrup Holm to Louise Arner Boyd, December 19, 1927, Marin History Museum.

2. Letter from Louise Arner Boyd to unknown recipient, July 31, 1928, Marin History Museum.

3. Letter from Rolf Tandberg to Mrs. G. Skjerda, September 6, 1966, Marin History Museum.
4. "Miss Boyd at Spitsbergen," *New York Times,* July 9, 1928.
5. Untitled document by Louise Arner Boyd, 1928, 5, Marin History Museum.
6. Ibid., 6.
7. Untitled, undated document by Louise Arner Boyd, Marin History Museum.
8. Untitled document by Louise Arner Boyd, 1928, 7, Marin History Museum.
9. Ibid.
10. Louise Arner Boyd, "The Yollying Swedes," n.d., Louise Arner Boyd Archive, San Rafael Public Library.
11. Notes to film reels for the 1928 Expedition, Louise Arner Boyd Archive, San Rafael Public Library.
12. Hjalmar Riiser-Larsen, *Femti Är For Kongen* (Oslo: Gylendal Norsk Forlag, 1957),161.
13. Untitled, undated document by Louise Arner Boyd, RO-1, Marin History Museum.
14. Letter from Louise Arner Boyd to unknown recipient, August 5, 1928, Marin History Museum.
15. Hjalmar Riiser-Larsen, *Femti Är For Kongen* (Oslo: Gylendal Norsk Forlag, 1957), 158.
16. Letter from Louise Arner Boyd to an unknown recipient, July 12, 1928, Marin History Museum.
17. Lincoln Ellsworth, "Air Pioneering in the Arctic," *Boys Life,* September, 1928, 64.
18. Letter from Louise Arner Boyd to unknown recipient, August 5, 1928, Marin History Museum.
19. Untitled, undated document by Louise Arner Boyd, Marin History Museum.
20. Unpublished notes to film reels for the 1928 Expedition, Louise Arner Boyd Archive, San Rafael Public Library.
21. Hjalmar Riiser-Larsen, *Femti Är For Kongen* (Oslo: Gylendal Norsk Forlag, 1957), 156.
22. Ibid., 159.

23. Letter from Rolf Tandberg to Mrs. G. Skjerda, September 6, 1966, Marin History Museum.

24. Hjalmar Riiser-Larsen, *Femti År For Kongen* (Oslo: Gylendal Norsk Forlag, 1957), 160.

25. Letter from Louise Arner Boyd to unknown recipient, n.d., Marin History Museum.

26. Hjalmar Riiser-Larsen, *Femti År For Kongen* (Oslo: Gylendal Norsk Forlag, 1957), 161.

27. Letter from Admiral Herr to Louise Arner Boyd, September 15, 1928, Louise Arner Boyd Archive, San Rafael Public Library.

CHAPTER FIVE: THE ICE QUEEN COMETH

1. "To the Royal Geographical Society," *Punch, or The London Charivari*, June 10, 1893, 269.

2. Letter from Frank J. Rogers to Louise Arner Boyd, May 12, 1931, Marin History Museum.

3. Letter from W.R. Bruce to Louise Arner Boyd, April 22, 1931, Marin History Museum.

4. Letter from Isaiah Bowman to Louise Arner Boyd, March 25, 1931, Archives of the American Geographical Society, University of Wisconsin–Milwaukee.

5. Letter from Louise Arner Boyd to Astrup Holm, January 1, 1930, Marin History Museum.

6. Sverker Sörlin, "The Burial of an Era: The Home-Coming of Andrée as a National Event," in *The Centennial of S.A. Andrée's Polar Expedition,* edited by Urbank Wrakberg (Stockholm: Royal Swedish Academy of Science, 1999), 100.

7. More recent scholarship by James Loeffler in the September 2013 issue of the *Journal of American History* reveals a darker side to Isaiah Bowman. Loeffler asserts that Bowman held deep-seated anti-Semitic views, and as chancellor of Johns Hopkins University supported a quota on Jewish faculty and students. He also opposed both admitting Jewish refugees to the United States and the creation of the state of Israel.

8. Letter from Louise Arner Boyd to Isaiah Bowman, February 6,

1931, Archives of the American Geographical Society, University of Wisconsin–Milwaukee.

9. Letter from Isaiah Bowman to Louise Arner Boyd, February 23, 1931, Archives of the American Geographical Society, University of Wisconsin–Milwaukee.

10. Letter from Isaiah Bowman to Louise Arner Boyd, February 24, 1931, Archives of the American Geographical Society, University of Wisconsin–Milwaukee.

11. Ibid.

12. Letter from Louise Arner Boyd to Isaiah Bowman, February 28, 1931, Archives of the American Geographical Society, University of Wisconsin–Milwaukee.

13. Winnifred Menzies, unpublished 1931 manuscript, Menzies family collection.

14. C.J. Anrick, "A Summer Voyage to East Greenland," lecture given at Swedish Association for Anthropology and Geography on January 22, 1932.

15. Untitled article, *Aftenpost*, June 27, 1931.

16. Erik Bratseth, unpublished 1931 diary, Bratseth family collection.

17. Ibid.

18. C.J. Anrick, "A Summer Voyage to East Greenland," lecture given at Swedish Association for Anthropology and Geography on January 22, 1932.

19. Erik Bratseth, unpublished 1931 diary, Bratseth family collection.

20. Louise Arner Boyd, "The Louise A. Boyd Seven Arctic Expeditions." *Photogrammetric Engineering and Remote Sensing* (December 1950): 652.

21. C.J. Anrick, "A Summer Voyage to East Greenland." lecture given at Swedish Association for Anthropology and Geography on January 22, 1932.

22. Winnifred Menzies, unpublished 1931 manuscript, Menzies family collection.

23. "Halvard Devold forteller om okkupasjonen," *Sunnmørsposten*, July 22, 1931.

24. Erik Bratseth, unpublished 1931 diary, Bratseth family collection.

25. Hallvard Devold, *Polar Liv* (Oslo: Gylendal Norsk Forlag, 1940), 137.

26. Erik Bratseth, unpublished 1931 diary, Bratseth family collection.

27. John Giæver, quoted in "Norway and Past International Polar Years — An Historical Account," *Polar Research* 26 (2007): 200.

28. John Giæver, *In the Land of the Musk-Ox* (London: Jarrold Publishers, 1958), 184.

29. C.J. Anrick, "A Summer Voyage to East Greenland," lecture given at Swedish Association for Anthropology and Geography on January 22, 1932.

30. Louise Arner Boyd, "The Louise A. Boyd Seven Arctic Expeditions," *Photogrammetric Engineering and Remote Sensing* (December 1950): 652.

31. C.J. Anrick, "A Summer Voyage to East Greenland," lecture given at Swedish Association for Anthropology and Geography on January 22, 1932.

32. Ibid.

33. Winnifred Menzies, "Unknown Ice-bound Tracts of Greenland Coasts Yield Secrets to Women Pioneers," *Christian Science Monitor*, August 22, 1932, 5.

34. Winnifred Menzies, "Short Days, Long Winters No Bar to Contentment for Lonely Greenland Villagers," *Christian Science Monitor*, August 23, 1932, 5.

35. Ibid., 1.

36. Rufus Steele, "The March of the Nations," *Christian Science Monitor*, August 22, 1932.

CHAPTER SIX: GREENLAND BECKONS

1. Letter from Louise Arner Boyd to Isaiah Bowman, March 25, 1932, Marin History Museum.

2. Letter from Vilhjalmur Stefansson to Louise Arner Boyd, June 3, 1932, Stefansson Archives, Dartmouth College.

3. Louise Arner Boyd, *The Fiord Region of East Greenland* (New York: American Geographical Society, 1935), 4.

4. Ibid.

5. Letter from Harlen Bretz to Isaiah Bowman, December 21, 1932, J. Harlen Bretz Archive, University of Chicago.

6. Letter from Louise Arner Boyd to Lauge Koch, November 29, 1932, Marin History Museum.

7. E.O. Shebbeare, quoted in Wade Davis, *Into the Silence: The Great War, Mallory, and the Conquest of Everest* (New York: Alfred A. Knopf, 2011).

8. Letter from Louise Arner Boyd to William Drew, December 24, 1932, Gray Herbarium Archives, Harvard University.

9. William B. Drew, unpublished paper on the 1931 expedition, Drew family collection.

10. Louise Arner Boyd, "The Louise A. Boyd Seven Arctic Expeditions," *Photogrammetric Engineering and Remote Sensing* (December 1950): 651.

11. Louise Arner Boyd, *The Fiord Region of East Greenland* (New York: American Geographical Society, 1935), 301.

12. "A Big Day for the Children of Steinvagen, Skutvika and Skjorva," *Sunnmørposten,* n.d.

13. J. Harlen Bretz, unpublished diary, "Greenland In and To and From," J. Harlen Bretz Archives, University of Chicago.

14. Louise Arner Boyd, *The Fiord Region of East Greenland* (New York: American Geographical Society, 1935), 6.

15. Noel Odell, "The Mountains of North-East Greenland," in *Cambridge University Mountaineering 1934*, edited by J.A. Ramsay (Cambridge: Cambridge University Mountain Club, 1934).

16. J. Harlen Bretz, unpublished diary, "Greenland In and To and From," J. Harlen Bretz Archives, University of Chicago.

17. Untitled, undated document by Louise Arner Boyd, Marin History Museum.

18. Louise Arner Boyd, *The Fiord Region of East Greenland* (New York: American Geographical Society, 1935), 11.

19. J. Harlen Bretz, unpublished diary, "Greenland In and To and From," J. Harlen Bretz Archives, University of Chicago.

20. Ibid., 161.

21. Louise Arner Boyd, "An Arctic S.O.S.," n.d., Marin History Museum.

22. J. Harlen Bretz, unpublished diary, "Greenland In and To and From," J. Harlen Bretz Archives, University of Chicago.

23. Ibid., 205.

24. Ibid., 288.

25. Letter from Louise Arner Boyd to Mait Miller, n.d., Marin History Museum.

26. Ibid., 288.

27. Ibid., 247.

28. Louise Arner Boyd, *The Fiord Region of East Greenland* (New York, American Geographical Society, 1935), 30.

29. Ibid.

30. J. Harlen Bretz, unpublished diary, "Greenland In and To and From," J. Harlen Bretz Archives, University of Chicago.

31. Elizabeth Fagg Olds, *Women of the Four Winds* (Boston: Houghton Mifflin, 1999), 259.

32. Louise Arner Boyd, *The Fiord Region of East Greenland* (New York, American Geographical Society, 1935), 34.

33. Ibid., 38.

34. Ibid., 40.

35. J. Harlen Bretz, unpublished diary "Greenland In and To and From," J. Harlen Bretz Archives, University of Chicago.

36. Louise Arner Boyd, "The Louise A. Boyd Seven Arctic Expeditions," *Photogrammetric Engineering and Remote Sensing* (December 1950): 653.

CHAPTER SEVEN: AN OBSESSIVE PURSUIT

1. Letter from Louise Arner Boyd to Harlen Bretz, April 19, 1934, J. Harlen Bretz Archives, University of Chicago.

2. Louise Arner Boyd, unpublished travel diary to Norway, Finland, and Sweden, Louise Arner Boyd Archive, San Rafael Public Library.

3. Louise Arner Boyd, *Polish Countrysides Photographs and Narrative* (New York: American Geographical Society, 1937), 7.

4. Letter from G. Poivilliers to Louise Arner Boyd, April 22, 1935, Archives of the American Geographical Society, University of Wisconsin–Milwaukee.

5. Letter from J.B. Charcot to Louise Arner Boyd, February 7, 1935, Marin History Museum.

6. Letter from Mait Miller to Louise Arner Boyd, January 4, 1936, Archives of the American Geographical Society, University of Wisconsin–Milwaukee.

7. Louise Arner Boyd, *The Coast of Greenland with Hydrographic Studies in the Greenland Sea. The Louise A. Boyd Arctic Expeditions of 1937 and 1938* (New York: American Geographical Society, 1948), xi.

8 Letter from Isaiah Bowman to Harlen Bretz, July 26, 1934, J. Harlen Bretz Archives, University of Chicago.

9. Letter from Noel Odell to Harlen Bretz, August 13, 1934, J. Harlen Bretz Archive, University of Chicago.

10. Letter from Harlen Bretz to Noel Odell, November 26, 1935, J. Harlen Bretz Archives, University of Chicago.

11. Telegram from William F. Humphrey to Adolf Hoel, January 18, 1936, Louise Arner Boyd Archive, San Rafael Public Library.

12. J. Harlen Bretz, unpublished expedition notes, J. Harlen Bretz Archives, University of Chicago.

13. Letter from Louise Arner Boyd to Harlen Bretz, April 13, 1936, J. Harlen Bretz Archives, University of Chicago.

14. Letter from Peder Strand to Louise Arner Boyd, February 19, 1935, Marin History Museum.

15. Louise Arner Boyd, *The Coast of Greenland with Hydrographic Studies in the Greenland Sea. The Louise A. Boyd Arctic Expeditions of 1937 and 1938* (New York: American Geographical Society, 1948), x.

16. Letter from Harlen Bretz to Louise Arner Boyd, November 6, 1936, J. Harlen Bretz Archives, University of Chicago.

17. Tahoe Washburn, *Under Polaris: An Arctic Quest* (Montreal and Kingston: McGill-Queen's University Press, 1999), 4.

18. "Woman Explorer Sailing for North," *New York Times,* May 5, 1937.

19. "Woman Explorer on Trip to Arctic," *Montreal Gazette,* May 26, 1937.

20. *Polar Record* 2, no. 14 (1937): 115.

21. Louise Arner Boyd, *The Coast of Greenland with Hydrographic Studies in the Greenland Sea. The Louise A. Boyd Arctic Expeditions of 1937 and 1938* (New York: American Geographical Society, 1948), 4.

22. Henry J. Oosting, unpublished diary, "Greenland in 105 Days Or Why Did I Ever Leave Home," Henry J. Oosting Archive, Duke University.

23. Louise Arner Boyd, *The Coast of Greenland with Hydrographic Studies in the Greenland Sea. The Louise A. Boyd Arctic Expeditions of 1937 and 1938* (New York: American Geographical Society, 1948), 9.

24. Henry J. Oosting, unpublished diary, "Greenland in 105 Days Or Why Did I Ever Leave Home," Henry J. Oosting Archive, Duke University, 32.

25. Ibid., 34.

26. Ibid., 37.

27. Ibid., 43.

28. Louise Arner Boyd, *The Coast of Greenland with Hydrographic Studies in the Greenland Sea. The Louise A. Boyd Arctic Expeditions of 1937 and 1938* (New York: American Geographical Society, 1948), 11.

29. Henry J. Oosting, unpublished diary, "Greenland In 105 Days Or Why Did I Ever Leave Home," Henry J. Oosting Archive, Duke University, 83.

30. Ibid, p. 90.

31. Ibid, p. 94.

32. Louise Arner Boyd, *The Coast of Greenland with Hydrographic Studies in the Greenland Sea: The Louise A. Boyd Arctic Expeditions of 1937 and 1938* (New York: American Geographical Society, 1948), 24.

33. Henry J. Oosting, unpublished diary, "Greenland in 105 Days Or Why Did I Ever Leave Home," Henry J. Oosting Archive, Duke University, 108.

34. Ibid., 103.

35. Ibid., 110.

36. Louise Arner Boyd, *The Coast of Greenland with Hydrographic Studies in the Greenland Sea. The Louise A. Boyd Arctic Expeditions of 1937 and 1938* (New York: American Geographical Society, 1948), 40.

37. Ibid.

38. Ibid., 46.

CHAPTER EIGHT: CONTRIBUTING TO SCIENCE

1. Russell Owen, "Woman Makes Her Mark," *New York Times*, May 1, 1938, 124.

2. Ibid.

3. "Miss Boyd Pictures Rigors of Exploring Arctic Fiord Region," *Daily Princetonian* 62, no. 5.

4. "Memo of a Conversation with L.A.B," June 5, 1939, Archives of the American Geographical Society, University of Wisconsin–Milwaukee.

5. K.C. Edwards, "Review of 'Polish Countrysides,'" unknown journal 3, no. 7 (September 1937): 537.

6. W. Elmer Ekblaw, "Polish Countrysides," *Economic Geography* 13, no. 4 (1937): 431–32.

7. Viyella Wilson, "American Women Explorers Carry Torch of Science All Over the World," *Washington Post,* May 29, 1938.

8. Letter from Henry J. Oosting to Mrs. R. Roche, October 26, 1937, Henry J. Oosting Archives, Duke University.

9. Telegram from Louise Arner Boyd to Henry J. Oosting, November 24, 1937, Marin History Museum.

10. Letter from Louise Arner Boyd to Elling Aarseth, April 14, 1938, Marin History Museum.

11. Letter from Finn E. Bronner to Louise Arner Boyd, April 22, 1938, Bronner family collection.

12. Letter from Finn E. Bronner to unspecified brother, June 13, 1938, Bronner family collection.

13. Louise Arner Boyd, *The Coast of Greenland with Hydrographic Studies in the Greenland Sea. The Louise A. Boyd Arctic Expeditions of 1937 and 1938* (New York: American Geographical Society, 1948), 48.

14. Joseph Mulvaney, "Queen of Arctic Explorers Seeks to Aid Science," *San Antonio Light,* January 8, 1939.

15. Letter from Finn E. Bronner to Iain Brownlie Roy, December 1, 1997, Iain Brownlie Roy collection.

16. Louise Arner Boyd, *The Coast of Greenland with Hydrographic Studies in the Greenland Sea. The Louise A. Boyd Arctic Expeditions of 1937 and 1938* (New York: American Geographical Society, 1948), 51.

17. Ibid.

18. Letter from Finn E. Bronner to Iain Brownlie Roy, December 1, 1997, Iain Brownlie Roy collection.

19. Ibid.

20. "Completed Expeditions — Miss Louise A. Boyd's Arctic Expedition 1938," *Polar Record* 3, no. 17 (January): 25.

21. Louise Arner Boyd, *The Coast of Greenland with Hydrographic Studies in the Greenland Sea. The Louise A. Boyd Arctic Expeditions of 1937 and 1938* (New York: American Geographical Society, 1948), 62.

22. Ibid., 66.

23. Louise Arner Boyd, "The Louise A. Boyd Seven Arctic Expeditions," *Photogrammetric Engineering and Remote Sensing* (December 1950): 656.

24. Willie Knutsen and Will C. Knutsen, *The Arctic Sun on My Path* (Guilford: Lyon Press, 2005), 116.

25. Louise Arner Boyd, *The Coast of Greenland with Hydrographic Studies in the Greenland Sea. The Louise A. Boyd Arctic Expeditions of 1937 and 1938* (New York: American Geographical Society, 1948), 72.

26. Ibid.

27. Ibid.

28. Ibid., 77.

29. "Boyd Expedition Sets Arctic Mark," *New York Times,* September 9, 1938, 23.

30. Edwin C. Hill, untitled. *San Francisco Call-Bulletin,* December 20, 1938.

31. Louise Arner Boyd, text of untitled speech, December 20, 1938, Archives of the American Geographical Society, University of Wisconsin–Milwaukee.

32. Letter from Finn E. Bronner to Louise Arner Boyd, Bronner family collection.

33. Lynn T. White, untitled, undated note, Marin History Museum.

34. Joseph Mulvaney, "Queen of Arctic Explorers Seeks to Aid Science," *San Antonio Light,* January 8, 1938.

35. Louise Arner Boyd, *The Fiord Region of East Greenland* (New York: American Geographical Society, 1935), 39.

36. Letter from Everett R. Peters to Louise Arner Boyd, June 6, 1939, Louise Arner Boyd Archive, San Rafael Public Library.

37. Letter from Richard B. Beam to Louise Arner Boyd, 1939, Louise Arner Boyd Archive, San Rafael Public Library.

38. Letter from Joseph Eden to Louise Arner Boyd, February 4, 1939, Louise Arner Boyd Archive, San Rafael Public Library.

39. Lecture notes for a presentation to the San Rafael Chamber of Commerce, January 5, 1939, Louise Arner Boyd Archive, San Rafael Public Library.

40. Letter from Louise Arner Boyd to Captain Johan Olsen, July 20, 1939, Marin History Museum.

CHAPTER NINE: HONOUR AND GLORY

1. Elizabeth Bradfield, *Approaching Ice: Poems* (New York: Persea Books, 2010), 72.

2. J.H. Dellinger, quoted in W.F. Snyder and Charles L. Bragaw, *Achievement in Radio: Seventy Years of Radio Science, Technology, Standards, and Measurement at the National Bureau of Standards* (Boulder: National Bureau of Standards, 1986), 225.

3. Louise Arner Boyd, *The Coast of Greenland with Hydrographic Studies in the Greenland Sea. The Louise A. Boyd Arctic Expeditions of 1937 and 1938* (New York: American Geographical Society, 1948), ix.

4. "War Department Notification of Personnel Action — Civilian Personnel Circular — Louise Arner Boyd," September 29, 1944, Louise Arner Boyd Archive, San Rafael Public Library.

5. Letter from Louise Arner Boyd to Robert Bartlett, November 1, 1940, Louise Arner Boyd Archive, San Rafael Public Library.

6. Hugh Stewart, "Robert A. Bartlett," *Arctic* 39, no. 2 (1986): 188.

7. Robert Bartlett, untitled document, March 27, 1941, Robert A. Bartlett Papers, George J. Mitchell Department of Special Collections & Archives, Bowdoin College Library, Brunswick, Maine.

8. Letter from Louise Arner Boyd to Robert Bartlett, November 1, 1940, Louise Arner Boyd Archive, San Rafael Public Library.

9. Letter from Robert Bartlett to Louise Arner Boyd, November 9, 1940, Louise Arner Boyd Archive, San Rafael Public Library.

10. Letter from Louise Arner Boyd to Barbara Gothie, May 21, 1941, Marin History Museum.

11. J.H. Dellinger, "Memorandum on the Louise Arner Boyd Arctic Expedition 1941," November 5, 1941, Marin History Museum.

12. Alexander Forbes, *Quest for a Northern Air Route* (Cambridge: Harvard University Press, 1953), 67.

13. John A. Schilling, unpublished journal, "Expedition on the *Morrissey* June through October 1941," Schilling family collection.

14. "Press Release," March 27, 1941, Robert A. Bartlett Papers, George J. Mitchell Department of Special Collections & Archives, Bowdoin College Library, Brunswick, Maine.

15. Letter from Acting Secretary of the Navy to Robert Bartlett, June 7, 1941, Robert A. Bartlett Papers, George J. Mitchell Department of Special Collections & Archives, Bowdoin College Library, Brunswick, Maine.

16. Letter from Vilhjalmur Stefansson to Louise Arner Boyd, June 15, 1941, Stefansson Archive, Dartmouth College.

17. Robert Peary, *Secrets of Polar Travel* (New York: Century Club, 1917), 8.

18. John A. Schilling, unpublished journal, "Expedition on the *Morrissey* June through October 1941," Schilling family collection.

19. Ibid.

20. Letter from Louise Arner Boyd to Barbara Gothie, May 10, 1941, Marin History Museum.

21. John A. Schilling, unpublished journal, "Expedition on the *Morrissey* June through October 1941," Schilling family collection.

22. Ibid. As did most scientists who participated in the Louise Arner Boyd expeditions, Dr. John A. Schilling went on to have an illustrious career. He participated in a study of flash burns as part of the Manhattan Project, became chief of the first full-time department of surgery at the University of Oklahoma, and worked tirelessly throughout his life in the field of academic surgery.

23. Archer S. Taylor, unpublished journal, "1941 Greenland Logbook," Taylor family collection.

24. Ibid.

25. Ibid.

26. John A. Schilling, unpublished journal, "Expedition on the *Morrissey* June through October 1941," Schilling family collection.

27. Letter from Frank Meals to Louise Arner Boyd, November 13, 1963, Louise Arner Boyd Archive, San Rafael Public Library.

28. Letter from Louise Arner Boyd to Frank Meals, January 11, 1964, Louise Arner Boyd Archive, San Rafael Public Library.

29. Letter from B.F. Giles to Louise Arner Boyd, September 12, 1941, Marin History Museum.

30. Letter from Barbara Gothie to Louise Arner Boyd, September 16, 1941, Marin History Museum.

31. John A. Schilling, unpublished journal, "Expedition on the *Morrissey* June through October 1941," Schilling family collection.

32. Letter from Louise Arner Boyd to Barbara Gothie, September 16, 1941, Marin History Museum.

33. John A. Schilling, unpublished journal, "Expedition on the *Morrissey* June through October 1941," Schilling family collection.

34. Ibid.

35. Ibid.

36. Archer S. Taylor, unpublished journal, "1941 Greenland Logbook," Taylor family collection.

37. John A. Schilling, unpublished journal, "Expedition on the *Morrissey* June through October 1941," Schilling family collection.

38. Archer S. Taylor, unpublished journal, "1941 Greenland Logbook," Taylor family collection.

39. Ibid.

40. Letter from Louise Arner Boyd to unknown colleague (likely secretary Barbara Gothie), n.d., Marin History Museum.

41. Louise A. Boyd, "The Louise A. Boyd Seven Arctic Expeditions," *Photogrammetric Engineering and Remote Sensing* (December 1950): 656.

42. Henrik Knudsen, "Battling the Aurora Borealis: The Transnational Coproduction of Ionospheric Research in Early Cold War Greenland," in *Exploring Greenland: Cold War Science and Technology*, edited by R.E. Doel, Kristine C. Harper, and Matthias Heymann (Basingstoke: Palgrave Macmillan, 2016), 147.

43. Louise Arner Boyd, *The Coast of Greenland with Hydrographic Studies in the Greenland Sea. The Louise A. Boyd Arctic Expeditions of 1937 and 1938* (New York: American Geographical Society, 1948).

CHAPTER TEN: THE NORTH POLE AND BEYOND

1. "War Department Notification of Personnel Action — Civilian Personnel Circular — Louise Arner Boyd," September 29, 1944, Louise Arner Boyd Archive, San Rafael Public Library.

2. Letter from Louise Arner Boyd to Cordell Hull, January 22, 1942. Louise Arner Boyd Archive, San Rafael Public Library.

3. Letter from Louise Arner Boyd to Vilhjalmur Stefansson, July 30, 1942, Stefansson Collection, Dartmouth College.

4. Letter from Finn E. Bronner to Director of Intelligence, September 11, 1948, Marin History Museum.

5. Letter from Hamilton Maguire to Louise Arner Boyd, July 15, 1942, Marin History Museum.

6. Letter from S.P. Poole to Louise Arner Boyd, July 14, 1942, Marin History Museum.

7. Letter from Louise Arner Boyd to Sanford Smith, October 29, 1941, Marin History Museum.

8. Text concerning award of the King Christian X Medal to Louise Arner Boyd, September 12, 1947, Marin History Museum.

9. From undated memo probably written by John Wright, American Geographical Society Library, University of Wisconsin–Milwaukee.

10. Text of the citation for the Certificate of Appreciation for Louise Arner Boyd, 1949, Marin History Museum.

11. "Woman Explorer Honored by Army," *New York Times*, March 19, 1949.

12. Ibid.

13. "Louise Arner Boyd," *Encyclopedia Arctica*, unpublished manuscript, Dartmouth College Library.

14. "The Lady Who Prefers Hardships of the Arctic to the Leisure of 'High Life,'" unknown newspaper, summer, 1939.

15. Jean Fay, "An Old Estate Goes Modern," *San Francisco Chronicle*, July 20, 1952, 55.

16. Letter from Louise Arner Boyd to unnamed individual, n.d., Archives of the American Geographical Society, University of Wisconsin–Milwaukee.

17. Eileen Summers, "Arctic Call Is Strong," *Washington Post*, December 4, 1954, 29.

18. Letter from Louise Arner Boyd to Richard Light, January 23, 1953, Louise Arner Boyd Archive, San Rafael Public Library.

19. Letter from Louise Arner Boyd to Harald Sverdrup, November 13, 1954, Marin History Museum.

THE POLAR ADVENTURES OF A RICH AMERICAN DAME

20. Letter from Louise Arner Boyd to Cathe and Nino Mowinckel, June 26, 1955, author's collection.

21. Louise Arner Boyd, "A View from 9,000 ft," Long Beach *Independent Press-Telegram, Parade: The Sunday Picture Magazine*, February 2, 1958, 2.

22. Letter from Ethel Smith to Louise Arner Boyd, June 28, 1955, Louise Arner Boyd Archive, San Rafael Public Library.

23. Letter from Louise Arner Boyd to Cathe and Nino Mowinkel, June 26, 1955, author's collection.

24. Letter from Lillian Brentnall to Louise Arner Boyd, June 17, 1955, Louise Arner Boyd Archive, San Rafael Public Library.

25. Letter from B. Herr to Louise Arner Boyd, June 24, 1955. Louise Arner Boyd Archive, San Rafael Public Library.

26. "Deserved Recognition," *Oakland Tribune*, February 27, 1960, 12.

27. Letter from Richard Light to Louise Arner Boyd, February 28, 1960, Louise Arner Boyd Archive, San Rafael Public Library.

28. Robert Peary was an early celebrity endorser of products (Eastman Kodak), as were Robert Falcon Scott (Fry's Cocoa and Chocolate), Ernest Shackleton (Kendall Mint Cakes), Richard Byrd (Sergeant Dog Remedies), Sir Hubert Wilkins (Lord Calvert Whiskey), and Captain Bob Bartlett (Wheaties, Pullman and Rail, and Winchester). Even fellow female American explorer Osa Johnson endorsed Vitality Tea. For more information, see Kerry Segrave's *Endorsements in Advertising: A Social History* (Jefferson, NC: McFarland, 2005).

29. "Elks Get Offer of Boyd Mansion," *Daily Independent Journal*, November 2, 1962, 4.

30. Letter from Louise Arner Boyd to Carl Clark March 29, 1963, author's collection.

31. Louise Arner Boyd, unpublished travel diary for Alaska 1967, Marjorie Fountain family collection.

32. "Another Award for Miss Boyd," *San Francisco Chronicle,* April 28, 1969.

33. Letter from Louise Arner Boyd to Virginia Pope, January 9, 1971, Marjorie Fountain family collection.

34. Letter from Burton Atkinson to Ansel Adams, February 16, 1972, Archives of the American Geographical Society, University of Wisconsin–Milwaukee.

35. Letter from Louise Arner Boyd to Virginia Pope, January 9, 1971, Marjorie Fountain family collection.

36. Letter from Finn E. Bronner to Lincoln Washburn, September 29, 1972, Iain Brownlie Roy collection.

37. Letter from Otis Taylor to Marjorie Fountain, 1973, Marjorie Fountain family collection.

38. "Obituary," *Polar Record* 16, no. 105 (1973): 873.

39. Letter from Finn E. Bronner to Lincoln Washburn, September 29, 1972, Iain Brownlie Roy collection.

EPILOGUE: THE LEGACY OF LOUISE ARNER BOYD

1. Letter written by Finn E. Bronner to Lincoln Washburn, September 29, 1972, Iain Brownlie Roy collection.

2. Text of radio program "It Can Be Done," prepared by Batten, Barton, Durstine and Osborn, Inc. for the Columbia Broadcasting System, May 3, 1939, 19.

3. Anna Maria Gillis, "A Socialite Conquers an Arctic Wilderness," *Washington Post*, April 10, 1996.

4. Letter written by Lincoln Washburn to Iain Roy, December 26, 1997, Iain Brownlie Roy collection.

5. F.E. Nelson, S.M. Peschel, and D.K. Hall, "Of Images, Archives, and Anonymity: Glacier Photographs from Louise Arner Boyd's East Greenland Expeditions, 1933, 1937, and 1938," *American Geophysical Union Fall Meeting Abstract*, December, 2010.

6. Author communication with Anders Anker Bjørk on January 18, 2016.

BIBLIOGRAPHY

NEWSPAPERS

Bergens Arbeiderblad
Christian Science Monitor
Chicago Daily Tribune
Daily Alta California
Daily Free Press
Daily Tribune
Davenport Democrat
Galveston Daily News
Hamilton Journal
Lincoln Journal
Los Angeles Times
Marin Journal
Montreal Gazette
New York Herald
New York Times
Oakland Tribune
Ojai Valley News
Pacific Rural Press
Prescott Evening Courier

Reno Evening Gazette
Reno Weekly Gazette and Stockman
Rochester Daily Union Advertiser
San Francisco Call/Call-Bulletin
San Francisco Chronicle
San Francisco Examiner
San Rafael Daily Independent
Sausalito News
Sunnmørsposten
Svalbardposten
Washington Post

MANUSCRIPT COLLECTIONS

Adams, Ansel. Papers. Center for Creative Photography, University of Arizona, Tucson, Arizona.

Bartlett, Robert Abram. Papers. George J. Mitchell Department of Special Collections & Archives, Bowdoin College Library, Brunswick, Maine.

———. Papers. Dartmouth College, Hanover, New Hampshire.

———. Papers. Newfoundland Provincial Archives, St. John's, Newfoundland.

Bowman, Isaiah. Papers. The American Geographical Society Library, University of Wisconsin–Milwaukee.

Boyd, Jack and Louise Arner. Papers. The Thacher School, Ojai, California.

Boyd, John Franklin and Louise Arner. Papers. California Historical Society, San Francisco, California.

Boyd, Louise Arner. Photographs and papers. The American Geographical Society Library, University of Wisconsin–Milwaukee Libraries, Milwaukee, Wisconsin.

———. Papers. California Academy of Sciences, San Francisco, California.

———. Papers. Gray Herbarium Archives, Harvard University, Cambridge, Massachusetts.

———. Papers. Marin History Museum, Novato, California.

———. Papers. National Institute of Standards and Technology, U.S. Department of Commerce, Gaithersburg, Maryland.

———. Papers. Norsk Polarinstitutt, Tromsø, Norway.

———. Papers. Ohio State University, Columbus, Ohio.

———. Papers. San Rafael Public Library, San Rafael, California.

———. Papers. Society of Woman Geographers Collection, Library of Congress, Washington D.C.

———. Papers. University of Bergen, Bergen, Norway.

———. Papers. University of Alaska Fairbanks, Fairbanks, Alaska.

Bratseth, Erik. Papers. Bratseth family collection, Norway.

Bretz, J. Harlen. Papers. University of Chicago, Chicago, Illinois.

Bronner, Finn Eyolf. Papers. Bronner family collection, United States.

Clark, Carl. Papers. Clark family collection, San Rafael, California.

Coleman, Janet. Papers. Coleman family collection, United States.

Cook, Seth. Papers. Contra Costa County Historical Society, Brentwood, California.

Drew, William. Papers. Drew family collection, United States.

Eastwood, Alice. Papers. California Academy of Sciences, San Francisco, California.

Fountain, Marjorie. Papers. Fountain family collection, United States.

Holm, Astrup. Papers. Statsarkivet, Tromsø, Norway.

Koch, Lauge. Papers. Rigsarkivet, Copenhagen, Denmark.

Millikan, Robert A. Papers. California Institute of Technology, Pasadena, California.

Olsen, Johan. Papers. Ishavsmuseet Aarvak, Brandal, Norway.

Oosting, Henry J. Papers. Duke University, Durham, North Carolina.

Reinhardt, Aurelia H. Papers, Special Collections, Olin Library, Mills College, California.

Roy, Iain Brownlie. Papers related to the British North-East Greenland Project and Louise Arner Boyd, Roy private collection, Scotland.

Schilling, John A. "Expedition on the *Morrissey* June through October 1941." Unpublished journal. Schilling family collection, United States.

Schooner *Ernestina-Morrissey* Archives at the Claire T. Carney University Library, University of Massachusetts Dartmouth, Dartmouth, Massachusetts.

Stefansson, Vilhjalmur. Papers. Stefansson Archive, Dartmouth College, Hanover, New Hampshire.

Tandberg, Rolf S. Papers related to the 1928 rescue attempt of Roald Amundsen, Library of Congress, Washington D.C.

Taylor, Archer S., Papers. Taylor family collection, United States.

AUDIO-VISUAL MATERIALS

Ice Man: The Life and Times of Captain Bob Bartlett. CBC Home Video. Toronto: CBC, 1998.

National Archives Gift Collection of Materials Relating to Polar Regions, Louise Arner Boyd Collection RG 401, RG 59, RG 165, RG 167, Library of Congress, Washington, D.C., including the Louise Arner Boyd Expedition films, 1926–1941.

White Thunder: The Story of Varick Frissell and the Viking Disaster. A film by Victoria King. National Film Board of Canada. 2004.

BOOKS AND ARTICLES

Ahlmann, Hans W. "Studies in North-East Greenland 1939–1940, Parts I-II." *Geografiska Annaler* 23 (1941): 145–209.

Amundsen, Roald, and Lincoln Ellsworth. *Our Polar Flight: The Amundsen-Ellsworth Polar Flight.* New York: Dodd, Mead, 1925.

Amundsen, Roald. *My Life as an Explorer.* Cambridge: Cambridge University Press, 2014.

Ancestry.com. "Passenger Manifest for the S.S. *Aquitaine*, 1920." Accessed July 15, 2013. www.ancestry.com.

Anda, Einar, Olav Orheim, and Jan Magerud. "Late Holocene Glacier Variations and Climate at Jan Mayen." *Polar Research* 3 (1985): 129–40.

Anema, Durlynn. *Louise Arner Boyd: Arctic Explorer.* Greensboro: Morgan Reynolds, 2000.

Anonymous. "Last Court." *Time,* July 6, 1925.

Anonymous. "Osborn Maitland Miller 1897–1979." *Geographical Journal* 146 (1980): 159.

Anonymous. "Science — Polar Pilgrims." *Time,* May 10, 1926.

Anrick, Carl-Julius. "En sommarresa till Ostgrönland." *Ymer* 2 (1932): 175–212.

Apollonio, Spencer. *Lands That Hold One Spellbound: A Story of East Greenland*. Calgary, AB: University of Calgary Press, 2008.

Barbour, M.G., and W.D. Billings. *North American Terrestrial Vegetation*. Cambridge: Cambridge University Press, 2000.

Barr, William. "The First Tourist Cruise in the Soviet Arctic." *Arctic 33* (1980): 671–85.

Barstow, Diantha Lamb. *The Colemans of California: A Family History Focusing On the Lives of John Crisp Coleman, Edward Coleman and Persis Sibley Coleman*. Baltimore: Gateway Press, 2003.

Bartlett, Robert A. *The Log of Bob Bartlett*. St. John's, NL: Flanker Press, 2006.

———. *Karluk's Last Voyage: An Epic of Death and Survival in the Arctic, 1913–1916*. New York: Cooper Square Press, 2001.

Bell, Morag, and Cheryl McEwan. "The Admission of Women Fellows to the Royal Geographical Society, 1892–1914: The Controversy and the Outcome." *The Geographical Journal* 162 (1996): 295–312.

Bennike, Ole. "Pingos at Nioghalvfjerdsfjorden, Eastern Greenland." *Geology of Greenland Survey Bulletin* 180 (1998): 159–62.

Berg, Kåre. *Heroes of the Polar Wastes: Pioneer Norwegian Explorers in the Arctic and the Antarctic*. Oslo: Andresen and Butenschøn, 2003.

Berg, Roald. "Gender in Polar Air: Roald Amundsen and His Aeronautics." *Acta Borealis* 23 (2006): 130–44.

Birmingham, Stephen. "San Francisco: The Grand Manner." *Holiday* 29(4): 98, 170–72, 174–76, 179–86.

Bjørk, Anders A., Kurt H. Kjaer, Niels J. Korsgaard, Shfaqat A. Khan, Kristian K. Kjeldsen, Camilla S. Andresen, Jason E. Box, Nicolaj K. Larsen, and Svend Funder. "An Aerial View of 80 Years of Climate-Related Glacier Fluctuations in Southeast Greenland." *Nature Geoscience* 5 (2012): 427–32.

Bjørk, Anders A., S. Aagaard, K. Kjaer, S.A. Khan, and J. Box. "110 Years of Local Glacier and Ice Cap Changes in Central- and North East Greenland." *American Geophysical Union* 12 (2014).

Blackmur, Arnold. *In Old Diablo: A Social History*. Redwood City, CA: Ampex Corporation, 1981.

Bliss, L.C., O.W. Heal, and J.J. Moore. *Tundra Ecosystems: A Comparative Analysis*. Cambridge: Cambridge University Press, 1981.

Bloom, Lisa. *Gender on Ice: American Ideologies of Polar Exploration.* Minneapolis: University of Minnesota Press, 1993.

Bones, Stian. "Norway and Past International Polar Years — a Historical Account." *Polar Research* 26 (2007): 195–203.

Bown, Stephen R. *The Last Viking.* Vancouver: Douglas & McIntyre, 2012.

Boyd, Louise A. *Through the French and Belgian Battlefields, Travel Diary 1920.* Unpublished. Marjorie Fountain Papers. Fountain family private collection.

————. *Through Normandy and Brittany, Travel Diary 1920–21.* Unpublished. Marjorie Fountain Papers. Fountain Family Private Collection.

————. *1928 Travel Diary (March 19–May 23, September 23–October 16).* Unpublished. Louise Arner Boyd Papers, San Rafael Public Library, San Rafael, California.

————. Unpublished, untitled, partial manuscript. Louise Arner Boyd Papers, San Rafael Public Library, San Rafael, California.

————. Lecture Notes. Unpublished and undated. Louise Arner Boyd Papers, San Rafael Public Library, San Rafael, California.

————. "Fiords of East Greenland: A Photographic Reconnaissance throughout the Franz Josef and King Oscar Fiords." *Geographical Review* 23 (1932): 529–61.

————. "Further Explorations in East Greenland, 1933." *Geographical Review* 26 (1933): 465–77.

————. *The Fiord Region of East Greenland. American Geographical Society Special Publication No. 18.* New York: American Geographical Society, 1935.

————. "The Marshes of Pińsk." *Geographical Review* 26 (1936): 376–95.

————. *Polish Countrysides: Photographs and Narrative. American Geographical Society Special Publication No. 20.* New York: American Geographical Society, 1937.

————. *The Coast of Northeast Greenland with Hydrographic Studies in the Greenland Sea. The Louise A. Boyd Arctic Expeditions of 1937 and 1938. American Geographical Society Special Publication No. 30.* New York: American Geographical Society, 1948.

———. "The Louise A. Boyd Seven Arctic Expeditions." *Photogrammetric Engineering and Remote Sensing* December (1950): 651–57.

———. *Kresy fotografie z 1934 roku*. Krakow: Wydawnictwo znak, 1991.

Bradfield, Elizabeth. *Approaching Ice: Poems*. New York: Persea Books, 2010.

Bravo, Michael, and Sverker Sörlin, eds. *Narrating the Arctic: A Cultural History of Nordic Scientific Practices*. Canton: Science History Publications, 2002.

Bretz, J. Harlen. "The Channeled Scabland of Eastern Washington." *Geographical Review* 18 (1928): 446–77.

Büntgen, Ulf, Lena Hellmann, Willy Tegel, Signe Normand, Isla Myers-Smith, Alexander V. Kirdyanov, Daniel Nievergelt, and Fritz H. Schweingruber. "Temperature-Induced Recruitment Pulses of Arctic Dwarf Shrub Communities." *Journal of Ecology* 103 (2015): 489–501.

Burn-Murdoch, William G. *Modern Whaling and Bear-Hunting: A Record of Present-Day Whaling with Up-To-Date Appliances in Many Parts of the World, and of Bear and Seal Hunting in the Arctic Regions*. Philadelphia: J.B. Lippincott, 1917.

Byington, Lewis Francis. *The History of San Francisco*. Three Volumes. Chicago: S.J. Clarke, 1931.

Cain, Ella. *The Story of Bodie*. San Francisco: Fearon Publishers, 1956.

California State Mining Bureau. *Ninth Annual Report of the State Mineralogist for the Year Ending December 1, 1889*. Sacramento: California State Mining Bureau, 1890.

Clark Historic Resource Consultants. *Historic Resource Evaluation Report for Maple Lawn/Elks Lodge 1312 Mission Ave., San Rafael, California*. San Rafael: City of San Rafael, 2006.

Coblentz, W., F. Gracely, and R. Stair. "Measurements of Ultraviolet Solar and Sky Radiation Intensities in High Latitudes. Research paper RP1469." *Journal of Research of the National Bureau of Standards* 28 (1942): 581–91.

Cox, Lynne. *South with the Sun: Roald Amundsen, His Polar Explorations and the Quest for Discovery*. New York: Random House, 2011.

Dakin, Susanna Bryant. *The Perennial Adventure: A Tribute to Alice Eastwood, 1859–1953*. San Francisco: California Academy of Sciences, 1954.

Davis, Wade. *Into the Silence: The Great War, Mallory, and the Conquest of Everest*. New York: Alfred A. Knopf, 2011.

Daysh, G.H.J., and C.P. Snodgrass. "International Geographical Congress — Warsaw 1934." *Scottish Geographical Magazine* 50 (1934): 386–90.

Decies, Gertrude. "London Is Mecca of Fashionables as the Shooting Season Ends." *Davenport Democrat*, October 3, 1926, 7.

DeLucia, Christine. *Schooner Ernestina: Historic American Engineering Record*. No. MA-168. Historic American Buildings Survey/Historic American Engineering Record Division (HABS/HAER) of the National Park Service. Washington: U.S. Department of the Interior, 2009.

Devey, David. *History of Coulterville*. Coulterville: Northern Mariposa County History Center, 1978.

Devold, Hallvard. *Polarliv*. Oslo: Gylendal Norsk Forlag, 1940.

Dick, Lyle. "Aboriginal-European Relations During the Great Age of North Polar Exploration." *Polar Geography* 26 (2002): 66–86.

Domosh, Mona. "Towards a Feminist Historiography of Geography." *Transactions of the Institute of British Geography* 16 (1991): 95–104.

Dorrance, John. "Lady of the Arctic." *San Francisco Magazine*, December, 1984: 41, 43–45, 151, 153–54.

Ellsworth, Lincoln. "Air Pioneering in the Arctic." *Boys Life* 7 (September 1928): 64–66.

———. and Edward H. Smith. "Report of the Preliminary Results of the Aeroarctic Expedition with 'Graf Zeppelin' 1931." *Geographical Review* 22 (1932): 61–82.

Fairchild, Wilma Belden. "Explorers: Men and Motives." *Geographical Review* 38 (1948): 414–25.

Farley, Rebecca. "'By Endurance We Conquer' Ernest Shackleton and Performances of White Male Hegemony." *International Journal of Cultural Studies* 8 (2005): 231–54.

Fitch, Col. Henry. *Pacific Coast Annual Mining Review and Stock Ledger*. San Francisco: Francis and Valentine, 1878.

Fleming, Fergus. *Ninety Degrees North: The Quest for the North Pole*. New York: Grove Press, 2001.

Fogelson, Nancy. "Greenland: Strategic Base on a Northern Defense Line." *Journal of Military History* 53 (1989): 51–63.

Forbes, Alexander. *Northernmost Labrador Mapped from the Air.* American Geographical Society Special Publication No. 22. New York: American Geographical Society, 1938.

———. *Quest for a Northern Air Route.* Cambridge: Harvard University Press, 1953.

Fowler, O.S. *Phrenological Character of John F. Boyd.* Boston: O.S. Fowler, 1871.

Funder, Svend, and Kaj Strand Petersen. *Glacitectonic Deformations in East Greenland. Bulletin of the Geological Society of Denmark 28.* Copenhagen: Geological Survey of Denmark, 1980.

Giæver, John. *To Mann I Möskosfjorden.* Oslo: Gyldendal Norskforlag, 1931.

———. *In the Land of the Musk-Ox: Tales of Wild Life in North-East Greenland.* London: Jarrold Publishers, 1958.

Gjertz, Ian, and Berit Mørkved. "Norwegian Arctic Expansionism, Victoria Island (Russia) and the Bratvaag Expedition." *Arctic* 51 (1998): 330–35.

Glines, Carroll V. *Bernt Balchen, Polar Aviator.* Washington: Smithsonian Institution Press, 1999.

Goldberg, Fred. *Drama in the Arctic S.O.S. Italia: The Search for Nobile and Amundsen, a Diary and Postal History.* Oslo: Fram Museum, 2003.

Guinn, J.M. *The History of State of California and Biographical Record of Coast Counties, California.* Chicago: Chapman, 1904.

Gulliksen, Bjørn. *Marine Investigations at Jan Mayen in 1972.* Trondheim: University of Trondheim, 1974.

Higgins, A.K., Jane Gilotti, and M. Paul Smith. *The Greenland Caledonides: Evolution of the Northeast Margin of Laurentia.* Reston: Geological Survey of America, 2008.

Historical Data Systems. *U.S. Civil War Soldier Records and Profiles.* Dudbury: Massachusetts, 2009.

Hoag, Charles C. *Our Society Blue Book.* San Francisco: Charles C. Hoag, 1899.

Hobbs, William. "The Defense of Greenland." *Annals of American Geographers* 31 (1941): 95–104.

Hoisington, William A. "In the Service of the Third French Republic: Jean-Baptiste Charcot (1867–1936) and the Antarctic." *Proceedings of the American Philosophical Society* 119 (1975): 315–24.

Holland, Clive, ed. *Farthest North: Endurance and Adventure in the Quest for the North Pole.* London: Robinson, 1994.

Holliday, J.S. *The World Rushed In: The California Gold Rush Experience.* Norman: University of Oklahoma Press, 2002.

Hornor, Jody, and Rick Hornor. *The Golden Quest and Nevada's Silver Heritage: Nineteenth-Century Lake Tahoe and Western Nevada Mining Districts.* Pilot Hill: Nineteenth Century Books, 2006.

Horwood, Harold. *Bartlett: The Great Explorer.* Toronto: Doubleday Canada, 1989.

Hovdenak, Gunnar, and Adolf Hoel. *Roald Amundsens Siste Ferd.* Oslo: Gylendal Norsk Forlag, 1934.

Hugo, C.F. "Report on the International Geographical Congress at Warsaw, August 23–31, 1934." *South African Geographical Journal* 17 (1934): 35–36.

Hulbe, C., W. Wang, and S. Ommanney. "Women in Glaciology: A Historical Perspective." *Journal of Glaciology* 56 (2010): 944–64.

Huntford, Roland. *The Last Place on Earth: Scott and Amundsen's Race to the South Pole.* New York: Random House, 1999.

Idaho State Historical Society. *Mining in Idaho. Idaho State Historical Society Reference Series Number Nine.* Boise: Idaho State Historical Society, 1985.

Joerg, W.L., ed. *Problems of Polar Research. A Series of Papers. American Geographical Society Special Publication No. 7.* New York: American Geographical Society, 1928.

Johnson, G. Leonard, and Oscar B. Eckhoff. "Bathymetry of the North Greenland Sea." *Deep Sea Research and Oceanographic Abstracts* 13 (1966): 1161–73.

Johnson, Russ and Anne Johnson. *The Ghost Town of Bodie: A California State Park.* Bishop: Community Printing and Publishing, 1998.

Kinsman, J.J., and J.W. Sheard. "Glaciers of Jan Mayen." *Journal of Glaciology* 4 (1963): 439–44.

Kjær, Kjell-G. "The Arctic Ship *Polarbjörn.*" *Polar Record* 42 (2006): 51–57.

Kjær, Kjell-G, and Magnus Sefland. "The Arctic Ship *Veslekari.*" *Polar Record* 41 (2005): 57–65.

Kjølås, Gerhard. *Skjegge Skjeldrup*. Trondheim: Rune Forlag, 1972.

Knappet, Melissa R. *Jewish Girls Coming of Age in America 1860–1920*. New York: New York University Press, 2005.

Henrik Knudsen, "Battling the Aurora Borealis: The Transnational Coproduction of Ionospheric Research in Early Cold War Greenland," in *Exploring Greenland: Cold War Science and Technology*, edited by R.E. Doel, Kristine C. Harper, and Matthias Heymann (Basingstoke: Palgrave Macmillan, 2016), 147.

Knoles, George H., ed. *Essays and Assays: California History Reappraised*. San Francisco: California Historical Society, 1973.

Knutsen, Willie, and Will C. Knutsen. *Arctic Sun on My Path: The True Story of America's Last Great Polar Explorer*. Guilford: Lyons Press, 2005.

Kugelmass, J. Alvin. *Roald Amundsen. A Saga of the Polar Seas*. New York: Julian Messner, 1955.

Lachman, Jill A. "Bodie, California: A Portfolio of Photographs." *California History* 73 (1994/5): 312–21.

Ladies of San Rafael. *San Rafael Cook Book*. San Rafael: Publisher not noted, 1898.

Lasca, N.P. "Postglacial Delevelling in Skeldal, Northeast Greenland." *Arctic* 19 (1966): 349–53.

Lemmon, S.J. *Record of the Red Cross Work on the Pacific Slope*. Oakland: Pacific Press Publishing Company, 1902.

Leviton, Alan, and Michele Aldrich. *The California Academy of Sciences, 1853–1906: A Narrative History*. San Francisco: California Academy of Sciences, 1997.

Lid, Johannes. *The Flora of Jan Mayen*. Skrifter Nr. 130. Oslo: Norsk Polarinstitutt, 1964.

Loose, Warren. *Bodie Bonanza: The True Story of a Flamboyant Past*. Las Vegas: Nevada Publications, 1989.

Lyons, Louis. "Young Women in Unselfish Devotion." *Who's Who Among The Women of California*. San Francisco and Los Angeles, 1922.

Makepeace, LeRoy McKim. *Sherman Thacher and His School*. New Haven: Yale University Press, 1941.

Marin County Historical Society. Bulletin. December 1–12, 1993.

Marin History Museum. *Early San Rafael.* San Francisco: Arcadia Publishing, 2008.

———. *Modern San Rafael.* San Francisco: Arcadia Publishing, 2012.

Marin County Free Library. Oral History Project. Martha Foster Abbott interviewed by Carla Ehat on January 27, 1977. Charles Tacchi interviewed by Carla Ehat and Anne Kent on May 9, 1980.

Martin, Geoffrey J. *The Life and Thought of Isaiah Bowman.* Hamden: Archon Books, 1980.

McLoone, Margo. *Women Explorers in Polar Regions: Louise Arner Boyd, Agnes Dean Cameron, Kate Marsden, Ida Pfeiffer.* North Mankato: Capstone Press, 1971.

Menzies, Winnifred Mackintosh. Unpublished manuscript. Undated. Menzies family papers.

———. "Unknown Ice-Bound Tracts of Greenland Coast Yield Secrets to Women Pioneers." *Christian Science Monitor,* August 22, 1932.

———. "Short days, Long Winters No Bar to Contentment for Lonely Greenland Villagers." *The Christian Science Monitor,* August 23, 1932.

Milburn, Geoff. "Noel Ewart Odell." *Climbers Club Journal 1986/87* (1987): 87–100.

Mitchell, Claudia, and Jacqueline Reid-Valsh. *Girl Culture: An Encyclopedia. Volume 1.* Santa Barbara: ABC-CLIO, 2008.

Monk, Janice. "Women's Worlds at the American Geographical Society." *Geographical Review* 93 (2003): 237–57.

Moss, Jocelyn. "The Call of the Arctic: Travels of Louise Boyd: Science and Society." *Marin County Historical Society Bulletin* 14 (1987–88): 3–11.

Moss, Sarah. *The Frozen Ship: The Histories and Tales of Polar Exploration.* New York: BlueBridge, 2006.

National Bureau of Standards. *Technical News Bulletin of the National Bureau of Standards. U.S. Department of Commerce* 291 (July 1941): 57.

National Society of the Colonial Dames of America website: www.nscda.org.

National Society of the Daughters of the American Revolution Lineage Book. Volume 20: 229. DAR ID # 19613 Mrs. Louise Arner Boyd.

National Society of the Daughters of the American Revolution website: www.dar.org.

Nelson, F.E., S.M. Peschel, and D.K. Hall. "Of Images, Archives, and Anonymity: Glacier Photographs from Louise Arner Boyd's East Greenland Expeditions, 1933, 1937, and 1938." *American Geophysical Union Fall Meeting Abstract* (2010).

Nicol, Susan. "Women Over-Winterers in Svalbard, 1898–1941." *Polar Record* 43 (2007): 49–53.

Nichols, Jane H. *A Historical Sketch: Rochester Female Academy, 1837–1912.* http://libraryweb.org/~digitized/books/Historical_Sketch_Rochester_Female_Academy_1837-1912.pdf.

Nuttall, Mark, ed. *Encyclopedia of the Arctic.* New York: Routledge, 2005.

Odell, Noel. "The Glaciers and Morphology of the Franz Josef Fjord Region of North-East Region of North-East Greenland." *Geographical Journal* 90 (1937): 111–25, 233–34.

Olds, Elizabeth Fagg. *Women of the Four Winds: The Adventures of Four of America's First Women Explorers.* Boston: Houghton Mifflin, 1999.

Oterhals, Leo. "Polhav — om personligheter I skruisen." Trykk: AiT Norbok, 1997.

Ottesen, Johan. "Ishavs-skuter III Selfangarar frå Sunnmøre 1920–1945." Fotoarkivet, 2001.

Oulie, Marthe. *Charcot of the Antarctic.* London: John Murray, 1938.

Payer, Julius, and Karl Weyprecht. *New Lands Within the Arctic Circle.* New York: D. Appleton, 1877.

Peck, Robert McCracken. "To the Ends of the Earth for Science: Research Expeditions of the Academy of Natural Sciences — the First 150 Years, 1812–1962." *Proceedings of the Academy of Natural Sciences of Philadelphia* 150 (2000): 15–46.

Perry, Charles Edward. *Founders and Leaders of Connecticut 1633–1783.* Alcester: READ Books, 2007.

Piatt, Michael. *Bodie: "The Mines Are Looking Well."* El Sobrante, CA: North Bay Books, 2003.

Pinther, Miklos. "The History of Cartography at the American Geographical Society." *Ubique* 21(2002): 1–8.

Quivik, Fredric. "The Standard Mill at Bodie, California." *Industrial Archaeology* 29 (2003): 1–29.

Ribadavia, Comte. *Chasses et Aventures dans les Régions Polaires*. Paris: Maisonneuve, 1927.

Richards, Dorothy Pilley. "Gwladys Mona Odell (1891–1977)." *Alpine Journal* (1978): 270–71.

Richardson, Mary Cabell, ed. *Order of the Descendants of Colonial Governors Prior to 1750: Roll of Members in the State of California*. [San Francisco?]: Order of the Descendants of Colonial Governors Prior to 1750, 1899.

Riffenburgh, Beau. *The Myth of the Explorer: The Press, Sensationalism and Geographical Discovery*. Oxford: Oxford University Press, 1994.

Riiser-Larsen, Hjalmar. *Femti År for Kongen*. Oslo: Gylendal Norsk Forlag, 1957.

Robinson, Michael F. *The Coldest Crucible: Arctic Exploration and American Culture*. Chicago and London: University of Chicago Press, 2006.

Roy, Iain Brownlie. "After Boyd: Photographing the Inner Kaiser Franz Josef Fjord Region Sixty-Six Years after Louise Arner Boyd's First Greenland Expedition." In *British National Expedition to Greenland, Report*. Unpublished. 1997.

———. *Beyond the Imaginary Gates: Journeys in the Fjord Region of North East Greenland*. Stockport: Dewi Lewis Publishing, 2004.

San Francisco Opera Association. Founder's list, 1923.

Schledermann, Peter. "Einar Mikkelsen (1880–1971)." *Arctic* 44 (1991): 351–55.

Simpson, Joseph Cairn. "Horses of California from the Days of the Missions to the Present. Seventh Paper — Oakwood Park Farm." *Sunset Magazine* 9 (1902): 29–40.

Skarstein, Frode. "Erik the Red's Land: The Land That Never Was." *Polar Research* 25 (2006): 173–79.

———. "'A Cursed Affair' — How a Norwegian Expedition to Greenland Became the USA's First Maritime Capture in World War II." *Polar Research* 26: 181–94. 2007.

Smith, Grant H., and Joseph Tingley. *The History of the Comstock Lode*. Reno: University of Nevada Press, 1998.

Smith, Neil. *American Empire: Roosevelt's Geographer and the Prelude to Globalization*. Berkeley: University of California Press, 2003.

Smithsonian Institution. Horticulture Collections Management and Education

Archives of American Gardens. Archives of American Gardens Information Sheet AAG Garden # CA361 Maple Lawn, San Rafael, California.

Snyder, Wilbert, and Charles Bragaw. *Achievement in Radio: Seventy Years of Radio Science, Technology, Standards and Measurement at the National Bureau of Standards*. Boulder: National Bureau of Standards, 1986.

Spitz, Barry. *Marin: A History*. San Anselmo, CA: Potrero Meadow Publishing, 2006.

Sprague, Marguerite. *Bodie's Gold: Tall Tales and True History from a California Mining Town*. Reno and Las Vegas: University of Nevada Press, 2003.

Starr, Kevin. *Endangered Dreams: The Great Depression in California*. New York: Oxford University Press, 1996.

Stefansson, Vilhjalmur. "1947." *Encyclopedia Arctica*. Unpublished manuscript. Dartmouth College.

Stone, James. *Diablo's Legacy: Recollections and Reflections, 1912–Present*. San Francisco: Miller-Freeman, 1994.

Sverdrup, Harald. "Roald Amundsen." *Arctic* 12 (1928): 221–36.

Swithinbank, C. "The Origin of Dirt Cones on Glaciers." *Journal of Glaciology* 1 (1950): 461–69.

Tate, Cassandra. "J. Harlen Bretz (1882–1981)." *Pleistocene Post* (Summer 2008): 2–4.

Thomas, Lowell. *Sir Hubert Wilkins. His World of Adventure*. Toronto: McGraw-Hill, 1961.

Trussell, Margaret. "Five Western Women Pioneer Geographers." *Association of Pacific Coast Geographers Yearbook* 49 (1987): 8–33.

United States of America. Official passport application for Louise Arner Boyd. 1920.

Unknown. *The Book of Common Prayer*. Oxford: Oxford University Press. Date unknown.

Vanderbilt, William M. *Mount Tamalpais Military Academy, 1890–1925*. San Rafael: Marin County Historical Society, 1993.

Victor, Paul-Émile. *Man and His Conquest of the Poles*. London: Hamish Hamilton, 1964.

Wade, F. Alton. "Wartime Investigation of the Greenland Icecap and Its Possibilities." *Geographical Review* (July 1946): 452–73.

Walker, David H. *Pioneers of Prosperity*. San Francisco: [David H. Walker?], 1895.

Washburn, Tahoe Talbot. *Under Polaris: An Arctic Quest*. Montreal and Kingston: McGill-Queen's University Press, 1999.

Wasson, Joseph. *Bodie and Esmeralda*. San Francisco: Spaulding, Barto, 1878.

Wedertz, Frank S. *Bodie, 1859–1900*. Bishop: Sierra Media, 1969.

Weems, John Edward. *Peary: The Explorer and the Man*. Los Angeles: Jeremy Tarcher, 1967.

Weidick, A. *Greenland Satellite Image Atlas of Glaciers of the World. U.S. Geological Survey Professional Paper 1386-C*. Washington: United States Government Printing Office, 1995.

Whitney, Harry. *Hunting with the Eskimos*. London: T. Fisher Unwin, 1910.

Who's Who. *Who's Who Among the Women of California*. San Francisco: Who's Who. 1922.

Wick, Marilyn. "From Bodie to B Street: The Making of the Boyd Fortune." *Science and Society. Marin Historical Society Magazine* 14 (1987–88): 12–22.

Willman, Michele. "Seeing with a New Lens: Louise Arner Boyd's Polar Expeditions." In *Politics, Identity, and Mobility in Travel Writing*, edited by Miguel A. Cabañas, Jeanne Dubino, Veronica Salles-Reese, and Gary Totten (New York: Routledge, 2016), 183.

Wilson, J. Warren. "The Initiation of Dirt Cones on Snow." *Journal of Glaciology* 2 (1953): 281–87.

Wright, John K. *Geography in the Making. The American Geographical Society 1851–1951*. New York: American Geographical Society, 1952.

Wright, John K., and George F. Carter. *Isaiah Bowman 1878–1950: A Biographical Memoir*. Washington: National Academy of Sciences, 1959.

NEWSPAPER REPORTS

"Aged Millionaire Near Death in Fall." *San Francisco Examiner*, April 29, 1920.

"American Girl Shot 11 Bears in Arctic." *New York Times*, September 26, 1926.

"American Woman Searching For Amundsen." *New York Herald*, Paris edition, August 9, 1928.

"Baker-McGavin Wedding." *Marin Journal*, November 11, 1909.

"Boyd Center Marks Centennial." *Ojai Valley News*, April 4, 2003.

"Boyd Memorial Park Dedicated with Appropriate Ceremonies." *Independent*, May 2, 1905.

"Boyd-Arner." *San Francisco Examiner*, April 29, 1883.

"Citizens Indignant at Mask Slackers." *Marin Journal*, October 31, 1918.

"Death Calls for Mrs. John F. Boyd." *Marin Journal*, October 2, 1919.

"Edward M. Greenway's Birthday Dance Opens the Season with Brilliancy." *San Francisco Call*, November 21, 1906.

"Fair to Be Given for Episcopal Church." *San Francisco Call*, September 23, 1910.

"Five Arrested as Flu Mask Slackers." *Marin Journal*, October 17, 1918.

"Flu Masks Discarded Wednesday at Midnight." *Marin Journal*, November 28, 1918.

"Heiress Plans Polar Venture." *Los Angeles Times*, January 26, 1931.

"Heiress to Lead Expedition to Arctic Region." *Chicago Daily Tribune*, March 8, 1931.

"Hotel Rafael Property Taken for Flu Cases." *Marin Journal*, October 31, 1918.

"Last Court of Season Held at Buckingham." *New York Times*, June 27, 1925.

"Louise Boyd Quits Society to Start on Jaunt to Arctic." *Tribune-Republican*, March 14, 1931.

"Mask Violators to Be Arrested." *Marin Journal*, January 23, 1919.

"Menzies, Importer, Dies at 88." *Oakland Tribune*, April 13, 1964.

"Miss Boyd at Spitsbergen." *New York Times*, July 9, 1928.

"Miss Boyd Confident of Rescue Outlook." *New York Times*, June 30, 1928.

"Miss Boyd in Far North." *Marin Journal*, July 19, 1928.

"Miss Louise Boyd Honored by Italy." *Marin Journal*, October 3, 1929.

"Monroe County Medical Society — 38th Annual Meeting." *Rochester Daily Union Advertiser*, June 9, 1859.

"Mrs. John F. Boyd Passes Away." *Sausalito News*, October 4, 1919.

"New Amundsen Search." *Washington Post*, June 28, 1928.

"News from Miss Louise Boyd." *Marin Journal*, August 2, 1928.

"Nine Searching Ships in North." *New York Times*, July 19, 1928.

"The Opening of the Ball." *Oakland Tribune*, November 24, 1906.

"Polimestrene I Eirik Raudes land hilser Polarbjørn velkommen." *Sunmorsposten*, August 3, 1931.

"Praises for Work of San Rafael Ladies." *Marin Journal*, September 13, 1906.

"Precautions Taken to Stamp Out Epidemic." *Marin Journal*, October 24, 1918.

"Present Their Daughter to Marin County Society." *San Francisco Call*, August 18, 1906.

"Respected Citizen Called by Death." *Marin Journal*, May 6, 1920.

"The Ruins As Seen By Ed Soules." *Marin Journal*, April 24, 1906.

"S.F. Woman in Arctic Hunt." *San Francisco Chronicle*, July 31, 1926.

"The Smart Set." *San Francisco Call*, January 17, 1907.

"The Smart Set." *San Francisco Call*, February 18, 1908.

"Society Events in Marin County." *San Francisco Call*, November 1, 1908.

"Two Warships Begin Hunt for Amundsen." *New York Times*, June 28, 1928.

"Warm Welcome for Mrs. Lansdale on Return from East; Social Notes." *San Francisco Call*, December 17, 1913.

"Wife of Pioneer Broker Dies Here." *San Francisco Examiner*, October 5, 1919.

"Woman Joins Arctic Search." *Lincoln Journal*, July 3, 1928.

Photo Credits

71   Courtesy of the author

74   Associated Press (file #100101016655)

79   Marin History Museum

81   The American Geographical Society Library, University of Wisconsin-Milwaukee Libraries

83   Knoller family collection

99   Norsk Polarinstitutt (NPO1686)

102 Norsk Polarinstitutt (NPO56693), photographer Rolf S. Tandberg

106 Norsk Polarinstitutt (NPO56610), photographer Henrik Warming

107 Norsk Polarinstitutt (NPO56643), photographer Henrik Warming

108 Norsk Polarinstitutt (NPO56678), photographer Rolf S. Tandberg

110 Associated Press (file #100101119681)

112 Norsk Polarinstitutt (NPO18311)

118 Polarmuseet, Tromsø, Norway, photograph courtesy of the author

121 Courtesy of the author

123 Marin History Museum

129 Courtesy of the author

133 Norsk Polarinstitutt (NPO50922), photographer Engnes

135 Norsk Polarinstitutt (NPO39399), photographer Adolf Hoel

141 The American Geographical Society Library, University of Wisconsin-Milwaukee Libraries

142 Polarmuseet, Tromsø, Norway, photograph courtesy of the author

143 The American Geographical Society Library, University of Wisconsin-Milwaukee Libraries

144 Norsk Polarinstitutt (NP004326)

146 Norsk Polarinstitutt (NPO18276), photographer John Giæver

149 The American Geographical Society Library, University of Wisconsin-Milwaukee Libraries

152 Courtesy of the author

157 Marin History Museum, photograph courtesy of the author

158 Norsk Polarinstitutt (NPO039435), photographer Paul Røer

163 Courtesy of the author

164 Courtesy of the author

166 Courtesy of the author

172 Norsk Polarinstitutt (NPO24778), photographer Oscar Bang

174 Norsk Polarinstitutt (NPO39393), photographer Hydle

176 Norsk Polarinstitutt (NPO19625), photographer Haakon Dahl

183 The American Geographical Society Library, University of Wisconsin-Milwaukee Libraries

185 Marin History Museum

191 The American Geographical Society Library, University of Wisconsin-Milwaukee Libraries

195 Courtesy of the author

204 Norsk Polarinstitutt (NPO50386), photographer Oscar Bang

207 (Left and right) Center for Creative Photography, University of Arizona, Tucson: Ansel Adams Archive

211 Associated Press (file #381201154)

216 Courtesy of the author

224 Norsk Polarinstitutt (NPO24778), photographer Oscar Bang

226 San Rafael Public Library, photographed by Andreas Vischer

229 Bronner family collection

231 Bronner family collection

232 Norsk Polarinstitutt (NPO24779), photographer Oscar Bang

236 Bronner family collection

238 (Top) Courtesy of the author; (bottom) Marin History Museum, photograph courtesy of the author

241 Courtesy of the author

248 Courtesy of the author

251 The Schooner *Ernestina-Morrissey* Archives at the University of Massachusetts Dartmouth

254 The Schooner *Ernestina-Morrissey* Archives at the University of Massachusetts Dartmouth

256 Courtesy of the author

258 Marin History Museum

261 The Schooner *Ernestina-Morrissey* Archives at the University of Massachusetts Dartmouth

270 Courtesy of the author

272 Louise Arner Boyd Archive, San Rafael Public Library

279 Courtesy of the author

280 Anne T. Kent California Room, Marin County Free Library, San Rafael, California

285 Marin History Museum

287 Associated Press (file #550620013)

290 Marjorie Fountain family collection

291 Marjorie Fountain family collection

294 Courtesy of the author

296 Courtesy of the author

302 Courtesy of the author

303 Courtesy of the author

304 Courtesy of the author

305 Courtesy of the author

307 Courtesy of the author

312 California Academy of Sciences

INDEX